*The Saving Lie*

ALSO BY F. G. BAILEY

# The Saving Lie

## Truth and Method in the Social Sciences

F. G. BAILEY

**PENN**

University of Pennsylvania Press

Philadelphia

10  9  8  7  6  5  4  3  2  1

Published by
University of Pennsylvania Press
Philadelphia, Pennsylvania 19104-4011

Library of Congress Cataloging-in-Publication Data
Bailey, F. G. (Frederick George)
    The saving lie: truth and method in the social sciences / F. G. Bailey.
        p. cm.
    Includes bibliographical references and index.
    ISBN 0-8122-3730-7 (cloth : alk. paper)
    1. Social sciences—Methodology. I. Title.

H61.B234 2003
300'.1—dc21                                                           2003047323

*For Mary*

# Contents

viii    Contents

# Preface

> *The world, so far from being a solid matter of fact, is rather a fabric of conventions, which . . . it has suited us in the past to manufacture and support.*
>
> —*I. A. Richards,* The Philosophy of Rhetoric

The idea that the world is a "fabric of conventions," although it seems to defy common sense, is not all that unusual. A more compact version—and more complicated, because it includes the notion of contraries—appears in William Blake's *The Everlasting Gospel:*

> Do what you will, this Life's a Fiction
> And is made up of Contradiction.

Common sense says that the world is an ordered physical reality, a "solid matter of fact," not a fiction or a mess of contradictions. Blake, however, and Richards—despite the words "Life" and "world"—were not talking about physical things but about ideas, which are fabricated. How they are fabricated is neatly conveyed in this fragment of epistemology taken from one of John Barth's novels:

> . . . the same feeling one has when a filling-station attendant or a cabdriver launches into his life-story: As a rule, and especially when one is in a hurry or is grouchy, one wishes the man to be nothing more difficult that The Obliging Filling-Station Attendant or The Adroit Cabdriver. These are the essences you have assigned them, at least temporarily, for your own purposes, as a taleteller makes a man The Handsome Young Poet or The Jealous Old Husband; and while you know very well that no historical human being was ever just an Obliging Filling-Station Attendant or a Handsome Young Poet, you are never-theless prepared to ignore your man's charming complexities—*must* ignore

them, in fact, if you are to get on with the plot, or get things done according to schedule. (1960, 31)

John Barth speaks for us all. We too, if we are to "get on with the plot" or get things done on time, must cut through life's "charming complexities" by assigning "essences" to people and to situations and so make everything simpler than we know it really is. There is no other way to make sense of what goes on or decide what to do. And, like Barth, we are usually put out when someone refuses to play the simplifying game and restores the complexities, not only because they hold up what we want done, but also because complexity brings with it uncertainty and apprehension. It forces us to realize that our chosen simplifying notion has rivals, and—worse—that it may be misleading or inadequate or even dangerous.

The simplifications reviewed in this book are certain fundamental ideas variously called *presuppositions* or *predications* or *philosophical underpinnings* that we use to explore the nature of human society. My bedrock presupposition (not everyone's) is that, at least to some degree, the world makes sense and is amenable to reason. I cannot imagine living a life so utterly and entirely unpredictable that I did not try to—and believe that I could—anticipate the consequences of my actions. Of course I know that I make mistakes; things often do not turn out as I expected, thus confronting me with an instance of life's charming complexities. But even a run of unforeseen calamities will not destroy my faith that at least some of the time I will find enough regularity in the world to make sense of what happens to me and to other people. In practice we live by the principle of determinism, whether we admit it or not, and to believe that there is no order whatsoever in the world and that all is chaos and confusion, and therefore to ask neither what is going on nor why things turn out as they do, is, in a rather literal way, to have gone out of one's mind.[1]

No other presupposition need be held as certain and indisputable. Out of the many that we can use to make sense of our dealings with one another, I will discuss two that, although not bedrock, are relatively foundational. The first (*expected utility* or *rational choice* or *methodological individualism*) is that a society is to be seen as a collection of individuals who are motivated to act for their own advantage. The second (*moral order* or *methodological holism*) is that a society's elements are

1. Tolstoy appeared to see things differently. At the end of Chapter 2 in the First Epilogue to *War and Peace* he wrote, "If we admit that human life can be ruled by reason, the possibility of life is destroyed" (1957, 3: 422). This is not, however, the direct contradiction that it seems to be, because Tolstoy was not concerned, as I am, with methodology (how to do things) but with ontology (how things really are).

not its individuals but its groups, because individuals mostly do what the group expects of them and are moved by thoughts not of personal advantage but of moral obligation. Through most of the books that I have written, both those on India and the more general studies of politics, I have threaded that single theme: the tension between action done for the advantage of the doer and action done, even when disadvantageous, for reasons of duty or conscience. But I have learned, teaching graduate seminars, that this apparently straightforward contrast between rational-choice models and holistic models is a source of confusion and a prompter of pointless altercation, because people uphold one or other side of the contrast as a concrete reality, as the unique truth about how the world works.

Choice of one to the exclusion of the other is not the way to go. These two predications should not be viewed ontologically—as being about the way things really are—and thus seen only as mutually contradictory propositions to be adjudicated true or false. Treat them, instead, both as methods (investigative procedures or tools) and as weapons. They are investigative tools that allow us to make sense of what we experience; at the same time they can be deployed to define situations and so exercise control over other people. As theories they are Blake's contraries and incompatible; as practices both are significant motivators and are not contradictory but complementary, each filling the gap that the other leaves. Like John Barth's "essences" they are analytic tools or, as I will call them, *saving lies* that enable us to make sense of human society and to cooperate or compete with one another and so get on with our lives. In that scenario there is no point in arguing that one or the other of them has exclusive access to *the* truth. The task, instead, is first to reveal what each essence conceals, and second, to find out how it is deployed in practice. When deployed, it serves as a weapon that people use to compete for the power that goes with deciding what essence will define a situation.

The book's three central parts follow that pattern. The first is about expected utility, the second is about holism, and the third is about rhetorical strategies used to affirm or dispute presuppositions that define situations, govern interaction, and so determine who will be in control.

The ideas that shape the book were developed in a ten-week social anthropology class for graduate students, most of whom were new to the discipline. I chose to focus on politics, which I take to be any act or process that concerns the distribution of power, and I set out to uncover whatever presuppositions underlie the analysis of power distribution, not only in other cultures but also in our own.

Teaching, in the present relatively unparadigmatic state of the discipline, focuses less on received ethnographic truth—"solid matters of fact"—than on methodology and on fostering an intellectual attitude of which the first element, for me, is the bedrock presupposition presented above: when confronted with a jumble of incomprehensible events or bewildering people, one must have faith that patterns will be found to make them comprehensible. Essences, in other words, can be assigned. Second, since an essence is a matter of opinion, it is necessary to test whatever is recommended as the significant essence by recalling complexities discarded in the process of selecting it and asking why that particular essence was preferred. The answer, I will suggest, is very often not some intrinsic merit that the chosen pattern has (for example, its "truth") but rather the advantage that someone sees in defining the situation in that particular way. As I write this, there is a simple instance before us. Why is the al-Qaida affair in Afghanistan and elsewhere so insistently defined as a "war" by the same people who refuse to make a formal declaration of war or to treat their captives as prisoners of war? Why is this not a police action against criminals? One could ask a similar question about the "war" on drugs. Who benefits from the definition? How do they do so? What are the hidden (and not always "charming") complexities?

This systematic scepticism towards any notion that is promoted as *the* truth goes along with presuppositions about the practice of anthropology and about the variousness of cultures within a single society. Once upon a time anthropology was ethnography. The dictionary meaning *(OED)* of that word is: "The scientific description of nations or races of men, with their customs, habits, and points of difference," which can be reasonably glossed as the study of other cultures, which exist in other societies ("nations" or "races"). But the concept of other cultures does not entail other societies. Otherness can be found in the next street (same town), in another department (same university), in a generation up or down (same family), across the genders, across classes, across dialects—in any situation in which a discontinuity of whatever kind can be assigned to mark an essence, in the process discarding other essences that ignore the discontinuity and proclaiming a unity. The discarded or hidden essences then become "other cultures." In other words, cultures are John Barth's "essences" writ large, and, like essences, they are assigned.

Here is an example. When anthropologists who investigate the corporate world use the term *ethnography* to describe what they do, they are referring to the method of investigation. We might call it "looking behind the curtain." In practice it means an insistent questioning of assigned essences and an uncovering of the complexity that is hidden behind them. In the context of formal organizations, ethnographic inquiry is a close investigation of conduct that is not officially recognized. The organization's articles of incorporation, written protocols, programmed rules and regulations, flowcharts and the like, all of which are logically consistent and relatively uncomplex, are penetrated in order to uncover values that structure an informal world where people do what suits them, so far as that is possible, and in the process reinterpret or disregard the organization's formal rules. What do such people think? What essences do they assign to their colleagues and to the work situation? Why do they select those essences?

I should say at once that I intend nothing prescriptive and exclusionary. There are many other ways to do anthropology. I am describing the method that I use in this book and, for sure, it will not be to everyone's taste, certainly not to those of my colleagues who shy away from the often intractable complexity that is entailed in hands-on, close-to-experience ethnography and are interested neither in its practice nor in its findings. Instead they devote their energies to constructing essences (highly abstract holistic models) that delight the mind and fortify the psyche exactly because they fabricate a unity that is beyond the reach of any empirical test that might put it in doubt. Thus complexity is airbrushed out of the scene. The task that I envision here is to uncover and at least reconsider the sociocultural complexities that are dumped in the act of assigning particular essences to persons, or, as in the case of expected-utility models and holistic models, to complex situations.

Just as no answer makes sense until you know what the question was, so also no book can be understood until the ideas and values that underlie and control it have been identified. Presuppositions in the study of society tend to come in clusters of related (but not identical) items selected from contrasted pairs: holism vs. individualism; structure vs. agency; morality vs. expected utility; moral science (normative laws) vs. natural science (positive laws); interpretivism vs. positivism; romantic vs. classical; postmodern vs. modern; normative rules vs. pragmatic rules; commitment vs. scientific detachment; and various others. Those social scientists who believe they have located their paradigms (virtually all economists, the majority of political scientists, and some sociologists) generally favor the second named in each of the contrasted pairs. Other social scientists, who take pride in being unparadigmatic and unpositivist, have adopted the first-named alternatives. Social anthropology once had straightforward positivist aspirations, but since about the middle of the twentieth century the positivist grand-theory goal—identifying a comprehensive scheme that cuts through diversity and complexity and discovers a basic "natural" patterning in social systems—has had an increasingly tenuous existence. It has likewise been mostly absent from the newer social studies disciplines, such as ethnic studies or women's studies. Practitioners in those fields, along with a postmodern "turn" in cultural anthropology, generally disdain positivism and are often more concerned to recommend what *should* be the case than to first understand what it actually *is*.

Where is this book located? I believe that we can make some sense of the social world and I consider the attempt to do so to be a moral imperative. If one needs to be sustained by a teleological pretense— that in the end it all hangs together because that is how the Creator designed things—no harm is done, providing time and energy are not spent trying to convert the methodological presupposition into a God-given truth. As I said, if we intend to use our minds, the premise of order is a methodological necessity. Whether or not order is also a divine artifact is a different issue that neither validates nor invalidates the methodology.

Beyond that, there is no presupposition that I can present as an absolute condition for understanding. Certainly I have preferences, some of which may come near to being foundational, but I cannot pretend that they are absolutes, because, again, they concern methodology. Methodology is always about if/then propositions; tools are effective or ineffective, not true or false. One such tool, already exemplified in what I said earlier about the complementarity of utilitarian and moral motivations, is the precept offered by an anonymous Greek sage: *mēden agān*—nothing too much, nothing in excess. Use the rational-choice scheme as far as it is effective in understanding what people do, and do the same with the holistic frame. "Nothing too much" has a whiff of morality about it (excess is evil) but in fact the recommendation is purely methodological. If you want to increase the stock of knowledge, then do not pursue a presupposition to excess and to the exclusion of other presuppositions that might be useful. Do not, to repeat the example, convert methodological predications about the nature of human society into scriptural truths that are beyond questioning and criticism. Closed minds close off knowledge.

Moral issues—judgments about good and evil—enter this book at two levels. First there are moralities entailed in the philosophies that I describe and analyze; I can try to present them without making moral judgments about them. Second, there are my own values. My presiding value is conveyed in Evans-Pritchard's declaration, "Knowledge of man and of society is an end in itself and its pursuit a moral exercise" (1948, 14–15). For me that is a directive, an absolute value. I do not try to prove it; I predicate it, and I am entirely comfortable with it. My own values, however, also enter the book in another way that is unfortunate, but probably inevitable. When I describe the logical underpinnings of the two controlling philosophies, methodological individualism and methodological holism, and review the use that has been made of them, I find myself (notably in Chapter 6, but in other places too) pulled beyond dispassionate description and analysis into making ethical assertions about good and bad social arrangements. Those assertions are a departure from the detached understanding (so hard to achieve in the social sciences) that I consider right for these endeavors.

In much of the book—and especially in its third part—I have tried to confine myself to positivist propositions about the ideas and attitudes that people have, why they have them, what they do with them, and what are the consequences. I describe what I consider to be the case, and I generally avoid ethical judgments about what should be the case. Most of the time will be spent in digging up complexities, complexifying assigned essences, and, on occasion, discovering unacknowledged agendas.

I will return to these and similar issues in the concluding chapter.

*Take away the saving lie from the average man and immediately you take away his happiness.*

—*Henrik Ibsen,* The Wild Duck

# Introduction:
# Ideas, Reality, and Saving Lies

*They said, "You have a blue guitar,*
*You do not play things as they are."*
*The man replied, "Things as they are*
*Are changed upon the blue guitar."*

—*Wallace Stevens, "The Man with the Blue Guitar"*

## Things as They Are

In the distinctly hyped paragraph that closes his *General Theory of Employment, Interest, and Money*, J. M. Keynes wrote, "[T]he ideas of economists and political philosophers, both when they are right and when they are wrong, are more powerful than is commonly understood. Indeed the world is ruled by little else. Practical men, who believe themselves to be quite exempt from any intellectual influences, are usually the slaves of some defunct economist. Madmen in authority, who hear voices in the air, are distilling their frenzy from some academic scribbler of a few years back . . . it is ideas, not vested interests, which are dangerous. . . ." Could he be wrong? Probably not, at least about ideas: they do matter. Ideas are like the blue guitar: they shape our world.[1]

They do not, however, shape it entirely. Reality also matters; events continually confound ideas. Moreover, we do not need ideas to feel the world's effects; viruses also strike those who know nothing of

---

1. Keynes 1947, 383–84. He published that book in 1936. The "madmen in authority," I surmise, were not only Hitler and Mussolini, as one might think looking back from after the Second World War, but also elected politicians and other men of influence who, at the time Keynes wrote, were trying to cope with the Great Depression, the financial and industrial slump that began in 1929 and continued into the late thirties.

"Academic scribblers" identifies people like himself or, a generation later, the three economists featured in the first part of this book, or any scholar who pretends to have an expertise that might change things in the world.

virology. The diphtheria bacillus, not the idea of diphtheria, killed children. But everything understandable—everything that we can talk about, argue about, or plan to deal with—requires an idea; from that perspective ideas also are a kind of reality, something that we experience. Without ideas we cannot understand the world. For that we need concepts, representations, models, structures, schemas, symbols, theories, world views, imaginaries, discourse, narratives, constructs, and the like, which, in some way not easy to define, connect us with part of the reality that is out there. For sure, much of the world—as we experience it—is not amenable to reason, but some of it is. Using ideas is like prospecting: sometimes you find what you want, yet much remains undiscovered, and there is always the risk of getting hurt or doing harm.

Ideas—to push the matter to an extreme—can also be thought of as lies of a special kind. Ibsen, in *The Wild Duck*, used a noun, *livsløgnen*, which is glossed as the "life lie" or the "saving lie," or the "lie that makes life possible." Some of the lies told by the characters in that play are what now is fancified as "the economical use of the truth" or "lawyers' truth"—lying by omission, people withholding facts that they do not want known. Other lies are willful misrepresentations of fact. But the life lie is different. It is the fiction that people build up about themselves—who they are, what they do—and about how their world works; they live inside the lie. Then the maker of tragedy may not be the one who misrepresents the truth but the honest person, the zealot, who believes that truth alone matters and should be laid open even when it destroys the life that the lie made possible. The saving lie is also known to us as faith, religion, or, especially, truth. Any idea, any belief, to the extent that it is pronounced "self-evident" and shielded from doubt and questioning, is a saving lie.

The ideas that we use to probe our experience—hypotheses, theories, and even what we accept as fact—have a similar contingent existence. They are abstractions, selections from a reality that is fuller than they are and may surface to prove them mistaken. Consequently, they are provisional, constructed for our convenience; they help us to understand what goes on. The real world is still there, however, and sometimes an idea that strays too far from it will bring disaster.[2] What that distance might be, why we habitually stay with ideas that are mani-

2. That, too, is a lesson in Ibsen's plays. In *An Enemy of the People*, Dr. Stockman, upholding the truth of science (that the town's water supply is contaminated) is worsted by various men of influence (including his brother, the mayor) who, fearing the financial loss that building a new system would involve, chose to believe that Dr. Stockman was wrong and to discredit him. The tone of the play is such that one knows, at the end, that reality must prevail and disaster will ensue.

festly out of touch with reality, and what *reality* should mean, are issues that will be argued through the book. In short, one axis of my inquiry is *abstraction*, which is the ever-shifting distance between the simplicity that ideas portray and the complexity that is experienced in reality. All truths are to be considered questionable, and anyone who claims to be objective, to be "telling it like it is," and to have access to *the* truth, is usually touting a truth that is only one in a field of competitors. "There may always be another reality / To make fiction of the truth we think we've arrived at," wrote Christopher Fry.

Then what does *reality* mean? Of course (to say it again) there is a real world; an empirical test will quickly invalidate the proposition that sticking your cold hands in a fire is an effective way to warm them. But claims to scientific objectivity cannot always be backed with such immediacy; they sometimes go entirely unbacked and serve instead to present an opinion (for example the unquestionable superiority of free-market economies) as if it were not just a fact but a superfact, an eternal verity, ultimately a religious truth, to deny which is a sin. Short of that extreme, any claim to scientific objectivity should be heard as a bid for intersubjectivity, an invitation to come on board. *Intersubjectivity* is what exists between two minds, and the word indicates not just existence but also agreement. In other words, a scientific fact is whatever those who follow scientific procedures agree is a fact. According to Karl Popper, these procedures include "free criticism" and "recognizing experience as the impartial arbiter of . . . controversies." "Free criticism" suggests that whatever is intersubjective is unlikely to be constant and secure; it is at the mercy of debate. It is also at the mercy of "experience," which implies that there exists, beyond the realm of intersubjectivity, a hard implacable objectivity, which one discovers through experience. But people can still disagree about what an experience means; therefore experience itself can only be validated through intersubjectivity; experience has to be pinned down by the meaning given to it. Experience must have a public character; that is, it must be intersubjective. In short "Scientific objectivity can be described as the intersubjectivity of scientific method" (Popper 1966, ii: 217–18).

If one puts intersubjectivity in the driver's seat, a social system is not a material reality that exists independently of any mind. *Social structure* and *social process* have to do with mental things, with ideas. That, it must again be emphasized, does not dispense with the idea of an objective reality; we encounter it when hard experience tells us that whatever was intersubjectively defined as "objectively" true in fact is not. But, short of those decisive moments, social life manifests a multiplicity of "truths," which compete with one another. It is a simple notion: a single situation can be defined—structured or modeled—in different and incompatible ways. Ideas are not facsimiles of what exists in the world. They are claims or propositions or models that *connect* us with it; they give us a window on it; they are tools that enable us to cope with life; they are designs for living. Their test is pragmatic: their "truth" is their effectiveness and we comprehend reality only in the failure (or success) of actions prompted by an idea.

Connection with reality would not matter if ideas were always used, as they often are, just for amusement—for making patterns that are intellectually pleasing, or merely to display, like a peacock's tail, the brilliance of a mind. Having the right connection does matter when ideas are put to use and knowledge is translated into know-how. Praxis disciplines the imagination because ideas mistakenly applied may have, as the intellectual tendency paraded in the first part of this book would say, a negative payoff. The world and society—other people—come to us not just as texts (to use another tendency's jargon) but also as unworded experience. We analyze and talk about social systems, but we also live them—enact them, enjoy them, and suffer them. The dialogues that enable us to make some sense of an encounter with reality take place between contending ideas; *sometimes* the referee that decides between them is the reality they purport to present. *Docet experientia*—we can learn from putting ideas into practice, from what happens to us, from our mistakes. Often, however, for a variety of reasons that I will consider later, experience does not have the last word, because its connection with ideas is overlooked or denied.

## Articulated and Unarticulated Knowledge

In fact, much of what we do is not represented at all in ideas. We do many things effectively without being able to present what we are doing in the form of ideas or models—that is, as abstract, organized knowledge. When Rubik's cube was in fashion, I watched a ten-year-old boy restore each face to a single color with truly impressive speed, while the adults around him were driven cross-eyed, unable to do it at all. I asked him to tell me how he did it, thinking that anyone who could perform so expertly would be able to analyze the performance and present it to me in words as an exact and critical sequence. In fact, he could *show* me what he did—he did it again and again—but he could not explain the reasoning behind the sequence of moves he made. He knew how to solve the problem of Rubik's cube. He had the know-how, but he could not impart it as discursive knowledge.

To turn his know-how into knowledge, he would have had to put it into words. He would have had to make a model—an abstract representation—of what he did, breaking the procedure down into its constituent parts, putting them in sequence, and, if he chose to elaborate, explaining what would go wrong at each step if the sequence was not followed. Evidently we do not capture *all* our conduct in articulated models. We have knowledge that we can use but cannot describe in a propositional form. Knowing how to do something is not the same as being able to explain what is being done and why it is done in that way.

There is nothing mysterious about this. People drive cars and change gear, ride bicycles, swim, shave, get dressed and undressed, tie their shoes, or clean their teeth, without ever articulating to themselves or anyone else what these quite complex sequential operations involve. Up to a point, social life runs that way too. Much of the etiquette that smoothes interaction with other people is second nature, not directly taught but just picked up and internalized from watching what goes on. We do many things—and we do them with consummate ease—without ever having the occasion to think out and put into words just what we are doing. That is how we speak our native language, while quite unable to recite the rules of grammar, still less the rules of phonetics. "Well blow me down!" said M. Jourdain, "Speaking prose for more than forty years, and I never knew it!" We can also do what is right without having to think about it. Much of our morality lies close to, if not inside, the tacit domain (and therefore is unquestioned). So also, sometimes, does the exercise of power. The perfect subjects, from a tyrant's point of view, are those who enact their subordination without ever thinking about it, let alone recognizing it as an imposition. In all these cases the knowledge of what to do is there, but it is tacit, unspoken, subliminal, beyond the reach of words, and therefore beyond the reach of critical thought.

There are many phrases that distinguish articulated knowledge from knowledge that is realized only in action. *Analytic knowledge, theory, abstract knowledge, reflexive knowledge, articulated knowledge, discursive knowledge,* or *propositional knowledge* is opposed to *practical consciousness, practical knowledge, habitus, praxis, know-how, savvy,* "smarts," *nous, skill,* and the like. The words in the second set are variously nuanced but all of them indicate the kind of knowledge required to take action in the real world where there are felt consequences. Ideas that are formulated but never enacted cannot have practical consequences. For this reason, the level of abstraction—the distance between the idea and an action or event—significantly influences the idea's chances of becoming a saving lie; the quicker and more regular the feedback, the more uncertain will be its existence as a life lie. Practical knowledge, since by definition it is not reflexive, cannot become a saving lie. (It can, of course, be mistakenly applied, and the result may cause the agent to bring it into the propositional domain and think about it critically by attaching it to one or another more general idea. Then it may be on the way to becoming a saving lie.) Propositional knowledge, on the other hand, more readily qualifies as a saving lie, and the more abstract it is, the more easily it is defended against evidence that negates it. That is the case with the pair of saving lies (expediency and morality) which shape the first two parts of this book.[3]

## Expediency and Morality

Besides helping us make sense of experience, ideas are also weapons, and their adversarial use is a second thread that runs through the book. Ideas, not vested interests, move the world, Keynes said, but an idea can also be a vested interest when it confers power. Any social situation—courtship, marriage, government and the law, the economy, organized religious life—is dominated by whoever gets to decide which ideas will regulate the interaction. Saving lies in these contexts are likely to be stated in highly abstract form, and their upholders protect the ideas by defying or concealing or falsifying evidence that would undermine them.

I will consider two such abstract ideas, or philosophies, in the first six chapters of this book, treating them as saving lies and looking both for their limitations and for the logical and rhetorical devices that their upholders use to protect them from critical scrutiny. The ideas are not new; the contradiction between utility and morality—what is expedient (utility) against what is right and just (morality)—has been a staple of social and philosophical inquiry for a long time.[4] Their contrast is encapsulated in a sentence from *Asinaria*, a comedy by Plautus: *Lupus est homo homini, non homo, quom qualis sit non novit.* The first part is often cited (in a short form) as *Homo homini lupus*, "A man is a wolf toward another man." My dictionary of proverbs gives only that and omits the second half, *quom qualis sit non novit*, which is a qualifier; it means, roughly, "when he doesn't know what kind of person the other

3. There is a third domain of knowledge: the unconscious that is identified in psychoanalytic theories. This domain contains desires and fears (and therefore ideas) that are either unavailable to the conscious mind or appear in it in a distorted form. Between practical and discursive knowledge there is no such strong emotional barrier. The significance of the unconscious mind for modeling social systems is beyond the scope of this book.
4. I should make clear at the outset the word *utility* has both a narrow and a wide meaning. Contrasted with *morality*, it has the narrow meaning of self-interest. Its wider catchall meaning, "anything that a person wants," clearly can include morality. On most occasions in this book *utility* will have the narrow meaning; I will indicate when the wider meaning is intended.

is." Each clause represents a different presupposition about human nature, and a different way to model the regularity that we perceive in human interaction—as an arena of predatory individuals—virtual animals—or as a community of people joined in mutual awareness and mutual consideration.

The arena is the economist's way; it models societies as *natural* systems. Economic man is the old Adam, unredeemed, without God's grace; he works for his own advantage.[5] But the outcome of his behavior, as he interacts with others like himself, is a natural, unintended order; it arises spontaneously. It is something that just happens; no one intentionally creates it. Indeed, the notion is that all social order (including morality itself) comes about in that fashion, arising gradually out of competitive encounters from which, by a process of natural selection, only those who happen to make the right choices survive (and along with them the choices themselves). The order that emerges can be perceived and to some extent understood, but it cannot have been planned, because the variables involved, even if they were known, would far exceed anyone's ability to compute them. In short, order emerges in society (culture, tradition, morality) in just the same way as it does in nature (pattern, regularity)—no one planned it, no one designed it; it is the product of natural selection. Virtually all economists and many political scientists use a version of that model. They take the individual and the manifold diversity of individual initiatives, hopes, fears, scruples, strengths, weaknesses, knowledge, and intentions out of the picture. How they do so will be explained in the following chapter.

Other social sciences, including sociology and social anthropology, generally favor the humanist or moral way, which models human beings as, in some respects, distinct from other manifestations of nature. It portrays their interaction as a *moral* system, taking into account the distinctions we make between right and wrong, our sense of being sometimes guided by conscience, notions like duty, integrity and virtue, and, of course, their contraries, self-seeking, dishonesty, and vice. In this scheme, order in society is not a natural phenomenon, it is designed. It emerges when the "new man" has been raised and the old Adam buried. It is the product of conscious restraint, planning, moral principles, and at least some degree of hierarchical control. The old Adam, however, is never entirely laid away, but stays around in the model as a continuing source of, and explanation for, disorder in society. Unlike the natural order, which is assumed to be inescapably present,

5. "O merciful God, grant that the old Adam in this Child may be so buried, that the new man may be raised up in him." An invocation for the baptism of infants in the *Book of Common Prayer*.

all-commanding, and inevitable, the moral order is contested, argued over, precarious and shifting, continually being broken apart and then rebuilt again.

The two sides—those who see society as a natural system and those who see it as a moral system—argue their cases in different ways. Economists, for the most part, stay within the framework of their own naturalistic assumptions, and therefore argue with each other. When they do directly address humanist models, they are likely to say that such models are of little use because they are not tractable. That is, they are fuzzy, imprecise, and platitudinous, they cannot be framed numerically and often are internally inconsistent, so that it is impossible to use them as a model should be used, which is to generate questions and come up with hypotheses that can be tested empirically.

The humanists have two forms of attack. First, they argue, there is a price to pay for insisting that a model must be tractable: economic models have a narrow focus, which causes them to leave out much of what we experience in the real world. We do not recognize ourselves in the culturally skeletal person portrayed in an economist's model, and a great part of what we want clarified in our dealings with each other is not even noticed, let alone explained. Such models work only in the imaginary world that economists create for themselves. They do not work in the real world—a nice irony since economists, as would-be scientists, are the ones who insist that theirs is a positive science, one that requires its theories to be tested empirically. Positive theories concern the way the world is, not the way it should be: a theory is valid if it correctly predicts the outcome of some change in circumstances, and whether the change is good or bad is a different concern. Unfortunately, this anxiety to deal only with empirically testable facts—to be positivist—seems to have blinded economists to the undoubted fact that the world that is includes people's ideas of how the world should be. Because economists ignore ethical values (and for some other reasons), their models are likely to fail the positivist test of application.

The second counterargument is addressed ad hominem: all scientists, including economists, are morally irresponsible. Scientific models convert human beings into things, making them objects of instrumental use and stripping them of their essential humanity. Even worse than a loss of dignity, the products of scientific work are often physically harmful. This is more often said of natural science than of social science, but it is the case that the advice given by economists often does have about it an air of indifference to consequential hardships. Sometimes the criticism is made against science itself, but that surely misses the point. It is not science that does good or evil but those who make use of scientific ideas; they deserve the credit or the blame. Science is a tool for the acquisition of propositional knowledge, and a tool, in itself, can only be judged effective or ineffective; it cannot be dignified with moral responsibility.

Humanists would agree, but say that the answer evades the issue. Models—intellectual tools—are used not only for understanding but also for advantage. They are, in other words, weapons that confer power and make it possible for those who control the weapon to exploit those who do not, or at least to justify their own hegemony. Moral models, of course, are no less open to such charges: oppression often masquerades as God's will or the public good. In both cases it is assumed that to evaluate a model one must also evaluate the uses to which it is put.

The term *evaluate* remains equivocal until a criterion for evaluation has been specified. Since I have defined models as tools and as weapons, the practical course is to use the equivocation rather than try to resolve it. A model, therefore, can be examined in two contexts, one intellectual and the other political. First ask: How well does it work? Does it sufficiently describe or explain or predict actions and events? Second, the notion of weapons leads directly to Cicero's inquiry: *Cui bono?* (Who benefits? Who has a piece of the action?) Is there, in this model's use, a hidden—perhaps unwitting—political agenda?

Part I (about neoclassical economics) and Part II (about structural functionalism) describe intellectual worlds made up of would-be incontestable verities, framed as abstract propositional knowledge. Part III, on agency, is a small voyage at the edge of a large ocean, a tryout for a longer journey. It models the connection between abstract knowledge and practical knowledge, first explaining how and why we want to— and must—think in terms of unchanging truth, and then considering the strategies we use to outmaneuver truth's fixity. The Conclusion presents the essence of my argument in the form of a mild polemic against the totality-itch, which is the notion that everything social and cultural can and must be encompassed within a single theoretical framework.

My discussions of particular issues are far from exhaustive: each marks a journey's beginning, not its end. Any reader who feels moved to do so can venture into the labyrinth of commentary that grew up around Friedman's 1953 essay (Chapter 1); or track down the article on social cost that earned Coase the other half of his Nobel prize (1960) and see if it has the same limitation as "The Nature of the Firm" (Chapter 2); or sample, in the correspondence columns of the journal *Man*, the mostly disbelieving reactions to Evans-Pritchard's revolutionary edict on the proper form of social anthropology (Chapters 4 and 5); or contemplate, critically, the patricidal debate about colonialism and the "end of anthropology" (Chapter 6); or review the spectacular corporate dishonesties uncovered in the presidency of the younger Bush and the consequent swift rewriting of essences assigned to business executives (Chapters 3 and 6); or seek out ways to deal with the problem of agency other than by sidestepping it (as critics will say I have done in Part III); or (Conclusion) attempt (as I do not) to resolve *theoretically* (it can be done in practice) the difference between "hedgehogs" and "foxes"; or— the heart of this book—to harvest from it, from other writings, and from experience, strategies that we use to persuade ourselves and each other how to make sense of the world and sometimes control it by "assigning essences" and defining situations.

# Part I
# Expediency

*How selfish soever man may be supposed, there are evidently some princi-*
*ples in his nature, which interest him in the fortune of others, and render*
*their happiness necessary to him, though he derives nothing from it, except*
*the pleasure of seeing it . . . for this sentiment, like all the other original*
*passions of human nature, is by no means confined to the virtuous and hu-*
*mane, though they may perhaps feel it with the most exquisite sensibility.*
*The greatest ruffian, the most hardened violator of the laws of society, is*
*not altogether without it.*

—*Adam Smith,* The Theory of Moral Sentiments

In the next three chapters I enter the domain of certain economists and examine their regnant expected-utility model, which presupposes that all actions—including what is done by the seemingly "virtuous and humane"—are motivated by self-interest. That model, for a century and more, has dominated not only our thinking about practical economic and political affairs but also much of our everyday dealings with one another. Nevertheless, it is in many ways patently out of touch with reality. Three chapters (1–3) chart a progressive acknowledging by economists of that problem but do not discover any satisfactory solution. The crucial difficulty is the complexity and uncertainty that is produced by our human capacity to make up our own minds. Are we to ignore that capacity and model a social system as a natural system? In that case, human choice—choice with intended consequences—is an illusion and we have no more ability to intentionally shape our destiny than does a flower or an insect. Nor can we be held responsible for what we do. Or should we model social systems as choice-theoretic, in part, at least, the product of our own volition?

The expected-utility model has a very powerful presence in social analysis. To show what it entails I will make a comparison between three economists, Milton Friedman, Ronald Coase, and Douglass North. All three happen to be Nobel laureates, but that is not why I selected them. They stand as representatives of particular points of view. In each case the discussion focuses on a single article or, in North's case, a short book. (The selected writings, I should make clear, do not represent the scholar and his life's work, but only the models he used on that occasion.) All three pieces are written in agreeably clear and forceful prose and are therefore accessible to those untrained in the mathematical language that most economists now use (thus, it is said, liberating themselves from the real world).

The order in which the three men became Nobel laureates happens to match the logical order of my argument, which is a descent from highly abstract general statements in the direction of empirically grounded particulars. The pattern is of a thesis, exemplified by Friedman (Chapter 1), followed by two recensions, one by Coase (Chapter 2) and one by North (Chapter 3), which are not out-and-out antitheses, but rather modifications intended to bring the original thesis somewhat closer to the world of action and experience.

*Chapter 1*
# A Very Beautiful Theory

*Anybody with the slightest mathematical bent can't help but view neoclassical, general equilibrium theory, with utility-maximization as a driving mechanism, as a very, very beautiful thing. . . . Economists are very reluctant to recognize and accept facts in the real world that seem to fly in the face of that beautiful theory, or undermine its basic assumptions.*

—*Herbert Simon, "The Failure of Armchair Economics"*

Kenneth Burke, in *A Grammar of Motives,* wrote, "In any term we can posit a world, in the sense that we can treat the world *in terms of* it, seeing all as emanations, near or far, of its light" (1969a, 105). He calls them "god-terms," indicating that they are sacred, all-powerful, and supposedly never to be questioned. The words themselves are simplified "reductions" of more complex matters, and "when we confront a simplicity we must forthwith ask ourselves what complexities are subsumed beneath it." That is what I propose to do with the "beautiful theory" that is driven by utility-maximization.

## Organizations and Markets

In November 1937 Ronald Coase published an essay, "The Nature of the Firm," in the journal *Economica*. It contains the following sentence (1937, 387): "If a workman moves from department Y to department X, he does not go because of a change in relative prices, but because he is ordered to do so." That mildly ironic statement does not seem to be the earth-shaker that, half a century later, it turned out to have been. Bosses give orders and workers obey; it is a familiar part of our culture, obvious to everyone except, it seems, to those who read *Economica* in 1937.

Coase was awarded a Nobel prize in 1991, in part for his work on the nature of the firm. On that occasion some ignoramus whose name

I do not recall, a columnist in the *Los Angeles Times*, poured scorn on the award, saying it was given for discovering something that was obvious to anyone who gave a second's thought to the matter. In the real world, workers and foremen and managers are all too familiar with ideas of command and hierarchy, and such concepts surely have an obtrusive reality that demands their inclusion in models of organizational behavior (including economic models). Why, then, did the world's economists, albeit belatedly, mark Coase's contribution as an intellectual invention of some importance?

They surely did not do so in 1937; they treated his article as a nonevent. The Nobel prize came to Coase half a century after the essay was written, and it was the early 1970s—a thirty-year delay—before the field that he had opened began to be exploited and the transaction-cost economics that he propounded began to grow. Why should an idea, which starts from a fact that seems so obvious and so much in the daylight, be left so long by economists in their dark unfathomed caves?

Coase was pointing out that *internally* firms rarely function on market principles. Within a firm or a corporation (or any kind of formal organization) much goes on that has more to do with the obedient servant than with the unremitting bargainer. Command and obedience evidently are forms of conduct that economists find problematical. Why this is so becomes clear in the contrast between neoclassical economics and its predecessor, political economy. Here follows a brief description of how chalk is not cheese.

Classical economists, often styled political economists, appear in a genealogy that includes Marx, J. S. Mill, Adam Smith, David Hume, Rousseau, Locke, Hobbes, and a legion of other political and moral philosophers. Neoclassical economic writing emerged here and there for most of the nineteenth century, in greater force about the 1870s, and began to dominate around the turn of the century, which marked a paradigmatic shift in the discipline from the study of how wealth is produced and distributed to a more narrow inquiry into the conditions that determined market equilibrium (the position at which supply and demand are balanced).

Political economists place economic activity in the context of political, religious, and familial institutions. Economic behavior is a function of institutions which both make it possible and limit its scope; thus, for example (further considered in Chapter 3), it is argued that the evolution of order-bringing institutions enabled an increase in the world's wealth. Reasoning in political economy is inductive. The method, roughly speaking, is to survey different institutions and find out what kind of economic behavior goes along with them.[1] There is also, running through the literature, a pervasive concern not only with what is now called development (how more wealth is created) but also with equity in distribution, and therefore with morality. Economic activity, in other words, is not to be explained sui generis, as a thing on its own, but as part of a larger social whole. If you wish to understand the production and distribution of wealth for the *oikos* (household) you must also understand where the state (*polis*) fits into the equation—hence *political economy*. To use more modern terms, political economy is *engaged* insofar as it is concerned with justice, and its framework models economic behavior as *embedded* in society.

The nineteenth-century neoclassical revolution in economics established a different orthodoxy, which, despite constant challenges, still dominates. It has two parts: first, microeconomic, which analyzes the relatively elemental domain of consumers, entrepreneurs, and firms; second, macroeconomic, which investigates what are assumed to be the aggregated consequences of microeconomic decisions (business cycles, national income, levels of unemployment, and the like) and which has come into the foreground since about the 1920s. My focus is mainly on microeconomic models.

In this orthodoxy, economic activity is no longer modeled as embedded; agents are imagined as unsocialized by anything except economic values. Its reasoning is deductive: one begins with a few simple assumptions about human nature and from them deduces propositions that explain or predict conduct. The assumptions are "so much the stuff of our everyday experience that they have only to be stated to be recognized as obvious" (Robbins 1937, 79). Some of these assumptions are indeed familiar parts of our everyday culture (slightly less familiar when translated into godling-terms): people want things because they derive satisfaction from them (things have *utility*); people want some things more than others (they have an *order of preference*); different things in different combinations are equally acceptable (discovered by *indifference analysis*); people use their heads to work out the most economical way to get what they want with the resources at their disposal (they are *rational economizers*); and, beyond a certain point, the more they have of something the less the incentive to get still more of it (*marginal utility*); things that have utility are by definition in short supply (economists have no interest in things that, being abundant, have no *scarcity value*), so there is *competition* for them; and this

1. That has to be an approximate description. No kind of reasoning can be purely inductive; an idea must be the starter.

competition is made orderly through *markets*, where suppliers and their customers bargain and so set prices.

These and other assumptions, put together, produce a model of *market equilibrium*, a self-adjusting economic system in which price balances supply and demand. In this way a market is an orderly system, but the order is *natural*: no one planned for it to happen. At the center of this model of a natural system is a most unnatural figure, the much derided "economic man," an omniscient market-wise individual who makes deals in his own best interests, acts in ways that he expects will maximize his utility (he *optimizes*), and has no other concerns whatsoever, being perfectly rational, unmoved by passion, and heedless alike to calls of duty or of conscience—indeed a cyborg-like creation, the fusion of a person with a yet-to-be-invented machine that cauterizes all trace of humanity.[2]

Assumptions about the market itself, although less familiar than those that concern economic man, are not entirely unknown; nor are they so readily taken as plain common sense. There is a vague awareness of Adam Smith's "invisible hand" that is said to steer the necessities of life to the poor.[3] (This is now vulgarized as *trickle-down theory*, and is applied, like a deodorant, to make the market's presence seem less unpleasant to the wretched of the earth; it also assuages the consciences of those who live high on the hog.) The modeler's concept of perfect competition, in which no one firm is large enough to dominate supply or demand and any firm can costlessly enter or leave the market, is not widely known, and, if it were, would seem like someone's fantasy (which it is). Also unfamiliar is the fact that the expected-utility model ignores the limits set on rationality by limited computational

2. I will generally identify this intellectual tool as the *expected-utility* model. The same concept, extended outside economics into other social sciences, is *rational choice*. Other common descriptors in economics are *neoclassical*, *self-interest*, *marginal utility*, *marginalist*, *market equilibrium*, and *Walrasian*. M. E. L. Walras, a Frenchman, was one of three economists who, in the 1870s, independently rediscovered the idea of marginal utility on which neoclassical economics is based. The others were W. S. Jevons, an Englishman, and an Austrian, Carl Menger. Consumer behavior modeled as marginal utility had been earlier (1847) propounded by a German, H. H. Gossen.

3. "The rich only select from the heap what is most precious and agreeable. . . . They consume little more than the poor, and in spite of their natural selfishness and rapacity . . . they divide with the poor the produce of all their improvements. They are led by an invisible hand to make nearly the same distribution of the necessaries of life which would have been made, had the earth been divided into equal portions among all its inhabitants" (Smith 1966, 264–65). A less nuanced version came from Andrew Mellon in the 1920s: "The prosperity of the lower and middle classes depends upon the good fortune and light taxes of the rich" (quoted in the *Los Angeles Times*, June 7, 1992).

For Adam Smith, who shared the benignly optimistic assumptions of most eighteenth-century Scottish moral philosophers, the "invisible hand" belonged not to the market but to God, the beneficent Creator of a well-ordered world. To speak then of what is "natural" was to speak of what God created and kept orderly. See Bryson 1968.

abilities, limited access to information, and limited diligence. The model presupposes that we are smarter and better informed and more determined than we know ourselves to be. Moral concerns—that is, a concern for the interests of other people—are excluded; so are any drives other than rational self-interest.[4] The ethical indifference of neoclassical economizing is vaguely realized outside the discipline, but is treated with resolute ambivalence, as the verdict "Business is business!" testifies. That sentence is both praise and blame, both a justification (faintly apologetic) and a condemnation.

Imagined in this way, economic behavior is *not* embedded. Moral scruples and institutional variation are in effect excluded from the model by giving them a constant value; they are put aside as "other things" that are perpetually "equal" and therefore without consequence for the model. All exchanges are transactions, all roles are economic—no parent, child, friend, foe, lover, scholar, poet, sailor, statesman, or musician, but only buyer, seller, entrepreneur, businessman, arbitrageur, broker, and the like.[5] Utility-maximization, moreover, being purportedly anchored in human nature, is found everywhere at all times. Human nature is a constant, and there is no need to factor in psychological or cultural differences. This model, excluding also the political element that was present in political economy, gives economic behavior a conceptual existence insulated from other kinds of behavior. Market equilibrium—how the price mechanism adjusts supply and demand—is the central concern, and price is a central mover in economic behavior.

Against that background, it is clear why Coase's observation that a firm consists mainly of people giving and taking orders and is not a scene of perpetual and ubiquitous bargaining, the workmen moving

4. *Rational* is used in at least three senses in this book, the context making clear which is intended. In the present instance it has the narrow meaning given it in neoclassical economics: a rational actor is one who calculates the most effective use of scarce resources to maximize returns. *Rational*, in a wider sense, refers to a fundamental philosophical assumption, which I described in the preface to this book, that there is regularity in both the natural and the social worlds, and that reason will provide an understanding of the principles governing the way those worlds work. Third, the term may be used, especially in its negative form and in argument, to dismiss a point of view on the grounds that it is not consistent with the regnant paradigm. For example, those who did not agree with Lord Robbins that his assumptions were "the stuff of our everyday experience" could be dismissed as irrational.

The assumption of omnipresent rationality (first sense) in "economic man," because it is so palpably absurd, always seems to equivocate between the status of "what is" and "what would be if the world were rational," which begs the question. I will return to this issue later.

5. A transaction is an exchange focused entirely on the goods and services involved and not at all on the status of the persons making the exchange. I will come back to this distinction later.

around "in response to changes in relative prices," might constitute at least an embarrassment for the orthodox (and dominant) segment of his fellow economists. That sentence about why workers move from one department to another highlights conduct that appears to negate the market postulate on which the expected-utility model is founded and to put the price mechanism partly out of business. It invokes institutions and organizations[6] (as opposed to markets) and is potentially a regression—or, as others might see it, an overdue reconversion—from an exclusively neoclassical economic perspective to the inelegant but more realistic inductive confusions of sociology, history, and political economy.

But, as I said, in 1937 the cat was not set among the pigeons. Coase recalls that two of his senior colleagues at the London School of Economics congratulated him the day the article appeared, but never discussed it with him. Neither Robbins, the head of the department, nor Hayek, another great luminary at that time, ever mentioned the article to him. One can assume that most 1937 economists, if they read the essay, did not see anything of great significance in it. Evidently the question that it addressed was not then in fashion.

Established authors get the kind of attention that is denied to beginners, and Coase was a beginner. In 1937, when he published the essay, he was on the first rung of the academic ladder, an assistant lecturer in economics. He may also have been seen as something of an outsider, although he does remark that his relations with his senior colleagues were "quite cordial." He had come into the discipline through the back door (a degree in commerce that trained people for "works and factory management"). He also did and said things that must have marked him as unfashionable. He had, for example, a penchant for economic ethnography: "During my time in the United States I attended very few classes and . . . most of my time was spent in visiting businesses and industrial plants" (Williamson and Winter 1991, 39).[7]

It might have been more than a mild case of academic halitosis. Ideas are sometimes dismissed because they are old hat; other ideas, which face the future or confront the present, may be rejected because

6. Both these words refer to regular ways of cooperating. *Organizations* are groups deliberately set up to accomplish something specific—a judicial system, a university, a sports club, a bank, a firm, and so on. *Institutions* are sets of values and beliefs that underlie cooperative activity and give rise to groups that are conventionally seen to have intrinsic value, as is the case with families or communities, which also are sometimes called institutions.

7. There is a hint of an "attitude" in an aside made in a 1987 lecture. Recalling two books that Joan Robinson had published in 1933, Coase said: "This new theoretical apparatus had the advantage that one could cover the blackboard with diagrams and fill the hour of one's lectures without the need to find out anything about what happened in the real world" (Williamson and Winter 1991, 52).

they make people feel uneasy. "The Nature of the Firm" seems to have had a faint odor of subversion. It opens with a statement (quoting Joan Robinson) to the effect that one should ask of a "set of assumptions in economics" not only "Are they tractable?" (that is, suitable for logico-numerical manipulation) but also "Do they correspond with the real world?" In a lecture delivered in 1987, Coase remarks, "Most readers will pass over these opening sentences (Putterman omits them when reprinting my article), and others will excuse what they read as a youthful mistake, believing, as so many modern economists do, that we should choose our theories on the basis of the accuracy of their predictions, the realism of their assumptions being utterly irrelevant." Coase promptly rejects that view and adds, somewhat caustically, "In effect what this comes down to is that when economists find that they are unable to analyze what is happening in the real world, they invent an imaginary world which they are capable of handling" (Williamson and Winter 1991, 52).[8]

Coase's venture into the real world to find out why firms exist produced an explanation that (from outside neoclassical confines) looks as disarmingly simple as the primary observation (workers take orders) that started the question. Neoclassical economists, Coase points out, had constructed their models of market equilibrium on the assumption that transactions had no cost. Materials had a cost, labor had a cost, capital had a cost, but the cost of getting information to get access to materials, labor, and capital could be ignored. On the contrary, Coase insists, these costs are significant, and they are the reason why firms come into being. Information is not free. "There is a cost of using the price mechanism," because, at the very least, you have the expense of finding out what the price is (1937, 390). Negotiating a deal has a cost. To put the matter very simply, firms exist because, certain other conditions being the case, it is more economical to make a contract with, say, employees to pay an agreed wage for an agreed range of tasks, than to bargain with them every time something has to be done. In other words, management is open to economies of scale of that particular kind. Package deals are cheaper; that is why firms come into being and that is how hierarchical behavior can be built into economic models.[9]

8. The reference could include his colleague at the University of Chicago, another Nobel laureate, Milton Friedman. The latter's vigorous apologia for "unrealistic" assumptions will be considered later.

Joan Robinson had sold the pass with the remark that tractable models were generally not realistic, and realistic models were rarely tractable.

9. One elaboration of Coase's arguments, begun in the 1970s, has focused not so much on employer-employee interactions as on the vertical integration of firms, interpreted

Notice that this contractual frame of reference, besides being obvious to the layman in a world of publicized negotiations between corporations and unions, does not eliminate the central character in neoclassical microeconomics—the rational, self-interested bargainer. There is no need to factor morality as a motive into the model: enlightened self-interest does the job sufficiently. People are moved by what they calculate will be best for themselves. A stage of bargaining between employer and employee is concluded when each considers they have the best deal possible. In this model, market behavior is still the moving force. A firm is, so to speak, nothing more than a market legally (and temporarily) stabilized at a point of equilibrium. Not only is the economic perspective still in place, but its grasp appears to have been extended by converting an organization (the firm) into a rational bargainer in a marketplace and/or itself into an intermittent marketplace for negotiating contracts between the boss and his underlings.

In this light, the Coase recension (transaction-cost economics) seems quite modest. The recipe he offered should have been attractive enough to his fellow economists. But more than thirty years went by before it got into the cookbooks, and even now transaction-cost economics is often found in the exotica section, along with behavioral economics, evolutionary economics, institutional economics, and the like.

Then why did the process take so long? Evidently (to stay with the idiom), a change would have incurred transaction costs. The political costs that go with altering a paradigm are well known. Horses may win races not because they are fastest but because their owners have influence off the track. The owners of existing paradigms have a vested interest in them; they penalize heterodoxy, if only by ignoring it or insulting it. Lionel Robbins used the following phrases in speaking of the institutional economics of his time and of various other related matters that roused his ire: "incredible banalities," "spineless platitudes," "tedious discussions," "amateur technology," "thoroughly unscientific and question-begging," "trite generalizations," "insufferable dreariness and mediocrity," and a variety of other pejoratives.[10]

Exogenous factors (such as the prestige and temperament of Lord Robbins) are obviously important, and on occasions they are decisive,

---

as a device to exclude the uncertainty of market operations from production (and so lower the cost). See Williamson and Winter 1991 and Moe 1984.

10. Taken from the first edition of Robbins 1932 and quoted by Coase in Williamson and Winter 1991 (52–53). See pp. 65 and 70 of the later edition (Robbins 1937), from which the author had "endeavoured to eliminate certain manifestations of high spirits no longer in harmony with present moods" (1937, xiii). The "high spirits" could hardly be written off as youthful exuberance; he was thirty-seven when he first published that book.

but they are not my present concern. My focus is on the neoclassical model and what is subsumed in it that might explain why Coase's essay failed to start an immediate debate. One possibility is that his work threatened to uncover unmentionables that had been hidden behind the fig leaf of "other things being equal." *Ceteris paribus* signifies things known to vary and to have an effect in the real world, but intentionally held constant (and therefore without input) when constructing a model. The implication of the phrase is that, in other cases, the value could be different. But in fact those other cases are never considered. In the construction of a straightforward expected-utility model, variables that concern, for example, ethics, or the distribution of information, or human frailty do not have the status of variables held equal but are perpetually excluded. At the same time, the formulaic and magical phrase "other things being equal" draws attention away from the fact of exclusion. (It is a way to create the economists' "imaginary world" that Coase derided.) Nineteenth-century economists, when theories failed to make correct predictions because certain factors had escaped notice, domesticated them as "disturbing causes" (Blaug 1992, 75).

To put it another way, the conditional status of ceteris paribus is easily forgotten, and things that are held equal for the model are quietly transformed and presented as things that actually are equal. In other words, they are marked as external factors that in reality (so it is assumed) have nothing to do with the process being modeled. These complexities, concealed in god-terms, would, if generally advertised, discredit the model by questioning its right to be considered positive science. The god-terms themselves, subsuming what might have been questionable, serve as protective devices.

Transaction costs were a complexity that neoclassical economists chose to disregard, until Coase came onto the scene. Their models were constructed on the presupposition that transactions are cost-free. This raises a general question. Should presuppositions be realistic, as Coase insisted? Or is that irrelevant, which is the position of "so many modern economists"? At issue is the status of economics as a positive science, a maker of propositions that can be tested by experience.

## Unrealistic Assumptions and Positive Science

Coase talked of an "imaginary world" that is created for orthodox economic theory when that theory fails to work in the real world. Its predictions fail, he argued, when its assumptions are unrealistic. His target was the axiom of costless transactions; businessmen know that transactions have costs and, when they think it will pay them, they set up firms in order to lessen those costs. If you assume that transactions are costless, you cannot account for the existence of firms.

The argument that unrealistic assumptions disqualify a theory was vigorously contested (not with direct reference to Coase, but in general) by Milton Friedman in an essay published in 1953, "The Methodology of Positive Economics."[11] This essay is a programmatic rather than substantive exercise, and it carries the message that "positive economics is, or can be, an 'objective' science, in precisely the same sense as any of the physical sciences" (4). Friedman wrote: ". . . the only relevant test of the *validity* of a hypothesis is comparison of its predictions with experience" (8–9). "Truly important and significant hypotheses will be found to have 'assumptions' that are wildly inaccurate descriptive representations of reality . . ." (14). How is it possible for "wildly inaccurate descriptive representations of reality" to produce accurate predictions for that same reality? Friedman has an answer. A model (Friedman uses *hypothesis*) is a generalizing instrument. It assigns an essence to a variety of particular situations, and its value, as a tool for reasoning, lies in this generality. The variety of particular instances is homogenized and transformed into a generalization by *abstracting* from particular situations the elements or forces that are relevant to whatever is to be explained. An abstraction is, by definition, an incomplete and therefore unrealistic description of reality. The logic of this (Friedman does not state it in so many words) is that *all* assumptions must be unrealistic, and if models are generated from assumptions, and some models lead to correct and others to incorrect predictions, then the realism of assumptions could not predetermine which model would be correct and which would not. Therefore unrealistic assumptions can capture the essence of reality.

This is a rhetorical shell game. The trick is done by amphiboly—by exploiting the ambiguity between *unrealistic* in the sense of *abstract* (a selective and therefore incomplete version of some reality), and *unrealistic* in the sense of *false* (misleading), highlighting the former and suppressing the latter. All assumptions (like all statements) are unrealistic in that they are abstracted from a more extensive reality. Essences, to go back to John Barth, have to be assigned; otherwise there can be no communication. So features that are present in reality (Friedman's favorite example is the color of a businessman's eyes) may be omitted from the model, because prima facie eye color has nothing to do with economic decisions. But ethical scruples, which also are present in reality, are omitted from the expected-utility model, al-

11. Some departments of economics, I am told, still use this essay for their students as a kind of catechism, a set of basic principles to be learned by every young economist before he or she can be confirmed in the neoclassical faith.

though prima facie considerations of honesty or concern for the welfare of others could have something to do with how decisions to deploy economic resources are made. The assumption that economic decisions are invariably made without reference to such matters is not just incomplete (an abstraction from a more complex reality); it may also be misleading, because, unlike eye color, ethical feelings may be relevant to understanding the decisions that a businessman makes.

How do we know that eye color is not relevant? Friedman would answer, presumably, in a positivist manner, saying that its lack of predictive capacities is open to empirical testing. But that is not the issue. The issue is what consequences follow from disregarding attributes (like considerations of right and wrong) that prima facie do have predictive relevance to the problem being investigated. Do unrealistic assumptions impair the usefulness of a model for which they are the basis?

It depends on what the problem is. If the issue is solely the link between a particular decision and its *consequences*, then any assumptions about how the decision was reached are irrelevant. The businessman's motives are not an element in the problem. If, however, the problem is to find out what determines one decision rather than another, then a realistic assessment of understandings and motivation is required. Friedman makes a distinction between *validity* and *applicability*, arguing that the significance of assumptions is not that they predetermine the validity of a model; what they do is decide where it will apply and where it will not. That is correct, but there is a consequence that Friedman does not draw. Robbins (1937, 39) put it neatly: "[A theory's] applicability to the interpretation of any particular situation depends upon the existence in that situation of the elements postulated." If a theory based on an assumption of self-interest is applied to a situation in which altruism reigns, then the theory will not produce an accurate prediction. That does not mean, Friedman argues, that the theory is invalid, only that it has been incorrectly applied. The failure lies in the application. Only a fool tries to knock in a nail with a saw.

But, it should also be said, if the "elements postulated" are unrealistic (in the sense of being a misleading fantasy or an empirical falsity), they do not exist and could not be used to determine the applicability of the theory to which they belong. If a theory rests on the assumption of a perfectly informed, perfectly rational businessman, and if there is no such entity, then the theory can never be tested because the element postulated nowhere exists. Theories that rest on the assumption of perfect information, costless transactions, or the unremitting effort implied in "maximizing," could similarly never be discredited, because there is nowhere to test them. Theories then would be unsinkable.

Every time they appeared to get a prediction wrong, that would be because they had been inappropriately applied. Of course they could still be pronounced valid, providing one separates validity from applicability (which my dictionaries do not—more on this later).

Friedman's argument is thus flawed, so far as it concerns a *positive* science (a science in which propositions are empirically testable). Having distinguished between validity and applicability, he then confuses the issue and thus conceals the plain irrelevance to positive science of a theory that is theoretically "valid" but can nowhere be demonstrated to be applicable. If the assumptions are manifestly unrealistic (in the sense of being false) and yet the theory which is based on them appears to produce accurate predictions, then either (1) the logic connecting assumptions with outcome is erroneous, or (2) some other assumptions hold in that situation (which means the theory has not been put to the test), or (3) a miracle has occurred, or (4) the assumptions were not unrealistic after all.

The logic of Coase's position is that if the assumptions are unrealistic, the model is never applicable and therefore never testable, and any theoretical validity it has is of no practical significance. Friedman is formally correct in saying that application in the wrong place does indeed leave the theory intact. But it is intact only so long as it is never given substance and used for prediction or explanation in the real world. If it is not empirically testable, however, it does not fall within the definition of positive economics. It would remain "pure" economics— that is, the economics of an imaginary world, in which propositions could be falsified only on the grounds of mistaken logic.[12]

Friedman's defense of unrealistic postulates is derived from the common distinction between positive economics, which makes propositions that are empirically testable in the real world, and economics as an "art" (the word has nothing to do with aesthetics but refers to the practical application of rules generated by positive theories). Positive

12. In a strident, confused, and frequently boorish review of a book on economic anthropology, Frank H. Knight writes that economics is an "exposition of principles . . . which have little more relation to empirical data of any sort than do those of elementary mathematics." Principles are required for "any intelligent or useful exposition of facts" but facts need not have "actuality," so long as they are "realistically illustrative" (in Herskovits 1960 [1952], 516). What the difference is between "actuality" and "realistically" is not made clear.

Robbins, Friedman, and especially Knight, in separating "principles" from the reality they organize and make comprehensible, seem sometimes to be regretting the necessity for economics to be a positive science, which inevitably requires a descent from pure form. J. M. Keynes, more influential in his time than any of those three, was not in the least confused about the issue. He wrote (in 1938) of economics as "a branch of logic," and "a way of thinking," and dismissed attempts to turn the discipline into a "pseudo-natural science." "[E]conomics is essentially a moral science and not a natural science. That is to say, it employs introspection and judgments of value" (quoted in Blaug 1992, 79).

economics, he writes, work with *as if* assumptions, which by definition need not be realistic, although the predictions or explanations derived from them may be realistic. But there is no way of knowing that the predictions are realistic except by empirical means, that is by experiment, which is itself a form of economic "art."[13] That procedure brings the "as if" into the real world, where it may be shown to be misleading (people are not, to repeat the examples, always self-interested and transactions are never costless) and to be the reason why a prediction was in error.

There is a final fallback defense for the usefulness of unrealistic assumptions, which takes the discussion to another level where economic behavior is modeled as truly a natural system. Friedman remarks, derisively, that he does not believe that businessmen apply their minds to "multivariable functions showing marginal cost and marginal revenue" (15) and so maximize their returns. He must be correct; most of them probably work out unit cost and add a percentage. But, Friedman continues, what businessmen say goes on in their minds is neither here nor there. The point is that if they did not maximize revenue over costs they would not be able to stay in business. Since some of them do stay in business, they must be following the maximizing principle, even if they cannot be articulate about it. This is *substantive* rationality; it models the results of a decision without regard to the *procedures* followed to make it.[14] The market (as modeled) is such that competition leaves a businessman only the choice between bankruptcy and maximizing. A process of natural selection eliminates those who do not maximize; therefore maximization, even if it does not have psychological reality in the minds of entrepreneurs, does have an objective or positive reality.[15] It is a description of what goes on in the real world, and what goes on in the minds of businessmen is irrelevant (22).

The short answer is that this is *not* what goes on in the real world. Some people stay in business for reasons other than fortuitous maximization of returns. They bribe, or they have political power, or they are born into the right caste, or for a variety of reasons they may

13. In the word "art" I think he has in mind the role of economists advising politicians, administrators, and businessmen. Validation (or falsification), which separates positive from pure theory, also arranges an encounter between a theory and the real world, but under conditions in which the parameters can be better controlled than in the world of practical politics: experiments in vitro, so to speak, rather than in vivo. I will return to questions of practice and theory in the final chapter.

14. The distinction between *substantive* and *procedural* rationality is taken from Simon 1976.

15. In other words, successful businessmen are like M. Jourdain: they tacitly enact the model that Friedman makes articulate.

choose to continue operating the enterprise even when its marginal
economic returns are negative. We must agree with the tautology: the
survivors are likely to be those who, whether knowingly or not, do
whatever is needed to survive. But the question is not only about the
consequences of decisions, it is also about how those decisions came to
be made. Accepting the natural selection argument effectively puts microeconomics and the rational entrepreneur out of business. The
theory grants that there may indeed be decision makers but gives
their process of reasoning no significance in predicting what will happen or in explaining what has happened.

This is surely the ultimate natural science framework. It transforms
*persons* making decisions and acting on those decisions into *things* that
move, willy-nilly, in the direction of survival or extinction at the behest
of implacable and uncaring natural forces. The actors may imagine
they are free agents, that they and their fellows have designed and can
rationally redesign the institutions under which they live, but the
reality (according to this model) is that institutions are to be understood as the chance outcome of a process of natural selection. They
are not the result of rational planning.[16]

That may be the case. But it is also the case that we behave as if our
decisions and our designs have consequences, as if there is a real
world in which people make sense of their experiences and decide
what should be done. In going about our daily lives we believe that
human intentions count for something, even if we are patently not
masters of our fate. To an extent, that too may be the case. Certainly it
can safely, but vacuously, be asserted that, other things being equal,
the nonmaximizer is more likely to go bust than is the maximizer. Until one knows what the other things are, the proposition has no application in the real world. It can also be argued that economic systems
are not as exposed to the hazards of natural selection as biological organisms. Economic actors, at least in the short run, learn from experience how to manipulate a collective destiny. What they learn, how
they acquire and process information, and how they use it are elements disregarded both in the simple evolutionary model and in the
optimizer model.

Since the rise of the neoclassical paradigm to hegemony in the discipline of economics, there have been, both within and outside the neoclassical ramparts, debates about its adequacy. There is, in fact, a large

16. Ex cathedra statements of this position, briefly discussed in my concluding chapter, are found in many of Hayek's writings. See 1988 and 1991.

combative literature.[17] Political commentary on issues of power and questions about who benefited from the use of the utility-maximizing model came mainly from beyond the neoclassical boundary; so also did doubts about one-dimensional "economic man," the person motivated solely by his own advantage. I will come to that later.

The issues that have been raised from within the pale (renegades excepted—see note 17) have mainly been directed at *substantive rationality*: How much can one assume that entrepreneurs know about the world in which they operate, how accurate is their information, how do they get access to it, how efficiently do they process it, and what competitive use do they make of it? The Coase recension is of that kind, and in the next two chapters I will follow some of the trails which it opened.

17. The "distance-from-reality" criticism is splendidly illustrated in a debate between Milton Friedman and Walter Heller (Friedman and Heller 1969). Here are some examples: "[I]f Milton's policy prescription were made in a frictionless Friedmanesque world—a world of his own making—it would be more admissible" (26). Friedman himself sat firmly astride the fence. Here is his comment on a paper about tax cuts: "It's a very interesting paper; it's a fine thing to have done. I think we ought to have more such examinations. But if you examine what he did, you will find what he has is an illustrative calculation of, not evidence on, the importance of the tax cut" (55). Or "[T]he widespread faith in the potency of fiscal policy . . . rests on no evidence whatsoever. It is based on pure assumption. It is based on a priori reasoning" (53).

Convenient access to insider debates is through Blaug 1992. Renegades are well represented by McCloskey (1985 and 1998), who provides, from within the neoclassical camp, a superb example of antipositivist attack rhetoric.

# Chapter 2

# The Coase Recension and Its Lineage

> *The solution . . . was very simple. All that was needed was to recognize that there were costs to carrying out market transactions . . . something which economists had failed to do.*
>
> —Ronald Coase, *"The Nature of the Firm: Meaning"*

## The New Economics of Organization

Coase, in the epigraph above, identifies one specific way in which the neoclassical expected-utility scheme failed to confront reality. He proposed a remedy, which is the idea of contract, and out of this grew a branch of economics that was later identified as the New Economics of Organization (NEO).[1] In this chapter I will explain the remedy and ask what failings it, in turn, has. To a small and largely unadmitted extent, when Coase introduced the idea of contract, he put in question the stark amorality of the imagined rational economizer. Contract implies conduct directed not only by wealth maximization but also by ideas of right and wrong. Morality thus makes a small incursion into the domain of neoclassical economics.

To show this, let me first recall the principal features of the expected-utility model. Robbins, with masterful brevity, defined neoclassical economics as "the science which studies human behavior as a relationship between ends and scarce means which have alternative uses" (1937, 16). The definition takes for granted the discipline's epistemological status: it is a positive science, which aims not only to be exact, but also to account for experience in the real world. It is value-free; its propositions are about means to ends, and the ends are already given.

The model assumes a natural system. Natural science is organized knowledge about *things*. Things do not think, choose, or feel emotions.

---

1. I have taken this appellation from the title of an essay by Terry Moe (1984).

The framework can be adapted for the study of people, so long as it excludes certain features that are manifestly experienced in the real world, for example, our limited computational capacity. We are not omniscient; we make decisions not only without thinking matters through, but also without having the information to do so, even if we had the computational capacity or were determined enough to make the effort. In the behavioral recension of neoclassical economics, limited computational capacity came to be called *bounded rationality*.

Other parts of our experience also are ignored. The conduct of economic optimizers is not influenced by conscience (in particular by a concern for the well-being of others). Nor do they worry about dignity or self-respect or have any wish to be recognized as persons, intrinsically valued (as distinct from things, which are instrumentally valued). They have no need for companionship. Love has no place in the model; neither does malevolence nor the desire for revenge. In fundamentalist neoclassical models all these features, indicators of our humanity, are ignored. The expected-utility model, which is the Zeus-concept of the neoclassical pantheon, posits an agent from whom no significant information is hidden, who uses information rationally and tirelessly, and whose single motivation is self-interest interpreted usually as material well-being or control over material assets. An individual's conduct can be sufficiently understood without taking into account moral choice, self-respect, affections, animosities, weariness, or limited information. Agents, all omniscient, are moved *only* by a drive to compete for prizes, such as power, prestige, or (most often) wealth.

If that is so, behavior can be modeled as a function of the opportunities available for gaining those prizes. But that very model—the economic automaton—opens the way to its own denial. One has only to ascend from the rational flatlands of self-regulating equilibrium systems a little way up the magic mountain, which represents reality, to realize that one could control agents' behavior by controlling their information about opportunities, or, in other words, by making sure they knew enough about carrots and sticks. To think of control is, ipso facto, to think of institutions or organizations, of Coase's firm, and of workers doing what the boss tells them to do. To think that way is also to admit that the model of a self-regulating market economy as a natural system does not correspond with reality. The market is at the mercy of those who control opportunities—themselves opportunists, manipulators, free spirits, intentioned human beings—whose conduct is not subsumable under any natural system. It is also to center attention on the distribution of information, on the costs of transacting, and, through the notion of control, on hierarchy and organization.

"Transaction cost economics examines alternative forms of economic organization with reference to their capacity to economize on bounded rationality while simultaneously safeguarding the transactions in question against the hazards of opportunism" (Williamson and Winter 1991, 105).

Thus emerges NEO, which is also called the *contractual model of organizations*. Its central concern, in a crude and limiting translation of the definition given above, is how to run a business successfully when you, the boss, don't know enough about what the workers are up to and the workers, by definition, are unimpeded by conscience or a sense of duty (in the neoclassical terminology, they are *rational*). Or, in another organizational setting, how are shareholders going to keep watch over a manager, when they do not have the expertise or the information to prevent him cutting himself a bigger share of the profits than they think he deserves?

To make sense of such situations, models were constructed of the interaction between two sticklike figures, *principal* and *agent*. The principal stands for the organization itself; the agent is its servant or employee. Thus the relationship between them is hierarchical and, in the model, it is based on a *contract*. Principal and agent bargain with each other over the description of the agent's job, penalties for unsatisfactory performance, the principal's obligations concerning conditions of work and remuneration, and the like, all of them quite complicated matters. The encounter is marketplace-adversarial, but only until a bargain is struck and a contract agreed. At that point (in the model) each party has achieved what it hopes is the best deal possible, and then they both are expected to cooperate in accomplishing whatever it is that the organization exists to do. In that hypothetical postcontractual quiescence, principals act (they make decisions) and the agents merely move as the principals indicate, having covenanted to do so "within certain limits" (Coase 1937, 391).

Principal and agent, as I said, are in an hierarchical relationship. *Hierarchy* in the economist's world is strangely used; it is not something that has to do with duty, conscience, or morality. A *command* relationship (in this context a less misleading term than *hierarchy*, which strongly—and ironically in the context of economics—connotes the sacred) is the outcome of a bargain that furthers the interests of each contracting party. The relationship is thus not an end in itself, not a matter of duty. The agents, who receive the orders, obey them to the extent that they believe it pays them to do so. Thus, by modeling the relationship as a form of contract, one puts a protective fence around the presupposition of economic individualism (with the principal standing in, as a quasi-individual, for the organization). Individualism—

the old Adam—is preserved, moreover, not only in bargaining to make contracts but also in cheating on them.

## Holes in the Fence: Contract

It would follow (cheating apart—I will come to that later) that a properly adjusted organization could function internally on market principles. A contract, which is the outcome of bargaining, would make that possible. An organization, in other words, could work as a natural system, impersonally, like a machine. The machine's parts (agents) would perform their functions not for ethical reasons (because they had promised to do so) but because they were hardwired to seek their own advantage and so, being rational, could not do (that is, could not afford to do) other than what they had concluded would benefit them most. Management of personnel then becomes basically a matter of adjusting rewards, negative and positive; a managed-incentive context is functionally identical with a command. Because their options are limited, articulated in a single register, agents can readily be made to do what the principal wants them to do. In this scenario, morally neutered agents, being motivated by their own advantage, have again become things, not persons. They have wants in the same sense that a plant wants water or fire wants air. Ethics are entirely off the board. Agents are not doing what is right or wrong; they do what is expedient. They have no option (if they are rational) but to conform with a context that is set by others. In other words, their very rationality transforms them into things.

That portrayal certainly fits a large part of human conduct, and to that extent the model is applicable in everyday life. People are used as instruments, and they know it, and, to a greater or lesser degree, they acquiesce. They do what the boss tells them in order to get paid on payday and to avoid being sacked. Machinelike predictability, potentially disturbed by the image of manipulative principals, appears to have been restored at least in the case of the manipulated agent. So far, so good.

But if the model is to be convincing, it must explain why the idea of *duty* as a service performed without asking for payment should not also be applicable to the dealings between principal and agent. Economics, as a positivist science, purports to model processes that go on in the real world. To frame the exchange between principal and agent as a contract appears to eliminate ethical considerations; in effect, the model says, people may talk of conscience and duty, but in reality their minds are on self-interest. What is the evidence that this is the case? What "complexities" are subsumed in the term *contract*? That line of inquiry points in three directions, all of which, when followed, embarrass the expected-utility paradigm that still underlies the Coase recension. They do not invalidate it; they point up its limited applicability.

One inquiry leads to the institution of contract. A moment's reflection shows that a contract is more than a promise. It is a promise that, if broken, will bring in a third party as redresser and/or penalizer: contract entails enforcement. Enforcement, certainly, would not be required if conscience alone directed human interaction, and therefore, since enforcers are needed, the expected-utility framework must be at least partly correct in hypothesizing agents as self-interested and morally neutered. But further reflection, on who does the enforcing, leads to complexities. The law of contract inheres in the law of property, which inheres in constitutional law, which inheres in the state. Thus emerges a complex of institutional frameworks that are not within the reach of the expected-utility paradigm. The wall that encloses that paradigm and protects it from having to incorporate institutions as a variable has then been breached. The market model stands revealed as less than adequate, because institutions are inescapably involved in the process by which a contract is supposed to convert a sense of duty into some tractable form of utility.

All models, however, have limited application and there is always a point at which an inquiry may be handed over to another team. The legal framework in which contract is embedded can quite legitimately be shelved and left for another occasion or for another person to make another kind of inquiry that is different from, but complementary to, the problem addressed by the expected-utility model.

The contractual theory of organizations has other weaknesses. Certain variables that are involved in the purported conversion from duty to utility are left unconsidered. Contract, as I said, has two elements: a promise and its enforcement. The contractual theory of organizations contemplates only enforcement. But *promise* has a vapor trail of notions like conscience and self-respect, which clearly are in complementary distribution with the need for enforcement; the more of one the less the need for the other. Why do some promises need less backup than others? Surely it is because some people are known to keep their promises, even when they lose by doing so. But to think along those lines is to question one of the supposedly self-evident propositions from which the expected-utility model is deduced: that of the self-interested optimizer. There is a problem here that is concealed by the legal-rational connotations that the word *contract* has.[2]

---

2. *Contract* excludes, or at least minimizes, notions of the sacred. Agreements that are sanctioned not by the threat of litigation but by conscience or by the thought of divine

Third, contract in practice is not the quietus that the simple version of the model makes it out to be. There are continuing problems with *postcontractual opportunism*, which arises from *incomplete contracting*. Opportunism is defined by Oliver Williamson (an influential voice in the generation that followed Coase) as "a deep condition of self-interest seeking that contemplates guile" (Williamson and Winter 1991, 92). He adds: "Promises to behave responsibly that are unsupported by credible commitments will not, therefore, be reliably discharged."[3] The nature of these "credible commitments," as you will see in a moment, shows just how difficult NEO scholars find it to keep the rational optimizer unpolluted by moral sentiments.

The opportunities for "guile" arise from the nature of contracting. A contract is a forward-looking document that anticipates future events, not only specifying rewards and penalties for performance and nonperformance, but also taking into account contingencies that may make it difficult for one party or the other to hold to their promise. Uncertainties about the future, in other words, make it inevitable that all contracts, to a greater or lesser degree, must be tainted by being incomplete. Therefore some mechanism that will deal with these contingencies—fill in the gaps that come to light—is needed. This is provided by the concept of *residual rights of control*. Each party may claim residual rights to a service that would have been specified in the original contract, if only the parties had known (and agreed) that it would be needed.

Under what conditions is either party likely to grant the other residual rights? After all, the holder of those rights has "within limits" a blank check, for in the nature of the case the rights cannot be closely specified beforehand. There is a clear and obvious answer. Someone who has a reputation for fair dealing will more readily be granted the rights than will a shyster, a person known to be given to opportunism. With that sentence the discourse has outgrown the expected-utility framework and moved toward morality. The reputation that makes incomplete contracting acceptable is a reputation for keeping one's promises, doing one's duty, and following one's conscience.

One could, of course, open a faux debate and insist that a reputation is nothing but a form of capital and could even be measured in

retribution are *covenants*. The word, once used for any kind of formal agreement, has fallen out of use except when framed by the law or by religion. It is often marked by the adjective *solemn*.

3. Hobbes said it too, in 1651. "If a covenant be made, wherein neither of the parties perform presently, but trust one another; in the condition of mere nature, which is the condition of war of every man against every man, upon any reasonable suspicion, it is void: but if there be a common power set over them both, with right and force sufficient to compel performance, it is not void" (1946, 89).

monetary terms as equivalent to the bond that a person who lacked the reputation would have to put down. For sure, a good reputation is an asset; it is even, within limits, fungible: one can cash in on it. But it also has intrinsic value, and its defining feature is not that of a commodity: a reputation is not readily transferable from one person to another. Iago, a hypocrite for sure, nevertheless was right when he said, "Who steals my purse, steals trash . . . But he that filches from me my good name / Robs me of that which not enriches him, / And makes me poor indeed."

## Holes in the Fence: Principals

Agents, in practice, do not behave in a machinelike way. Agent motivations cannot realistically be homogenized as rational self-interest. There are significant residues of altruism and self-respect; ideas of fairness or obligation; sometimes an attitude of "couldn't care less"; and, no doubt, also feelings of resentment and animosity. Principals are even more flawed, for it is never clear in the model whether they serve themselves or the organization. It is clear, however, that *principal* and *agent* cannot refer to individuals They are roles that, like masks, can be put on and taken off by one and the same person.

Principals, who are the initiators of contracts, have *bounded rationality*; they cannot foresee, any more than agents can, all the contingencies that might arise. For them, too, contracting is always incomplete, and if the system is to work it requires continuous ad hoc decision making after the initial contract has been agreed. This lack of omniscience would be externalized in a pure neoclassical model, because attending to it would remove the model from the protective ambiance of its imaginary world and subject it to reality testing. In transaction-cost models, however, the same features are a central concern: How should the principal best cope with agents who are (by definition) motivated to act in their own interest (pursue their own *subgoals*) to the disadvantage of the principal and the organization?

NEO theorists write about principals and agents in the manner of an engineer advising a client on how to create conditions that will allow a machine to work efficiently. In doing so they appear to ally themselves with the principals against the agents, typically with the bosses against their underlings. Principals are advised how best to control agents. This is so whether the agents are workers on the shop floor putting in "the fix," or bureaucrats running rings round their political masters, or corrupt self-serving representatives dishing hapless voters, or CEOs giving themselves rewards that leave their shareholders aghast. *Incentive alignment*, putting *slack* to good use, and other devices (to be described later) that reward behavior desired by the principal (and good for the organization) are all intended to strengthen the hand of the manager (against the worker), the politician (against the bureaucrat), the constituent (against the politician), and the investor (against the manager) by limiting (in the thoroughly neoclassical fashion of material rewards and punishments) the options of "servants" who are behaving rationally, as the model assumes they will behave—looking after themselves at the expense of their masters.[4]

This is an unequivocal *practical* position, given that the theorists are on the side of those in authority. But as a *theoretical* position, it is distinctly equivocal. Market behavior and institutional behavior are defined as contraries and mutually incompatible; the theory advances them both. It advocates market-dependent tactics in order to engineer an equilibrium position that will eliminate further market behavior; equilibrium indicates that a deal has been struck, whether or not the market has cleared itself, and bargaining is at an end. The theorists are being loyal to the model of an impersonal self-regulating system by suggesting ways in which adjustments at the interface between the machine and its environment will make it work better. But in doing so they are admitting that the system is not impersonal, not *naturally* self-regulating; it requires supervision.

If one asks who benefits from enhanced productivity, the answer must be that the principal, standing for the firm or the organization, is the intended beneficiary of the tactics that are recommended. It is not, however, simply the case that principals are individuals who benefit materially. *Principal* is an ambiguous concept. The principal, sometimes construed as an individual and a competitor in a marketplace, at other times represents the hierarchy, the organization. The whole point of various tactics described below is to advance external control over, and remove autonomy from, the economizing individual, the old Adam (in effect removing his neoclassical "natural" right to cheat). To the extent that this succeeds, the effect is to diminish the expected-utility model and the hegemony of the market, while elevating regulatory institutions and the postulate of hierarchy.

The principal's tutelary position—the fact that *principal* must be a synonym for *organization* or *institution*—can be reached by deduction. The model of an organization as a machine is itself defective, because it ignores a defining feature of the concept: *machines do not build themselves.* Think of the hierarchy of principals and agents in an organization. The person who is a principal is himself an agent for the principal

---

4. The justification, paradoxically for a model that is rooted in raw old-Adam individualism, is that of any social-contract theorist: that everyone benefits if the system works in an orderly fashion and people obey the rules.

next above him in the chain of command, and so on, all the way to the top, where there must be a principal who is *not* part of the mechanism, but is the machine's designer.[5] Moreover, working downwards, at every step in the chain of command some redesigning and interpreting of a general rule to fit particular situations is likely to be needed, because things go wrong and people try to fix them. In that case every agent becomes part designer and therefore part person (in effect part principal), and ceases to be a mere thing. Discretionary power, the power to deal constructively with what has not been foreseen—a kind of power that is not found in a machine—is manifested at every level, and when it is not accommodated in the model the whole apparatus, predictions as well as postulates, is shifted into an imaginary world.

The NEO framework thus appears to allow for the exercise of discretionary power, that is, persons who control and adjust the machine. The NEO focus is on ways in which power might be used to make the system work more predictably and more efficiently than it otherwise would. The ideal natural system of the orthodox neoclassical framework has thus become a managed system and to that extent is no longer natural. The pendulum swings away from the "natural" equilibrium of a system to the ways in which controlling individuals can fix an "equilibrium" at a point which is advantageous to themselves. That they will attempt to do so is taken for granted in the concept of the rational economizing individual.

The contractual recension thus has its problems. It is internally incoherent. The term *principal* seems to contain a denial of economic rationality, and, as earlier became clear, there are corresponding difficulties with *contract*. Some of these features—more will emerge later—are Bentham's *res tegendae* (things that have to be hidden if the model is not to lose credibility).[6]

## How Holes Are Plugged

NEO theorists solved two neoclassical problems by abandoning the axiom of costless information and acknowledging bounded rationality. They did not, however, abandon (did not even modify) the axiom of the utility-expecting market-person. The axiom of self-interest remained intact, and its behavioral manifestations, together with their "remedies," became centers of NEO attention. Remedies are needed because people are opportunistic; they cheat. But there is no room for

5. This is a variant of the First Cause argument for the existence of God. *Principal*, as will become clear, is endowed in NEO discourse, surely inadvertently, with some quasi-divine features. The same is true of *economic man*, insofar as he has no human weaknesses.
6. See Larrabee 1952.

the concept of *cheating,* in the normal sense of that word, in a natural-systems model, which, from the outset, strips the scene of all ethical notions.

This lacuna is apparent in the concept *slack.* Slack is in use when a higher principal encourages a lesser principal to ride closer herd over agents by allowing him/her to keep for his/her own use (give them *marketable title* to) a percentage of the savings that the more efficient supervision generates. (An example, which antedates the present use of the term *slack,* is tax-farming.) Slack, regarded as an incentive, is wholly in accord with the neoclassical axiom that optimizers are unhampered by scruples. It is a purported solution for *information asymmetry* (more on that later), its object being to encourage more efficient monitoring. Slack recognizes, as does all NEO theory, that there is a problem with the distribution of information. But notice that slack leaves untouched the realm of duty and conscience; the word carries with it a casual dismissal of ethical considerations. The metaphor points in two directions. In one, the overseer is "taking up the slack" in the feedback mechanism; in the other, his superiors are "cutting him some slack" by letting him keep a percentage of what his efforts bring in. Neither version picks up moral implications, for example, that such devices can result in exploitation and other inequities. Those possibilities are externalized, that is, the costs that fall on those who do not profit from the activity—in the present case they may be actively victimized by it—are excluded from consideration in the model.[7]

The persuasive devices considered in the previous chapter are cerebral: they identify a problem and provide a form of reasoning in which the problem can be made to disappear. For example, if the economic system is a natural system, it is pointless to ask (with a view to taking action) who benefits from it, or who is responsible for it, or what is ethically correct conduct in it. Recall also the adroit use of ceteris paribus and of "disturbing causes" to draw attention away from the difference between what happens and what the model predicts should happen. What is being practiced is a version of pseudocasuistry: general principles are confronted with particular cases, but the case material is selected and adjusted in such a way that the principles always emerge undamaged from the encounter, and the argument serves not to give, but to prevent, a clear view of the issues.

Other devices appeal to a level of reasoning that is subcerebral. They are suggestive rather than explicit, a feature that is part of

---

7. Pollution resulting from manufacturing processes (and not charged to the manufacturer) is a standard example of an externalized cost.

Kenneth Burke's *tonality* (1969b, 98). The ambiance that selected terms and phrases suggest is itself a covert part of the argument, quietly leading the audience to a place where the facts appear to speak for themselves. Choosing words that will not trigger unwelcome questions is one way to keep matters off an agenda. The device is *tendentious selection*: the choice of terms to model a situation in such a way that attention is diverted from features that would embarrass the model. In the present case the embarrassing features are manifested in concrete situations; therefore the terms chosen tend to steer the discourse away from the concrete towards the abstract.

Consider the following four NEO godling-terms: *postcontractual opportunism, moral hazard, adverse selection,* and *asset specificity. Postcontractual opportunism* means going back on your promise when you see an advantage in doing so.[8] *Moral hazard* is the problem that a principal faces because his agents are less than honest. He has no sure way to find out what they are really doing, and so they do what suits them and not him—for instance they might *shirk. Adverse selection* refers to the fact that an insurer, for example, has less than perfect information about his clients, who conceal from him information that would benefit him and disadvantage them. The same is true of job applicants, who do not advertise their defects. *Asset specificity* is a situation in which, for example, a manufacturer contracts to sink a major part of his resources into making a specific product for another manufacturer in return for being the sole or main supplier of that product. Then, depending on circumstances, one or the other might renege on the terms of the contract, holding the other to ransom, so to speak, because the other has no alternative buyer/supplier.

The first thing to notice is that the action depicted in all these phrases, when considered in a concrete situation, raises moral questions. But morality has a direct lexical reference in only one of them, *moral hazard*, and even then the connotation of event-based contingency in *hazard* serves to neutralize the suggestion of ethical responsibility contained in *moral*. The noun dominates and the noun refers to an event, and events are not subject to ethical judgments of right and wrong. In two of the phrases (*adverse selection* and *moral hazard*) the fact that persons have decided to do something that is sufficiently dishonest to make them conceal it is itself concealed in the phrase. *Opportunism* does have a whiff of the unethical; it means taking advantage of circumstances, often in disregard of ethical principles. But it is also a judgment of cognitive capacity, of rationality (as defined in neoclassi-

---

8. A sellers' market for houses in Britain in the late 1960s, when vendors acquired the habit of raising the price *after* accepting an offer, popularized an unfamiliar verb for this particular form of postcontractual opportunism: the prospective buyer was *gazumped*.

cal economics), indicating someone smart enough to seize opportunities. *Shirk* is certainly not a term of praise, but as a reproach it is quite mild, indicating a passive rather than an active dishonesty, a suggestion that the blame lies as much with the circumstances as with the individual. In short, the absence of strong words like *cheat* or *steal* or *defraud* functions to divert attention from the ethical judgments that people in the real world attach to these actions. The choice of words helps to screen morality out of the data before it can infect the model.

Second, the fact that real people are involved in these situations is left unemphasized. People are there, but they are faceless rational economizers. Morality has no place in a model that uses the metaphor of a machine. All that can be said when things go wrong is that the machine is malfunctioning. Therefore one should expect rhetorical devices that rewrite moral turpitude as mechanical malfunction. The device is similar to the use in English of the impersonal passive or of an intransitive verb, which shifts an event from the ethical domain of praise and blame into a natural domain: not "She broke it" but "It came apart in her hands." All the nouns in those four NEO phrases are abstract and refer to types of action (*opportunism*, *selection*), or conditions (*hazard*), or things and their characteristics (*asset specificity*), not to agents, who in all four cases are cheats and their victims. People, it seems, can be adequately understood as a function of things. *Principal* and *agent*, of course, and nouns like *employer*, *employee*, *entrepreneur*, *buyer*, *seller*, and *arbitrageur* do appear, but again, they always are presented as affectively and ethically neutered. Abstraction, for sure, is a requirement in modeling, as, indeed, in all statements. But the chosen godling-terms function so as to suggest an atmosphere of impersonality, enticing the reader away from the concrete and the personal in the direction of what is abstract, mechanical, and impersonal.

Remedies likewise lack the moral dimension. Agents who shirk or otherwise cheat their principals are, in the model, brought back into line by the application of rewards and penalties. One name for this process is *incentive alignment*. The metaphor is thoroughly impersonal: *alignment* suggests a mechanic timing an engine or getting the right toe-in on a car's front wheels, or a builder lining up the foundations of a house. Cognition and motive and will, affect and self-respect and duty, which are important variables in the process as it works itself out in practice, are wholly absent from the metaphor.

There is a similar suggestion of an objective, adjustable (and measurable) world in one of the major workhorse deities in the NEO pantheon: *information asymmetry*. If the victim only knew as much as the cheater, there could be no cheating. Information is out of balance. Built into this metaphor is the unspoken assumption that the information passing up and down organizations is sufficiently homogenous to be quantified, measured in units, with at least enough precision to engineer an appropriate redistribution. The metaphor is a variation on the familiar neoclassical theme of equilibrium: problems vanish when things balance themselves out. Hidden in the phrase is the huge complexity of the concept *information*, not least the paradox that information also functions as disinformation. NEO folk are, of course, well aware of this, since the point of information asymmetry is (to name one setting) that agents are able to cheat because the principal does not know what the agents are getting up to and because they feed him disinformation.[9] But the metaphor, suggesting mechanical balance, also suggests that the problem in information asymmetry is not with lies and deception and bluff, how to recognize them, how they are differently used, and—more generally—the peculiar capacity of words and other forms of message to be ambiguous. Instead, the problem is implicitly presented as a relatively simple mechanical one of finding the optimal distribution of information, which is factual and objective, in principle quantifiable, and, given the concept of transaction costs, a commodity that moves according to market principles. A major problem, variation in quality (What different kinds of information are there?) is ignored and the theory made (at least notionally) tractable by ignoring heterogeneity and concentrating on quantity (Under what conditions will there be an equilibrium-distribution of information?). The purblinding technique, once again, is to standardize the content of an interaction (as when a multitude of different-order preferences are homogenized as *utility*) and then concentrate on the deductive possibilities of distribution patterns, which are imaginary, or at least no more than contingently linked with actual distributions. This is a vintage example of inventing a world to fit a model.

*Information asymmetry* can be dismantled in a slightly different manner, again revealing its capacity to obscure ethics. Principal and agent are not symmetrically positioned with regard to the objective truth: the agent has the closer and the more accurate view. The god-term thus implies the notion of *instrumental rationality*, which is the condition of those agents who are assumed to have an accurate and complete knowledge of the real world with which they are dealing (which is a postulate of the expected-utility model). Its contrast is *procedural rationality*: actors reason, but on the basis of mistaken or incomplete infor-

9. Even worse, from the point of view of efficient economizing, is the following situation: when the marginal product of each member of a team of agents cannot be measured separately, slackers may be paid more (and strivers less) than is economically appropriate.

mation.[10] Ideas of deceit and disinformation are then covertly built into the model through the concept of *proxy information*. Principals are at risk in the situations of adverse selection and moral hazard because they must rely on proxy information, such as letters of reference, supervisor's reports, and the like, which, being secondhand, are less accurate than direct observation (and are also subject to the hazard of the information conveyors' *subgoals*, that is, the axes they are grinding). The logic behind this is that it is in the nature of hierarchy to make it impossible for a principal to know all that his agents know; the best he can get is an abstract. The feature that is *not* lexically incorporated into the metaphor of asymmetry is that what the principal often does get is not a summary but blarney; thus, the issue that is not faced is the quality of information. That proxy information can be disinformation (as distinct from information that is abstracted but accurate) is hidden in the neutral adjective *proxy*.[11]

It is all curiously disingenuous. First there is a blanket assumption that hirelings (agents) maximize their own utility, if necessary at the expense of others. Adherence to that presupposition is required if one is to stay in the neoclassical economic community. Individuals, the model assumes, are standardized—preprogrammed—to behave in this way; that is, they are not individuals in the usual sense of that word, but automata. In everyday discourse what the hirelings do would be called cheating. But automata cannot cheat, because they do not have moral choices. To use the normal vocabulary of moral turpitude would be to concede the fact of moral agency and so admit that the foundational presupposition of expected-utility theorizing is flawed: it is the case that people can act out of a sense of duty and be guided by their consciences. To the extent that feature is acknowledged, the expected-utility model is rendered inoperable. Hence the ingenious use of words and phrases to create an amoral—natural—intellectual ambiance.[12]

10. Instrumental rationality can also be termed *objective rationality*. The distinction is a derivative from Simon's *substantive/procedural rationality* (1986, 19; and 1976).

11. This is the same rhetorical device (amphiboly) that Friedman used when he failed to acknowledge that some abstractions can also be false and misleading. See the previous chapter.

12. Morality has no place in this model because rational conduct in economics is by definition directed toward self-interest. It is striking how rarely economists feel moved to step aside and remark that economic man is a repulsive construct. Keynes, as often, had a wider vision. Putting up a front of optimism in the midst of the great depression, he wrote: "When the accumulation of wealth is no longer of high social importance, there will be great changes in the code of morals. We shall be able to rid ourselves of many of the pseudo-moral principles which have hag-ridden us for two hundred years, by which we have exalted some of the most distasteful of human qualities into the position of the highest virtues . . . the love of money as a possession . . . will be recognized for what it is, a somewhat disgusting morbidity, one of those semi-criminal, semi-pathological propensities which one hands over with a shudder to the specialists in

## Giving Ground

Concealment has its limits, and from time to time words slip out that are inescapably linked with ethical behavior. Williamson's definition of opportunism, quoted earlier, "a deep condition of self-interest seeking that contemplates guile" is surprising not only for the word "guile" but even more for the psychologically loaded phrase "deep condition." Elsewhere (1991, 151) he quotes the jurist H. L. A. Hart: " 'Sanctions' are . . . required not as the normal motive for obedience, but as the *guarantee* that those who would voluntarily obey shall not be sacrificed by those who would not." In other words, there are bad people and good people; people who contemplate guile and people who are honest; people who look to their own advantage and others who do their duty ("voluntarily obey"); and, I assume, people who switch motives on different occasions. Utility maximization (in its crass form of self-advantage) is no longer in the driver's seat. Hart's sentence, moreover, implies that "the normal motive for obedience" is not fear of punishment, but conscience. This is the same lesson that we learned from taking apart ideas about residual rights in contracting and the significance of reputations. Such thoughts lead in the direction of a complementary model that centers on conscience and duty.[13]

Other notions of this kind lie waiting to be developed. The process of long-term contracting that requires residual rights might be seen in a different way, less as sets of lawyerlike stipulations than as the emergence of trust and notions of duty. One might argue that when an activity requires cooperation over a long period, there is a threshold beyond which contractual enforcement becomes less and less important. There might be a positive learning curve—the parties learn to

mental disease. All kinds of social customs and economic practices, affecting the distribution of wealth and of economic rewards and penalties, which we now maintain at all costs, however distasteful and unjust they may be in themselves, because they are tremendously useful in promoting the accumulation of capital, we shall be free, at last, to discard" (1932, 369–70).

Perhaps Lord Robbins, whose vision was not wide, had this in mind when, not long afterwards, he wrote of "spineless platitudes" and "incredible banalities."

13. Friedman once again has a fallback argument. Commenting on "the perennial criticism of 'orthodox' economic theory as 'unrealistic' " and on the complaint that "economics is a 'dismal' science because it assumes man to be selfish and money-grubbing" (perhaps he too had read Keynes—see the previous note), he remarks that "criticism of this type is largely beside the point unless supplemented by evidence that a hypothesis differing in one or another of these respects from the theory being criticized yields better predictions for as wide a range of phenomena" (1953, 30–31). If aspirins don't cure my stomach ulcer, shall I go on taking them because there's nothing else in the medicine chest? Maybe. It's a human thing to do—kid oneself. But the aspirins won't fix the ulcer; they could make it worse. They might, of course, help cure a headache. Models are like aspirins; they are of use where they are applicable, and can be harmful if wrongly applied.

trust one another. In short, nakedly aggressive market behavior is replaced by contract, and contract gives way to trust, making enforcement unnecessary and producing a "deep condition" not of self-interested guile, but of the reverse, which is trust. That could be how institutions grow.

I will return, in Part III, to the process which connects interactions with institutions.

*Chapter 3*
# Gains from Trade

> *But the Chicago [S]chool just goes rolling along. Miraculously, all the evidence—I really mean, all the admissible evidence—strengthens their conviction, held for decades, that to err is human, and to live by rules is divine. . . . [T]he Chicago School still adheres to the proposition that we should put our trust in stable formulas, not in unstable men and institutions.*
>
> —Walter Heller, in Milton Friedman and Walter Heller, Monetary versus Fiscal Policy: A Dialogue

## The New Institutional Economics

The model examined in this chapter, although still anchored in neo-classical economics, comes closer to reality than those so far discussed. It is designed to explain, among other matters, how economies that are inefficient nevertheless remain—miraculously, the ironic Heller might say—in existence. The question only arises if one first assumes that a market economy is a self-regulating system, evolving always in the direction of efficiency. If that is the case, natural selection should weed out units that are less able to produce wealth and allow more efficient units to survive. What is true of units should also be true of economic systems, so that inefficient systems should be eliminated when they come into contact with efficient systems, and there should be a convergence of the world's economies towards whatever type best maximizes wealth. This has not happened, and, despite the claims for free-market capitalism, it still is not happening at the present day when techniques of managing and distributing information are more effective than ever before.

One reason economic systems do not converge towards the optimum is that they are not self-regulating natural systems. To a degree, they are regulated by institutions, which belong to culture, not to na-

ture. Institutions constrain the choices that entrepreneurs make and
are themselves controlled by people more intent (in this conceptual
framework) on their own advantage than on overall efficiency. For
that reason inefficient economic practices survive. In short (and a
paradox for the neoclassical paradigm) the old Adam, having a piece
of the action, is to blame for the inefficiency.

These ideas, which are more sophisticated than they appear in that
brief sketch, are set out in a book by Douglass North, *Institutions, Institutional Change and Economic Performance*. He argues that institutions
enhance trust, make trade possible, and thus, through specialization,
increase productivity. But institutions, insofar as they are tools that the
powerful can use for their own benefit, may also stand in the way of
capturing the gains from trade.

North retains the wealth-maximizing postulate (in most economic
writing the default version of utility maximizing). His model also is
"choice-theoretic." It is designed to show how different levels of productivity (the measure of efficiency) are functionally related to differences in institutions. Thus he stands away from Robbins and Knight
and Milton Friedman and closer to Coase and the traditions of classical political economy. He does not assume that equilibrium (the
point of maximum efficiency when markets are cleared) is automatically achieved. Instead, the process stops where someone stops it,
and those who construct a particular "equilibrium" do so in their own
interests.

Institutions are defined as values and beliefs that are made operational in sets of rules, both formal (as in legal rules) and informal (as in
customs). These rules specify goals, in pursuit of which people set up
organizations, such as business firms, banks, insurance, the judiciary,
the police, civil services, religious bodies, educational institutions, the
military, and, of course, the state. Differences in economic efficiency
(the ratio of wealth produced to resources committed), whether across
time or space (North makes frequent comparisons between Third
World and developed industrial nations) are to be explained by showing how institutions enhance or inhibit the production of wealth. For
example, the difference in overall economic performance between
North American and Latin American countries, North argues, is in
part a function of their different institutions; the highly personalized
client-encouraging systems derived from Spain and Portugal make it
more difficult to capture the gains from trade than does the relatively
impersonal rule of law found in the English tradition.

In this framework, the New Institutional Economics (NIE), there
are some clear departures from an orthodox neoclassical economic

model.[1] NIE is the domain of historians and is data-rich. It begins with data, for example, the amply documented mid-nineteenth-century antislavery campaign in the United States, which persuaded voters to forbid slave owning in the newly incorporated western territories, a measure which precipitated the Civil War. The task then is to use the wealth-maximizing postulate to make sense of that campaign's success: the majority of voters were not slave owners and "could express their abhorrence of slavery at relatively little cost to themselves . . ." (North 1990, 85). Events set the problem, which is to explain how they came to happen that way. The procedure is essentially that of the scientist who makes an observation, detects a problem, constructs an explanatory model, and then sets up experiments (in this case archival experiments, so to speak) to test it. Neoclassical economists like constructing theories more than testing them, and, as I explained, they have developed a rhetoric to conceal the imaginary status of the "reality" that is supposed to test their theories. That particular rhetoric is less salient in historically anchored NIE writing.[2]

I will first present a simplified version of the theory that explains how institutions have made some economies more productive than others. I then bring an assortment of skeletons out of the cupboard and discuss the rhetoric that emerges around them. The main rhetorical defense seems to be confession, or, to put it more generously, a realistic assessment of the framework's limitations. Less effort (than in orthodox neoclassical economic writing) goes into fantasizing an imaginary world, more goes into working out how the real world falls short of the model's perfection.

## Gains from Trade

The story of gains from trade is like Kipling's Just So tale of "How the Leopard Got His Spots." It is a piece of conjectural history, eighteenth-century style, that explains, ex post facto, how we have become materially better off now than we were in the past. It takes the form of a

1. The "old" institutional economists would be represented, among others, by Veblen, whom the irascible Frank Knight wrote off as more satirist than scientist (Herskovits 1960, 516). Institutional economics appeared during the first quarter of the twentieth century as a protest against the excessively high level of abstraction in orthodox economics, against its separation from other social sciences, and against its failure to be *positive*—to submit its findings to empirical testing. A brief evaluation is found in Blaug 1985, 708–11.

2. This does not mean that historians do not, to some degree, "invent" (impose a pattern on their presentation of) the past; see *The Invention of Tradition* (Hobsbawm and Ranger 1983). That title acquires its irony from the meaning of the word *tradition* (something handed down) and from the commonsensical image of the historian as a narrator of past events; historians are supposed to tell things as they were.

quasi-evolutionary narrative divided into stages, in each of which a problem is solved and its successor arises, to be solved at the next stage. The narrative is unified by the telos of a perfect wealth-maximizing economy, but there is no pretense that such a state of affairs could ever be attained.

The first step is the proposition that (other things, of course, being equal) specialization and the division of labor make production more efficient. Adam Smith opens *The Wealth of Nations* with this sentence: "The great improvement in the productive powers of labour, and the greater part of the skill, dexterity, and judgment with which it is any where directed, or applied, seem to have been the effects of the division of labour." Concentration on one particular productive task enhances skill, leads to improvements in the technology, and permits economies of scale. But specialized producers, being also consumers, need each other's products; therefore specialization requires trade. But trade entails trust, a word which, in this context, has no affective component and denotes only an unsentimental expectation about the future conduct of trading partners.

In the absence of that expectation there is less incentive to trade. Unless traders already know that the other party will live up to its word, they will be put to the expense of finding out for themselves how big are the risks of entering into the deals, or to the possibly greater expense of exacting recompense from—perhaps also penalizing—people who do not deliver what they promised. The cost of acquiring information, let alone going after retribution, might be enough to deter traders from doing business at all, thus stunting economic growth. If the trade is not direct but passes through several links, the risks increase.

An instant quid pro quo transaction of simple commodities—direct, one-to-one, not needing credit—would lessen the need for trust, but not dispense with it entirely, because there is still information asymmetry. Cheating is to be expected, since, in this model as in all positive economic models, people enter a deal in an adversarial frame of mind, unhampered by ethics, and intending to get the better of the other person. The trading partner might cheat on the deal, putting sand in the sugar or water in the milk, and the like. In any case, such simple exchanging is not characteristic of the complex economic systems that are to be explained, being unworkable except at a rudimentary level. Besides, that limited style of transacting would restrict trade.

In the gains-from-trade Just So story the first way out of that impasse begins with exchanges that focus not only on the goods or services being traded but also on the persons involved. This is the *presta-*

*tion* stage of market creation and expansion.[3] Exchanges are made with people who are reliable as trading partners because they are also kinsmen or neighbors or of the same religion, thus having a relationship that Max Gluckman called *multiplex*: it carries several different strands of activity.[4] Those who cheat over transactions find themselves in trouble on other fronts: shunned by neighbors or disowned by kin or bereft of the comforts of religion. Uncertainty injected into economic deals is paid back with interest by destroying the exchange structure that supports the rest of life. Thus the option to cheat is removed and with it uncertainty about the other person's future conduct. In that way the notionally isolated economic individual, being in fact a member of society and being rational, can expand the domain of trust, and therefore of trade, at least to the limit of those connected through kinship or religion or ethnicity or any other link, especially those that have some moral standing. Thus emerges *enlightened* self-interest.

The enlightenment lies in realizing that a society that knew no other mode of exchanging than transactions (that is, exchanges exclusively motivated by the thought of material gain, which economists consider "rational") could not exist. It would be, to quote the master word man Hobbes, "the war of every man against every man." That is why certain commodities, which are deemed to be significantly linked with status, are protected from market exchange. A well-known example is provided by a people in West Africa, the Tiv, who separated their exchanges into three spheres: subsistence things, such as foodstuffs, cooking pots, and the like; prestige items like cattle, metal rods, or slaves; and control over people, in particular marriageable women. Exchange within each of these spheres was allowed; exchange between them was forbidden. The function—and the purpose—of this arrangement was to maintain a status quo in which power stayed with older men.[5] Protecting the rights of selected categories of people from the perils of a free market is familiar to us in the form of rationing systems, which divert necessities towards those deemed to deserve them, or licensing systems that serve the end of collective, rather than private, utility.

The prestation stage, however, is only one chapter in a continuing evolutionary narrative. Prestations are still restrictive; they limit the range of trading possibilities, and the market is not "free." The evolutionary drive must eventually be away from prestations (which are

3. A *prestation* is an exchange in which attention is focused not on the thing exchanged but on the relative status of the persons making the exchange. A simple example is a gift that marks friendship. A prestation is the obverse of a *transaction*. More on this later.
4. Gluckman 1955a, 19–20.
5. See Bohannan 1955. Note that in this scheme slaves are not people.

personalized) in the direction of transactions (which are impersonal and amoral). If trade is to expand and production to be enhanced, the specialized producer must get beyond the limiting confines of kith and kin and fellow believers and be able to do business wherever it will show the most profit. Kinship and the like are unnecessary costs on economic efficiency,[6] and reliance on personal ties restricts the size of the market. What is required is a device like the Roman *ius in rem*, which is a right in a thing against the world, against anyone and everyone, whatever their status. Thus, in this scheme, economizing is fundamentally a nonsocial, nonmoral activity; the only identities that should matter are the ones involved in production and exchange.

At this stage the allegory makers augment their utility-motivational presuppositions—What must individuals want to make them behave that way?—with functional presuppositions—What interactional need does this custom or this institution serve? The evolutionary "need" is for exchanges that are focused on the thing exchanged; that are impersonal, uncluttered by status considerations, and motivated solely by a desire for personal benefit (usually simplified as profit); and yet at the same time command trust. Something is required that will make it mechanically impossible for trading partners, who are otherwise strangers, to have the option of cheating.

The solution (more or less mechanical) is to make the cost of cheating so high that it ceases to be an option. In theory this can be done in a straightforwardly "natural" fashion that leaves no choice for would-be renegers, providing they are rational. A deposit is one such device. A genuinely natural system is, as Goffman put it, "implacable" (1970, 117): cheating is not a possibility. But in fact a wholly implacable social equivalent of implacable nature (as in the inevitability of death) is not easily imagined, let alone contrived.[7]

The final solution, the story suggests, is specialization of another kind: regulatory organizations that stand over and are independent of the market, a third-party enforcer that, hopefully, will have all the impersonality and therefore the efficacy of a natural enforcer. Trademarks, guarantees, brand names, contracts, a banking system, chambers of commerce, trade unions, a legal system and courts of law, and ultimately the state—all these can lower transaction costs by guaranteeing

6. Small commerce in rural southern and eastern Africa, even down to the trade store in the bush, was in the hands of Indians partly because any African who set up shop was swiftly impoverished by freeloading kin. On the link between ethnic difference and commerce, see Foster 1974.

7. In any case, an implacable system would lack the flexibility that permits intentional adaptation to a changing environment.

the good faith of otherwise untrustworthy people engaged in transactions. We have that kind of apparatus, and thus, the story concludes, we benefit from trade and have become wealthier than our forebears. Trust in transactions is created by organizations that specialize in providing a service that would be prohibitively expensive if done separately by each trader for each transaction. Trust is thus domesticated into economic thought by making it essentially a commodity that is purchased from a regulatory organization. You buy instant certainty instead of waiting to see if the other party will live up to its promise, and you pay less that you would if every trader tried to be his or her own enforcer. Regulatory organizations are thus like Coase's firms: devices that lessen transaction costs.

Evolution apart, the evidence is around us in everyday dealings (and on such larger stages as the former Soviet states) that free-market economies work to the extent that property rights are sufficiently protected by law to create confidence. If title to a piece of property—a car or a house or a plot of land—is uncertain, its value is diminished, because others beside the would-be owner may claim the right to use it. Making a title secure requires the help of legal agencies (for title search, title insurance, registration, and so forth) and, behind them, enforcement agencies that underwrite title proceedings. All those are transaction costs on acquiring and securing title, but the point is that those agencies are, hopefully, cheaper and more certain than hiring one's own enforcers. Their existence makes possible transactions that otherwise would not have taken place.

The story, in short, says this. We have become materially richer than our ancestors, and gains from trade are one reason why this has been possible. Regulation by organizations facilitates the expansion of trade. Rules, enforced by an external authority, make it less likely that transaction partners will cheat, even when they have no direct link with one another except the deal itself. Raw self-interest and the instant gratification afforded by cheating, which would cause trading relationships to self-destruct, are mechanically neutralized through penalties and transformed into enlightened self-interest: people are smart enough to opt for an advantage guaranteed by an impartial organization. Trust expands (as always in this context, a matter of calculated probability, not sentiment) and economic dealings become less uncertain.

Thus we have a logical sequence of steps in building the model: first the desire for greater wealth (a higher standard of living), then the notion that wealth is enhanced by specialization and trade, then the need for trust, then trust provided by organizations, and finally organizations shaped according to values and beliefs (institutions or, to use the anthropologist's term, *culture*). Institutions, coming at the end of the chain, look as if they are the independent variable, the final cause, the explainer of all that came before it but which is not itself explained. The desire to maximize returns, once one steps outside the neoclassical economic model, is a function of the institutional setting. Different cultures, as is often pointed out, set different values on winning that particular race. Even in the same culture, the entrepreneurial heroes of one generation may later seem like robber barons, heroic only in the scale of the misery they caused. Trust also is clearly a function of the institutional setting; that is the point of the Just So story. Institutions determine, in other words, the magnitude of the problem that has to be solved by regulatory organizations. Finally (I will come back to this), the extent to which the regulators are likely to be corrupt is also a function of institutions—of how strongly they are infused with the sentiment that honest dealing is an unquestionable ethical imperative.

But to propose that some economies are more efficient than others because they have different institutions is to leave things in the air. Institutions themselves change, and can be modeled as dependent variables. The task then is to get beyond institutions as a final cause and explain why they vary. Why, to use the same example, are Hispanic cultures more given to client forms of organization than are the impersonal northern European cultures? More generally, why do cultures vary? How does a culture come to be the way it is? How does it change?

## Individual Choice and Imagined Entities

North's goal is to build "a theory of institutions on the foundation of individual choices" (1990, 5). In such a model, since cultures vary and institutions change, the variation and the change must be (in part, at least) the outcome of individual decisions. Institutions may appear to be a constraint on and independent of individual choices, but in fact they are themselves shaped (up to a point) by those choices. This process occurs through the medium of organizations.

> Institutions, together with the standard constraints of economic theory, determine the opportunities in a society. Organizations are created to take advantage of those opportunities, and, as the organizations evolve, they alter the institutions. The resultant path of institutional change is shaped by (1) the lock-in that comes from the symbiotic relationship between institutions and organizations that have evolved as a consequence of the incentive structure provided by those institutions and (2) the feedback process by which human beings perceive and react to changes in the opportunity set. (1990, 7)

An opportunity is the coinciding of something wanted and the re-sources ("standard constraints") that make it available. Institutions, presumably, define what is wanted—"incentive structures" in the passage quoted above. In other words, they define values. North goes on: "Incremental change comes from the perception of the entrepreneurs in political and economic organizations that they could do better by altering the existing institutional framework at some margin" (8). But, he adds, entrepreneurs do not have "true models" and they process the information through "mental constructs that can result in persistently inefficient paths" (8). This is surely correct; entrepreneurs do not have "true models," but only imagine or hope they do. Their rationality, in other words, is something attempted, *procedural rationality*, and not reasoning based on a perfect knowledge of an objective world, *instrumental rationality*. The process by which institutions change is therefore more than a little hit-and-miss, because entrepreneurs have only incomplete and inaccurate information; their intentions have only a haphazard link with outcomes. This again is surely a correct account of the way the world works: *Nam homo proponit, sed Deus disponit* (Man proposes, but God disposes—Thomas À Kempis).

If procedural rationality connects with the real world only in a hit-and-miss fashion, the reasoning involved cannot satisfactorily account for the process through which institutions have in fact evolved to capture the gains from trade. The idea of rationality—a calculated decision with foreseen consequences—is displaced by a random process, and the model that sets out to explain historical events can no longer be choice-theoretic. Procedural rationality—entrepreneurs cannily "altering the existing institutional framework at some margin"— sufficiently describes the way in which decisions are reached, but the link between plans and subsequent events has become uncertain. Even in the case of a wealth-maximization decision that actually is followed by expanded trade and enhanced productivity, the reasoning that went into that decision is connected with the outcome only by chance. Without instrumental rationality the designs people have and the decisions they take cannot be used to predict (or subsequently explain) what happens, because what happens is not necessarily the outcome of those decisions.

This problem arises because North wants a model that is choice-theoretic. A model based wholly on natural selection and ignoring the way decisions are reached would not have this difficulty. Firms that *happen* to conduct themselves in ways that suit their environment will be selected for survival; others, which *happen* to be out of accord with their environment, will go to the wall. In that scheme, as Hayek (1988) insists, institutions (his "traditions") are selected not by reason but by "success." Computational skills and access to information are not pertinent because "culture" is a natural system that finds its own outcomes. Just as an evolutionary biologist ignores the possibility that a plant or an animal might calculate the evolutionary consequences of its behavior, so also cultural change could be modeled without factoring in decision making or the ideas that people have about the way the world works.

The merits and demerits of this distant perspective are not the present issue. But, as already noted, such an evolutionary scheme would be a fundamental departure from the NIE model because it is not choice-theoretic; it has no place for the *rational* individual. It dispenses with the analysis of motivation and calculation and focuses only on contingent features and their relation to an environment. It rules out the possibility of planning and management. It rules out rationality, because the organism does not have the ability to connect means with an end and so direct its own evolutionary path. In fact, it rules out microeconomics altogether.

That extreme is unacceptable to neoclassically orthodox economists, who assume that information is sufficiently available to make it possible for some decisions to have the anticipated outcomes. Nor is it acceptable to the NIE writers because it negates from the outset the model of entrepreneurs receiving feedback and calculating advantage, altering organizational decisions "at some margin," and so eventually modifying the underlying institutions and thus shaping events in the world.

If one does not take the ultraevolutionary path and assumes that there is some connection between intentions and subsequent events, the problem of rationality manifests itself in another way. Suppose it is the case that an expanded range of trust has made available gains from trade, and that is why the world has become wealthier. Suppose also that the expanded trust is a function of regulatory organizations. The trust envisaged in NIE theory, like that in the NEO model, is not a matter of honor and self-respect. To admit that would be to admit altruism as a significant mover and to deny the basic postulate of the self-interested would-be maximizer. Trust is still of the Coase type; it arises from contracts and from the belief that contracts will be enforced. The theory depends crucially on the enforcers of trust, which gives rise to the problem of the ultimate enforcer, already encountered in asking who is the principal's ultimate principal.

North makes very clear that the creation of regulatory organizations does not necessarily produce an economic system that is constantly being realigned for maximum productivity, still less—to paraphrase Keynes again—for "the good of us all." The enforcer of contracts is the state (and its agencies), but "if the state has coercive force, then those who run the state will use that force in their own interests at the expense of the rest of the society" (59). At that point the theory has a problem. If the world has become wealthier, and if this is due to institutions that create trust and make possible the gains from trade, and if these institutions were deliberately created, then some of the time either (1) those who ran the state rose above their baser selves and acted in the public interest, or (2) their private interests happened (that is, by no one's design) to coincide with the public interest in producing an overall expansion in productivity. The latter case is a variant of the evolutionary scheme and the model is not choice-theoretic.

If the first alternative is true (regulators themselves regulated by conscience), why should the theory not suppose that such things happen among ordinary people in everyday life? In the Just So model that is not the case. Ordinary entrepreneurs are not conscience-driven; they have to be made to see that it is in their interest not to cheat because they will be punished if they do and rewarded if they do not. Why is that not the case with the regulators, too? If it is the case, and if the regulators have to be constrained like ordinary people, we are again in need of an argument for the existence of God: Who will police the police, watch over the watchmen, enforce good behavior from the enforcer?

Regulatory organizations are supposed to function impartially, like machines, but the makers of these machines, being rational (as an economist sees rationality), design and run them to benefit themselves. If everything were to work properly (which is the first alternative listed above—regulators regulated by conscience) a regulatory organization would constitute a reasonable transaction cost to pay as a discount against uncertainty. But, as North points out, "no one at this stage in our knowledge knows how to create such an entity" (59). Leviathan, the mythological and incorruptible entity that Hobbes constructed to control our selfishness, in reality turns out to be a person, and a flawed person at that—an old Adam in fact, the original sinner—scheming, calculating, going his own way—in that respect ethically no different from the subjects who are likewise scrambling for their own advantage. Leviathan is itself supposed *not* to be a competitor; it should work impersonally for the public good, favoring neither any contesting party nor itself. But again "choice-theoretic" subjectivity emerges and brings with it a contest over definitions. Who is to define the public good? The rival parties may all have their own versions, and so might Leviathan. Then Leviathan turns out to be not an implacable regulatory organization but at best an arena, or, worse, an unusual arena because the umpire is an active contestant in the game.

We are back in the world that has in it no principals, no regulators, only self-interested agents (politicians and officials) who masquerade as referees, shirk their duties, and cheat those with whose well-being they are charged. The model of how the gains from trade are captured thus reveals itself, at least in some respects, as workable only in an imaginary world that is made orderly by entities that "no one at this stage in our knowledge knows how to create."

Examples are everywhere. Officials in regulatory agencies in the United States line up with the leaders of the industry and make sure that regulations are implemented in such a way that the welfare of the consumer, supposedly protected by the agency, takes second place to the welfare of the industry. The boards that set up these units often contain members of the industry to be regulated, and it is in their interest (being in business, they are rational) to make sure that the agency does not work efficiently.[8] Legislators in developing countries (and elsewhere) make laws ostensibly designed to facilitate commerce and to safeguard the public interest, but either they do so with such draconian enthusiasm that commerce is inhibited, or else they quietly convert the public trust into a private business by selling licenses and permits. The public interest then becomes a rhetorical theme, a convenient facade behind which partisan advantage (*sub-group goals* in the NEO jargon) can be pursued. Even without intentional dishonesty or self-enrichment, organizations established to perform a particular task can become valued not as means to an end but as ends in themselves; then they do not work for the public good but simply to aggrandize themselves or at least to stay in business (this process is an example of *goal displacement*).

Even if the Leviathans were Teflon-proofed against opportunism, information asymmetry would still expose them to being deceived, and would prevent feedback from making their operations efficient. If the old Adam does surface in them, then, as instanced above, the very controls that are supposed to facilitate trade allow the controllers to enrich themselves, with money or with power, by promoting a Byzantine regulatory apparatus that in the end restricts trade. The media at the present time contradicts itself by providing both an inexhaustible supply of anecdotes about the difficulties of doing business in the non-Western world, where one has to cope with dishonest officials and politicians, and, at the same time, stories about the impossibility of making money in the contemporary United States in the face of public-interest regulations, which ensure—or should ensure—that officials and politicians remain honest.

---

8. A lucid account of how and why these things take place is found in Moe 1995.

The problem, as I said earlier, centers not on the enforcement side of contract but on its other half: on the kind of good faith that is resistant to opportunism, the regulator or the competitor who follows the rule without question because it is right, even when it is personally inexpedient. Conduct of this kind has no place in the neoclassical paradigm, and Coase, in his recension, kept it out by transforming duty into a commodity that can be bargained for in a contract negotiation. North, perhaps because a historian is more sensitive to the taunt of creating imaginary worlds, is less sure that he has the answer. Here is the passage in which the sentence quoted above is placed. "Third-party enforcement means the development of the state as a coercive force able to monitor property rights and enforce contracts effectively, but no one at this stage in our knowledge knows how to create such an entity. *Indeed, with a strictly wealth-maximizing behavioral assumption it is hard even to create such a model abstractly*" (59, italics added).[9] It is not hard; given the "wealth-maximizing assumption" it is impossible, because what is to be created is an institution, and the wealth-maximizing assumption cannot encompass institutionally directed conduct. This is a plain statement of where the neoclassical paradigm must have a stop.

Nor is that the only passage that marks the limit of the wealth-maximizing model. ". . . motivation is more complicated than the simple expected utility model [makes it out to be]. . . . [U]nder certain conditions traits like honesty, integrity, and living up to a reputation pay off in strictly wealth-maximizing terms. . . . *Still unexplained is a very large residual. We simply do not have any convincing theory of knowledge that accounts for the effectiveness (or ineffectiveness) of organized ideologies or accounts for choices made when the payoffs to honesty, integrity, working hard, or voting are negative*" (42, italics added).

North foregrounds these difficulties. He does not treat them as *res tegendae*—quite the reverse. His "primary message is to economists and economic historians" (vii–viii), and his aim is to provide a model that relates economic performance to a context of institutions, to bring the neoclassical paradigm closer to reality. Consequently, the book does not feature argumentative defenses (described earlier) that neutralize the model's weaknesses by externalizing them. The weaknesses are trumpeted, as in the several passages quoted above, or in this: "There is a persistent tension in the social sciences between the theories we construct and the evidence we compile about human interaction in the world around us. It is most striking in economics,

9. These frank admissions are to be contrasted with the we-will-not-give-an-inch hyperbole found in Milton Friedman's defense of unrealistic postulates, discussed earlier.

where the contrast between the logical implications of neoclassical theory and the performance of economies (however defined and measured) is startling" (11).

## At War 'Twixt Will and Will Not

Those forthright statements do not sit easily with certain other passages in North's book. While he is ready to mark the wealth-maximizing model's boundaries, he is, not unexpectedly, also strong in its defense. He commits himself at the outset to individualism: "The choice-theoretic approach is essential because a logically consistent, potentially testable set of hypotheses must be built on a theory of human behavior. . . . Institutions are a creation of human beings. They are evolved and altered by human beings; hence our theory must begin with the individual" (5). Agreed, but that is not the end of the matter. There is also the question of what moves individuals, and what shapes their motivations. On what theory of human behavior should we build testable hypotheses?

North's individual is still essentially amoral. In talking of the corruptibility of rulers, he writes "rules are, at least in good part, devised in the interests of private well-being rather than social well-being. . . . [R]ules are derived from self-interest" (48). Individual-based models, however, have the failing that North so unambiguously describes: the god-in-the-machine problem, the fair-minded regulator, the entity that "no one yet knows how to create." There is a hint of this difficulty in the phrase quoted above, "at least in good part," a qualifier which suggests that North is himself caught in a path dependency pattern that leads him into ambivalence; he is reluctant to go back and choose an option previously rejected, and so waste resources already committed. Models, no less than technologies or institutions, are subject to path dependency, and if one has set out with the assumption of wealth-maximizing amoral individuals, it is difficult to admit, as the journey ends where the asphalt stops and the dirt road begins, that the assumption is limiting and there are other roads that one might need to take.

The same ambivalence is revealed in North's discussion of the negative-sloped curve that describes a trade-off between moral conviction and self-interest: people do what they think is right when it does not cost them too much. "What determines how much people will pay to express and act on their convictions? We seldom know much about the elasticity of the function, but we do have abundant evidence that the function is negatively sloped and the price incurred for action on one's convictions is frequently very low (and hence convictions are

significant) in many institutional settings" (44). North is caught between his knowledge that people sometimes do what they think is
right even when it hurts them ("when the payoffs to honesty, integrity,
working hard, or voting are negative") and the expected-utility
model's postulate that people do not behave in that way. At least three
times in the first third of the book (20, 40, 43) we are alerted to the
negative-sloped curve, and the point is made again on pages 85–86.
North gives the example, as I mentioned, of the voters who banned
slave owning in the western states in antebellum America: ". . . the
structure of institutions, in this case the electoral process, makes it
possible for people to express their ideas and ideologies effectively at
very little cost to themselves." He adds that the votes might have been
otherwise if the voters in the North had foreseen "the price [they]
would pay in the Civil War" or if the slave owners had been able to
"bribe or pay off the voters" (85). Intuitively, that particular case
seems more than plausible.

The general implication of the negative-sloped curve is that, when
push comes to shove, what counts in making a decision is the effect on
the pocketbook. But what then is to be made of the amply documented instances of genuinely altruistic behavior? Perhaps North is
right and altruism is statistically uncommon. It is possible, however,
that the labeling of the coordinates that produces the negative-sloped
curve is itself an assumption, and North's own reference to honesty
observed even when the payoff is negative suggests that the proposition could have been expressed in a different way, making conviction
the independent variable: people factor in costs inversely to the ethical importance of the issue, believing that virtue should have no price
on it. That interpretation obviously would not accord with the com-
monsense "bottom line" cynicism that is the mark of all economic
thinking about human conduct.

In NIE discourse (at least in North's), moral scruples are no longer
exogenous, as they are in orthodox neoclassical models, but they enter
to determine decisions only at the margin of supposedly real necessities, which are interests. That may indeed be the modal case—every
man has his price and it isn't much. But questions remain. How is one
to explain different elasticities—in particular those convictions that
are inelastic enough to resist negative payoffs? Rabbis and ayatollahs
do not eat pork, but every man has his price and if you pay them
enough they will. Assuming that to be true, it is not the issue. What
has to be explained is why the price is higher for them than it would
be for a Baptist. How, in other words, is one to explain cases in which
conviction is clearly the determining variable and people refuse to let
cost deter them from ethical action?

Meanwhile, a rhetorical job has been done. North acknowledges the independent status of "organized ideologies," "culture," standards of "honesty, integrity, and hard work," and the like, and their capacity to withstand the negative payoff. But, against this, the several-times-mentioned negative demand slope serves to suggest that these things are, for the most part, secondary to the payoff. In North's writing, ethical convictions as determinants have the status of an agenda for the next meeting—matters that should not interfere with decisions reached today. My general argument is that in the NIE framework a residue of the inexplicable persists because the postulate of the amoral agent is still in command. Morality, I argued in the last chapter, is the concept concealed in the godling-term *principal*. In NIE discourse it is concealed in the term *institution*.

North's theory of institutions, stated in outline, is this. Given the expected-utility postulate, the mere existence of society in general, and in particular the increasing ability of (some) societies to capture the gains from trade through cooperation and trust, have to be explained. Leviathan (the archetypal regulatory institution) takes care of one part of this problem; people are compelled to see that it is in their own interest to modify their predatory tendencies and attend to the public good. But Leviathan itself also has those predatory tendencies, which explains why some societies have not captured the gains from trade as successfully as have others. But, I have argued (agreeing with North), the model does not explain why some societies have the kind of institutions that help them capture the gains from trade and other societies do not. Why does Leviathan sometimes (but not always and everywhere to the same degree) suffer from human imperfections, both computational incapacity (which prevents it from getting perfect feedback) and moral weakness (which causes the regulators to serve their own interests instead of the public interest)?

After Coase, the neoclassical postulate of perfect information has been modified by its contrary: the cost of transactions is not a constant (zero) but a variable. It seems reasonable to suggest that the axiom of an amoral maximizer should also be turned into a variable. North says this more or less directly in the sentence quoted above: "We simply do not have any convincing theory of knowledge that accounts for the effectiveness (or ineffectiveness) of organized ideologies or accounts for choices made when the payoffs to honesty, integrity, working hard, or voting are negative." This can only suggest that the ultimate unregulated part of the regulator has to be taken care of by conscience. In other words, the concept of a rational economizer also needs to be modified by its contrary, the ethical economizer (a concept which, outside the neoclassical stockade, is not an oxymoron), and turned into a variable. If that is true for the ultimate regulator, then it will also be true for every ordinary entrepreneur.

At the end of the line, unless one follows the ultraevolutionary path that sidesteps people's understandings, the postulate of amoral man has to be balanced against a concept of duty, morality, honesty, self-respect, or any other feature that can stand for the ultimate watchman. There is nothing unreasonable or revolutionary about this suggestion. Any paradigm that always and everywhere claims eminent domain has ceased to be a tool and become a god-frame. To reduce its status from scripture back to being a presupposition and to confront it with its rivals is no more than to restore its scientific standing.

We have witnessed, during the passage from a "very beautiful theory" (Robbins, Knight, and Friedman) to its transaction-cost recension (Coase) and to the new institutional economics (North), a progressive (albeit slight) intrusion of the ethical person into the machinelike paradigms of orthodox neoclassical economics. Alternatively, it is a move toward re-embedding the discipline into the world of experience, and a tacit admission that conduct is a function not only of wealth or power maximizing but also of ethical concerns.

# Part II
# Morality

*The scientific task is to understand, and not to explain.*

—*Louis Dumont, "On the Comparative Understanding of Non-Modern Civilizations"*

The antithesis to the economists' positive model is a structural or holistic model. The particular form of structuralism that I will examine was deployed—the episteme is no longer in fashion—in the middle decades of the twentieth century by social anthropologists who called themselves structural functionalists. In their domain, action is presumed to be motivated not by the prospect of personal gain but by a sense of duty. Given that presupposition, the intellectual task is to discover the principles that underlie the values and beliefs that govern conduct[1]—to discover, in other words, social structures.

The model recognizes morality, which expected-utility models do not, but it fails to encompass our obvious ability to take initiatives, to bend principles, and so also to create them. The result is that, by itself, it cannot make much sense of social change. Chapters 4 and 5 describe structural functionalism and its problems, and, toward the end of Chapter 5, I will introduce a recension, which is simple—almost a matter of common sense—but also radical, because it makes possible the use of structural models to analyze change in social systems.

The pattern resembles that of Part I. After describing some initial confusions over a "natural science of society," it moves from the elegant and abstract purity of monostructuralism toward the complexities that become apparent when a single-structure model is brought closer to reality. I will use a classical example of single-structure modeling (in a book by Evans-Pritchard) and follow it with the no less classical—and constructive—hatchetry done on structural functionalism and monostructuralism by Edmund Leach.

Chapter 6 describes the polemics and the adversarial posturing of two sets of critics, one intent on discrediting expected-utility models and the other attacking structural-functional models. It is an interlude, tidying away issues that emerged but had not been sufficiently confronted in the preceding chapters; it readies the transition to Part III.

---

1. *Conduct* is behavior in relation to moral standards expected of the agent. We can comment on the *behavior* of animals, but not on their conduct.

# Chapter 4

# Natural Systems and Moral Systems

> *When I find myself in the company of scientists, I feel like a shabby curate*
> *who has strayed by mistake into a drawing room full of dukes.*
>
> —W. H. Auden, "The Poet and the City"

## General Equilibrium Theory

Herbert Simon's dry comment on his fellow economists (Chapter 1's epigraph) contains a succinct description of their "beautiful theory": "general equilibrium theory, with utility-maximization as a driving mechanism."[1]

Few social anthropologists subscribed openly to the second of these god-terms, *utility maximization*, or made it the founding assumption of their analyses. The reason is obvious. Some of the assumptions on which it rests—what Robbins identified as "so much the stuff of our everyday experience that they have only to be stated to be recognized as obvious"—are not always the stuff of everyday experience that anthropologists noticed in other cultures, particularly those labeled *primitive*. When they wrote about the production, distribution, and consumption of wealth in primitive or peasant societies they often described conduct that is beyond the reach of the beautiful theory. A chicken sacrificed to an irascible deity in order to safeguard the crop in a rice field in Bisipara is, from a standard rational maximizer's point of view, at best procedurally rational, certainly not instrumentally so: it is a chicken wasted, a resource that might have been more profitably invested elsewhere.[2]

---

1. One should take a moment, first to savor the unsurpassable impersonality of these words, and then to recall that the modal interpretation of Simon's "driving mechanism" had been described by Keynes, a generation earlier, as "the most distasteful of human qualities . . . one of those semi-criminal, semi-pathological propensities which one hands over with a shudder to the specialists in mental disease."

2. *Standard* is intended to exclude proponents of catchall definitions of utility. The ethnographic reference is to Bailey 1994.

People who do that, Friedman would have said, will not stay long in business, and no doubt he would have thought the same about the relatively vast sums Bisipara people spent on weddings, funerals, and other ritual occasions.

In other words, the gross homogenizing involved in the economist's concept *utility* violates anthropology's prime directive, which is to find out, empirically, how people construe their world, precisely reversing Friedman's "random chance or whatnot" dismissal of businessmen's thoughts and calculations. Or, to put it another way, the anthropologist's task would be to take apart the term *utility*, as it applies in places like Bisipara, and identify its many and diverse manifestations. *Utility maximization* is not a presupposition on which anthropologists theorize, but a problem they investigate. It is their business to unpack *expected utility* and discover what kinds of utility—moral as well as material payoffs—are being expected. That procedure renders the beautiful theory intractable, but it does provide a more comprehensive representation of what actually goes on in the minds of people in Bisipara than one could get by deduction from a standardized profit-maximizing assumption.

The other and more comprehensive god-term, *general equilibrium theory*, made a better showing in social anthropology. For about twenty-five years, ending in the late fifties, structural functionalism was in vogue, and in that time general equilibrium theory (in a perfectly nontractable version) came near to having the directive status in social anthropology that it had among neoclassical economists. In this chapter I will discuss the different interpretations put on equilibrium theory at that time, and I will show the direction in which the discipline was pointed when the argument went off the boil and structural functionalism went out of fashion.

## Structural Functionalism

The definition of equilibrium in neoclassical economics is precise: an economy is in equilibrium when, for every good that enters the market, demand and supply are equal. Clearly this is not a state of affairs that ever existed anywhere; rather it is a model that makes it possible to think about how prices are set and how decisions are made about the production or consumption of goods. Equilibrium deals in tendencies; it implies movement around a position rather than the position itself. When the thermostat is set at seventy degrees Fahrenheit, that figure is notional; the room's actual temperature fluctuates a few degrees above and below it. Equilibrium, in short, is not a physical actuality, but a mental thing, an imagined norm, sometimes, as in the case of room temperature or body temperature, also a desideratum.

The neoclassical assumption, it will be recalled, is that the market—the economy—is a natural system; equilibrium is spontaneous. Buyers and sellers do not strive to bring it about; they have quite a different axe to grind. They are adversaries, each out to get the best deal at the other's expense, and the consequence of their striving, a pattern of oscillation around a norm, is unintended.

The notion of equilibrium in social anthropology was less precise, and closer to political economy than to neoclassical economics. Political economy embeds the production and distribution of wealth in the framework of other institutions—politics, religion, kinship—and takes into account the mutual influence these different institutions have on one another. Social anthropology likewise did not focus on a single institutional activity but on the conceptual whole that is constituted by the relationship between institutions. It asked how they are connected with, and depend upon, one another, and how the whole, so constituted, maintains itself in equilibrium. Second, anthropologists recoiled—but somewhat confusedly—from the idea that society is *entirely* a natural system; they preferred to see it as a moral order. But they also, at the time when structural functionalism was in the ascendant, paraded a scientific attitude. Consequently they did not address the issue of social justice or make forthright statements about inequity and exploitation. They wrote from the standpoint of moral relativism and used the metaphor of pathology to soften the directly ethical implications and, consequently, the hint of blame that would have been conveyed by words like *fairness* or *justice*. I cannot recall anywhere in the writings of that time a custom or an institution, let alone an individual, being directly and centrally condemned (by the writer) as evil. As scientists they were detached. It was not their job to fix the blame on wicked people, only to demonstrate that wickedness (as the "natives" defined it) indicated that the social structure was out of kilter. The task then was to identify the mechanism that would intervene to restore normality (equilibrium).

Structural-functional models were unhesitatingly labeled *scientific*. The second paragraph of Radcliffe-Brown's preface to *African Political Systems* (Fortes and Evans-Pritchard 1940, xi) reads like a manifesto:

The task of social anthropology, as a natural science of society, is the systematic investigation of the nature of social institutions. The method of natural science rests always on the comparison of observed phenomena, and the aim of such comparison is by careful examination of diversities to discover underlying uniformities. Applied to human societies the comparative method used as an instrument for inductive inference will enable us to discover the universal, essential, characters which belong to all human societies, past, present, and future. The progressive achievement of knowledge of this kind must be the aim of all who believe that a veritable science of human society is possible and desirable.


Of course the method of natural science does not rest *only* on "the comparison of observed phenomena." First one has to decide what is going to count as a phenomenon, selecting an essence from the welter of experience, abstracting it, making it into a concept. One also has to identify a problem: What is it that has to be explained? Third, no inquiry gets successfully off the ground without a basic theory. Fourth, with its help, explanatory hypotheses are generated, and, finally, put to the test.

The "observed phenomena" that Radcliffe-Brown identifies are institutions. In broadest terms his problem—the problem of structural functionalism—is contained in this question: How is it possible for human societies to exist? Why do they not fall apart? At first sight this looks like one of those tediously unanswerable questions that can be swiftly discarded because they are like asking why water is not dry. A society is, by definition, something that coheres, and if it does not cohere it is not a society. But a moment's reflection shows that cohesion is experienced as a variable. Societies do fall apart, some more readily than others. The question does pose a genuine problem: social cohesion is a state of affairs that could be—and frequently is—otherwise.

Radcliffe-Brown's basic theoretical assumption is *functional unity*, which is "a condition in which all parts of the social system work together with a sufficient degree of harmony or internal consistency, i.e. without producing persistent conflicts which can neither be resolved nor regulated" (1952, 181). Functional unity or "inner consistency" (183) is found in social systems insofar as they have the capacity to regulate deviance and resolve conflicts.

At a very abstract level, there is a formal resemblance between this and market equilibrium. Conflicts that are resolved or regulated suggest that, as in the case of markets, social equilibrium is not a state of affairs but an abstraction that denotes movement toward and away from a norm of perfect harmony, which is never achieved. This type of movement is certainly a part of "the stuff of our everyday experience," and in that respect the structural functional model is in the same general equilibrium category that can be found not only in neoclassical economics but also in the natural sciences.

But there the resemblance ends, certainly when the comparison is with the hard sciences, and in a more ambiguous way when the comparison is with neoclassical economics. The equilibrium that is envisaged in structural-functional models is an intended one, something that is valued: people attempt to resolve and regulate conflicts. It is—apparently—a norm in the moral sense of the word, not only a statistic, and it is likely to be both supported and contested. Planets move in regular orbits, and to the extent that the planetary system is in dynamic equilibrium, their movements can be predicted. But astronomy has yet to reveal any agency that surveys the system and takes action to remove irregularities. The complementary notion of a planet as a backslider or a troublemaker—a treasonous vassal of the kingly sun—is not entertainable, except as a poetic fantasy. But social systems have regulations and sanctions, ways of monitoring themselves, and they sometimes encounter rebellions and revolutions in which those who dominate and those who are dominated fight to decide whose version of "equilibrium" will prevail.

One can model social equilibrium as a natural phenomenon, void of content and nothing more than a steady state, but only by doing what the neoclassical economists do, which is to depersonalize the situation entirely, strip it of its cultural content and thus of its institutions, and so model society as a natural system. Some of the structural functionalists found it difficult to abandon that ideal, and in their writings, as the next section will show, the line dividing a natural equilibrium from one that was intended (a moral order) was not always clear.

### *African Political Systems* and *The Nuer*

There was, in short, some ambivalence about the structural-functional model's status, an ambivalence betrayed, perhaps, by the homiletic style of its devotees. Consider the following true believer's identification of the road to salvation. It occurs in the introduction, written by Fortes and Evans-Pritchard, to *African Political Systems*. "We speak for all social anthropologists when we say that a scientific study of political institutions must be inductive and comparative and aim solely at establishing and explaining the uniformities found among them and their interdependencies with other features of social organization" (1940, 5). Earlier (3) they had written: "A comparative study of political systems has to be on an abstract plane where social processes are stripped of their cultural idiom and are reduced to functional terms." One might think this statement was intended to clear the way for the kind of natural-systems model that neoclassical economists constructed by posing agents "stripped of their cultural idiom." But this was not the case. Discussing conquest theories of the origin of the state

(9–10) the authors spin off a series of hypotheses that connect political form with cultural difference. Furthermore, a lengthy discussion toward the end of their essay (16–22) separates the agents' "private interests," which concern "pragmatic and utilitarian" things, from "common interests," which are matters of "moral value and ideological significance." The fact that "moral value and ideological significance" is a matter of culture and sits uncomfortably with a natural science theory of human behavior was not, on that occasion, given notice. Before long it was, by Evans-Pritchard; I will come to that soon.

The introduction to *African Political Systems* precedes eight essays on various societies in different parts of sub-Saharan Africa. The eight social systems fall into two categories: five had centralized governments; three did not, but existed in a state of "ordered anarchy," as Evans-Pritchard put it. In these "acephalous" societies, an absence of government coexisted with an absence of chaos, which, at first sight, is no small paradox, because in our own society the primary association with order is regulation by government—laws, the police, and the courts.

So why do acephalous societies not fall apart? Why does any society not fall into chaos? The editors' first answer is this: "A relatively stable political system in Africa represents a balance between conflicting tendencies and between divergent interests" (11). The sentence is less clear than it might be. "Tendencies," I suspect, means no more than oscillation, being pulled now in one direction and now back again in the other. The system is "relatively stable" so long as a departure from the mean is countered by a reverse movement; the system, that is to say, correctly but also vacuously, is relatively stable so long as it is not unstable. On the other hand, the phrase "divergent interests" is perfectly clear: it is the basic notion that when there is not enough of something to satisfy everyone, conflict may ensue. That is the reason why societies might fall apart, so we are back to asking why they do not.

The editors have two answers. The first is "balance of forces" (11–15). In the case of the centralized states "it is a balance between the different parts of the administrative organization. The forces that maintain the supremacy of the paramount ruler are opposed by the forces that act as a check on his powers." The reader is advised not to think of this arrangement "as nothing more than an administrative device. A general principle of great importance is contained in these arrangements, which has the effect of giving every section and every major interest of the society direct or indirect representation in the conduct of government." The paramount ruler, for quite practical reasons, has to delegate power, and "without the cooperation of those who hold [subordinate] offices, it is extremely difficult, if not impossible, for the king to [rule]." Thus there is a "balance between divergent interests."

What kind of equilibrium is here being represented? The actors are modeled, expected-utility fashion, as in pursuit of what they think is their own best interest; and, just as in market economics, out of their adversarial stance comes an *unintended* equilibrium. The implication is that the paramount, and his subordinates, and everyone else, given their druthers, would prefer outright victory, and they strive for it. Everyone has both eyes on the spoils, not on equilibrium or "functional unity" or "inner consistency." Seen in that way, the equilibrium of structural-functionalist theory is no more expected or intended than market equilibrium. It is spontaneous, a natural feature of the social system, which is therefore, in that respect, a natural system.

Or is it? When the authors turn to acephalous societies, they find a "different kind of balance." "In the societies without an administrative organization, divergence of interests between the component segments is intrinsic to the political structure. Conflict between local segments necessarily means conflict between lineage segments, since the two are closely interlocked; and the stabilizing factor . . . is simply the sum total of inter-segment relations." Reading this, one has a sense of the writers struggling to find words, for the sentence, literally taken, must mean that the system ("totality of inter-segment relations") is its own "stabilizing factor," which is to say no more than that the system is a system. They intend, however, something quite simple and familiar: balance of power. As they put it later, "If force is resorted to in a dispute between segments it will be met with equal force." And, "In such a system, stability is maintained by an equilibrium at every line of cleavage and every point of divergent interests in the social structure." [3]

Is the foundational image still that of a natural system, a state of affairs that comes about spontaneously, no one intending it? Certainly the language—"equilibrium," "line of cleavage," "point of divergent interests"—suggests a would-be natural science framework. But in both cases—the acephalous society and the centralized state—the word "interests" opens the way to a model that portrays human society as, at least in part, the product of human intentions—in this case, calculations. The paramount ruler takes account of what might be in the mind of his subordinate rulers, and they keep a wary eye on those under them, because misrule "may even result in movement of secession

3. They might have added "other things being equal," since force will "be met with equal force" only if the segments are also equal in manpower. A genealogical model will not by itself accurately portray the demographic reality. Leach complained (see below) that the structural functionalists had trouble distinguishing *equilibrium* (a property of models) from *stability* (a property of societies); this is an instance of the confusion.

or revolt"(13). In sum, "The structure of an African state implies that kings and chiefs rule by consent" (12). Balance, therefore, is not spontaneous and unintended but the result of a calculation that the naked pursuit of one's own interest would be self-defeating. The same must be true of the acephalous systems. If these are considered to be natural systems, then force met by equal force must logically end in Hobbes's war "of every man against every man." Evidently, that is not what the authors intend; *realization* that force could be met by equal force provides the restraint. True, this does not—yet—eliminate the notion of social order as a spontaneous product, because the only motive attributed to the individual agent is still self-concern, albeit enlightened. But it certainly removes the hard-science "planetary system" version of society, even if it leaves intact, for the moment, the economist's version of a natural social order.

Subsequent commentary strengthened this identification of enlightened self-interest as a source of stability in acephalous societies.[4] In the same year that *African Political Systems* appeared (1940), Evans-Pritchard published a monograph on the Nuer, the people who were the subject of his essay in *African Political Systems*. His book, *The Nuer: A Description of the Modes of Livelihood and Political Institutions of a Nilotic People*, has become a classic, and sixty years later, as I write this, it still is in print. Among the many, many people who have commented on *The Nuer* is Max Gluckman, a friend and junior colleague of Evans-Pritchard. Explaining why Nuer society did not descend into chaos, Gluckman chose to enlarge on what Evans-Pritchard had somewhat taken for granted: basic material interests. The Nuer, cattle keepers who lived on a floodplain of the Nile river, moved between wet-season homes on higher ground, where they had millet gardens, and dry-season camps in low-lying land, where water was still available for the cattle and for themselves. Groups of people (the "segments" of the earlier quotations) "which are separated by miles of flood in one month, some time later may be camping together at a single waterhole; and to reach this they have had to drive their cattle through the territories of yet other groups. It is therefore essential for these various groups to be on some sort of friendly terms with one another, if they are to maintain their cattle, and themselves, alive. These ecological necessities force people to co-operate; and this helps to explain how the Nuer can be organized in tribes of 60,000 people and more, without any kind of instituted authority" (1955b, 5–6). Gluckman went on to list similar occasions on which enlightened self-interest led

4. Readers unfamiliar with these books are asked to remind themselves, whenever they see the present tense used, that this is an "ethnographic present" that refers to things as they were, in the case of the Nuer, more than seventy years ago.

people to help one another. Nuerland was not a land of plenty, and from time to time people went hungry and sought help from those who happened to be less in need. Outbreaks of rinderpest decimated cattle; people both helped the unfortunate to restart their herds and sometimes they dispersed their own herds to other kraals as a precaution against total loss. All these features were described in *The Nuer*, although not made salient.

In Gluckman's descriptions there is a refreshing intrusion of everyday matters, of people and what they do, and an air of actuality, all of which is a noticeable departure from the quasi-scientific abstractions of structural-functionalist editorial writings. The cold impersonality of "If force is resorted to in a dispute between segments it will be met with equal force" gives way, for example, to a real-world description (taken from an essay by Elizabeth Colson about the Tonga, who live in what now is Zambia) of the sheer inconvenience, not to say misery and even personal danger, that invests people who, living in one community, have ties in another that is feuding with their own. Such crosscutting ties, Gluckman points out, create a category of people who have a strong incentive to act as peacemakers and avert a conflict in which force is "met with equal force." More generally, any kind of prolonged dispute inside a small face-to-face community, where people depend on one another to get through the day, makes life difficult.[5] The returns to unrelenting contentiousness, to use the economists' idiom, are palpably negative.

Utility explanations of this kind—people do what they do because it pays them—are not highlighted in *The Nuer*, despite the fact that Evans-Pritchard opens the book with a wonderfully vivid account of the Nuer homeland and its resources and constraints, and follows it with a chapter on how the Nuer make a living. He details their productive preferences: they adore their cattle; they put up with gardening and fishing, because they cannot do without millet and beans and fish. They feud with one another; they steal cattle from other tribes and from each other. They are violent, warriors by inclination. Nuerland has neither iron nor stone, and even wood is scarce. Nuer do not trade much with their neighbors; they raid them. They have neither money, nor markets. The simplicity of their material culture shapes the social order. "Social ties are narrowed, as it were, and the people of village and camp are drawn together, in a moral sense, for they are in consequence highly interdependent and their activities tend to be joint undertakings." More than this: "Technology, from one point of view is an oecological process: an adaptation of human behavior to

5. See Colson 1962, 102–21, and 1974, 31–59; Gluckman 1955b, 1–26.

natural circumstances. From another point of view material culture may be regarded as part of social relations, for material objects are the chains along which social relationships run, and the more simple is the material culture the more numerous are the relationships expressed through it." That is to say, material things not only have utility, in the economist's sense; they also mark and express social relations. Personality, too, is a function of the "crudity and discomfort of their lives." "Courage, generosity, patience, pride, loyalty, stubbornness, and independence are the virtues the Nuer themselves extol" (1940, 88–90).

This passage, which essentially shows how the technology of production and distribution shapes both social relations and personalities, is followed immediately by a warning: the reader should not be tempted to make an economic analysis. Economic relations among the Nuer cannot be described apart from the social relations in which they are embedded. Even those Nuer who have special skills provide them in return for a small gift or gratis in the name of kinship. There are no economic classes. The individual cannot be modeled as an economic unit. Even families are not to be thought of as economic units; every productive activity is, to a degree, also a collective activity. "[A]ll the people of a village have common economic interests, forming a corporation which owns its particular gardens, water-supplies, fishing-pools, and grazing grounds; which herds its cattle in a compact camp in the drought; and operates jointly in defence, in herding, and in other activities; and in which, especially in the smaller villages, there is much cooperation in labour and sharing of food" (1940, 92). The boilerplate Nuer, in other words, is not an old Adam.

The disclaimer begins with this sentence: "It is unnecessary to write more on what are generally called economics" (1940, 90). That mildly dismissive phrase, "what are generally called economics," is intended, I suspect, to exclude specifically the type of "general equilibrium theory" that has "utility-maximization as a driving mechanism." In particular, the list of qualities—courage, generosity, pride, stubbornness, loyalty, and so on—all negate the model of the rational man in neoclassical economics, and if, at one point, Evans-Pritchard describes the typical Nuer as endowed with "pronounced individualism," he has in mind not a selfish, calculating maximizer, but rather qualities of self-respect, pride, and quickness to take and give offense.

The Nuer, of course, like everyone else, did economize: they deployed their scarce resources in such a way as to survive in a difficult terrain. Dispersing the herd so as to lessen the risk of it being wiped out by rinderpest is the act of a rational calculator. If one has virtually nothing to trade except cattle, then cattle raiding is a rational way to increase one's capital. Tacit permission to cross each other's territory in the twice-yearly migration pays off better than having to fight one's way. Obviously Evans-Pritchard was aware of this feature of Nuer life but took it for granted, leaving it at the margin of his analysis.

This is not the only instance in which the book sidelines, or even glosses over, evidence of rational calculation in a competitive arena. Time and again the author stresses, with evident admiration, every Nuer's prickly sense of being as good as every other Nuer. They were the least servile of people: they were "very proud in spirit" and "their derisive pride amazes a stranger" (90). Not only do they value equality, they actually have it: "There is little inequality of wealth and no class privilege" (91). Yet there is also a category of people whom the author calls "bulls" (179–80). Such a man, he writes, is a "social leader" and "the master of the hamlet." He is wealthy in cattle and "round [his] homestead are clustered the homesteads of his brothers and married sons and, often enough, the homesteads of his sisters' husbands and daughters' husbands." Then follows another swift disclaimer: "He has no defined status, powers, or sphere of leadership." Yet, "It is easy to see in village or camp who are its social leaders, and it is these people who have furnished the administration with most government chiefs. . . ." Again, "As the chief man of his family and joint family he takes the most prominent part in settling the affairs of these groups, but he cannot on that account be said to have political authority." In sum, "Leadership in a local community consists of an influential man deciding to do something and the people of other hamlets following suit at their convenience."

There is an odd to-and-fro quality about these passages. It is as if the author is stuck on a fence and unable to climb down on the side he prefers. The Nuer political system is acephalous, and clearly Evans-Pritchard is anxious that the reader should not confuse the "bull" (or any other Nuer category of prominent person) with the office-holding chiefs of centralized African kingdoms. Each time he describes actions that seem to indicate leadership, he promptly and assertively insists that these men are not leaders. Why the assertiveness? Certainly the rich man gathering a cluster of relatives around him tarnishes those eloquent portrayals of the feisty Nuer, all so "proud in spirit." But there is more at issue: expected utility has a foot in the door. The bull, perhaps, could be modeled as a political entrepreneur, a patron, feeding relatives and others in time of hunger, helping them provide the cattle needed to make a marriage, putting them in his debt in a variety of ways—in other words, turning them into his clients. Patrons are the rivals of other patrons, and, as one builds this model, there emerges a political system, analogous to a market, and of a radically different kind from the model that portrays "functional unity" as the "sum total of inter-segmental relations."

## A Pattern of Ideas

The driving mechanism in structural-functional equilibrium models is not utility maximization but its inverse—what people do because they think it their duty, even when it is to their disadvantage. In other words, conscience is the motor, and conscience is directed by the values that separate right from wrong. How these values are maintained and sufficiently internalized so that people will follow them, even when the payoff is negative, and do so without thought to reward or punishment, is therefore a central inquiry in a structural-functional analysis. The inquiries logically take off from precisely the point where expected-utility analysis, which assumes motivation only by "divergent interests," has reached its limits.

The penultimate section of the introduction to *African Political Systems* is entitled "The Mystical Values Associated with Political Office" (16–22). Force, the editors say, of course exists in African political systems and is "one of the main pillars of the indigenous type of state." Nor, they make clear, do African people live out their lives in mystically generated harmony and solidarity. There are "basic needs of existence" that are "the subject of private interests" (a small nod in the direction of expected utility). Those basic needs result in "tendencies towards political fission," which are counterbalanced by "common ritual values." "Mystical" indicates values that transcend rational choice and the calculation of costs and benefits. They deal with absolutes, things that are intrinsically valued.

An essential feature, therefore, of a social structure is its embodiment of common values. The structure persists to the extent that people know what these values are and continue to be emotionally attached to them. Ritual is the mechanism of attachment. "Members of an African society feel their unity and perceive their common interests in symbols, and it is their attachment to these symbols which more than anything else gives their society cohesion and persistence. . . . Myths, dogmas, ritual beliefs and activities make his social system intellectually tangible and coherent to an African and enable him to think and feel about it." The authors add: "Furthermore, these sacred symbols, which reflect the social system, endow it with mystical values which evoke acceptance of the social order that goes far beyond the obedience exacted by the secular sanction of force. The social system is, as it were, removed to a mystical plane, where it figures as a system of sacred values beyond criticism and revision." Reward and punishment, gain and loss, are not the immediate driving mechanism, as they are in expected-utility models. Private gain is subordinated to the public good. The symbols, nevertheless, are in the end utilitarian. They refer to "fertility, health, prosperity, peace, justice—to everything, in short, which gives life and happiness to a people," and they are associated with "the nodal institutions of the social structure." These common public interests are in constant tension with the divergent private interests "because, in the ordinary course of events, people are preoccupied with sectional and private interests and are apt to lose sight of the common interest and of their political interdependence." Therefore "periodical ceremonies are necessary to confirm and consolidate these values" (16–22). Thus the inquiry enters a world that is not recognized by neoclassical economists.[6]

Could the social system envisaged in the passage above nevertheless be understood as a natural (that is, unintended) phenomenon? The discourse on symbols, which climaxes the introduction to *African Political Systems*, explicitly founds itself on the study of morality, on the ideas that people have about right and wrong. Morality, furthermore, rather than force, or reward and punishment, is presented as the foundation on which all political systems, whether acephalous or centered—indeed all social systems—ultimately rest. All this seems to be a mile away from Friedman's businessman whose thoughts and intentions have no value in explaining how the economic system works. Therefore if a natural system is defined as one that goes its way, implacably, uninfluenced by human intervention, the structural-functional analyses in *African Political Systems* are apparently not in the natural-systems category.

But, again, there are other ways to ask the question, and they lead one to less clear conclusions. Natural science deals in problems; that is, the inquirer describes a state of affairs that could be otherwise and explains why it is not. Why do some cells become cancerous and others not? Why do firms exist at all? The essays in *African Political Systems* address similar positivist questions. Why do "tendencies to political fission" among the Nuer result in "ordered anarchy" instead of chaos and self-destruction? Why did even the most powerful African chiefs devolve power to subordinates? These are problems of the same form

6. That mystical domain might provide the answer to North's problem: "We simply do not have any convincing theory of knowledge that accounts for the effectiveness (or ineffectiveness) of organized ideologies or accounts for choices made when the payoffs to honesty, integrity, working hard, or voting are negative." North, however, as I noted earlier, might say that simply to describe "sacred values" that are "beyond criticism and revision" is not to offer any tractable theory. The question is how they attain (or lose) the status of being "beyond criticism and revision." I will come back to that question in Part III.

as those posed in the natural sciences, and they are presumably open to solution by the comparative method. One or another contextual variable or a combination of them must account for the onset of cancer. In the same way, a survey of chiefs, from those best able to centralize power to those most forced to devolve it, should uncover explanatory variables.

Are the people observed aware of the functional significance of what they do? If they are not, then at least to that extent Radcliffe-Brown's "inner consistency" is part of a natural system and not of a moral order. Certainly, it is implied, people believe that the absence of peace and justice imperils fertility, health, and prosperity. They also make a connection between rituals and "fertility, health, prosperity." But are they aware of the connection between all that and "functional unity" or "inner consistency"? No; just as businessmen do not target market equilibrium when deciding on a price, so no one is out to promote the social system's "inner consistency." No one has clear ideas about "functional unity." "The African does not see beyond the symbols; it might well be held that if he understood their objective meaning, they would lose the power they have over him" (18).[7] The analysis drifts away in the direction of scientific impersonality. As in the case of Friedman's businessman, the thinking of the actors has nothing directly to do with the way the system really works. It functions without reference to their thoughts and intentions, and their role is only to experience its effects.

Is this also the case with *The Nuer*? Certainly the first two chapters contain general statements that are Evans-Pritchard's scientific conclusions and are not part of Nuer culture. Nuer must have been aware of the physical constraints that their habitat put upon them, but they could hardly have articulated the principle that "material objects are the chains along which social relationships run, and the more simple is the material culture the more numerous are the relationships expressed through it." To do that they would require a scientific (comparative) framework, which they did not have.

Explanation abounds in the first two chapters of *The Nuer*. Nuer beliefs and values are framed in environmental constraints and resources that account for the form they have. The discourse, up to that point, is one of cause and effect, not function. But then the book changes form. Chapter 3 describes Nuer conceptions of time and space. Chapter 4 shows how they think about territory, and, together with the Chapter 5, which is on descent groups, explains how territorial concepts and descent concepts relate to one another. The final

---

7. "Objective meaning"—how the anthropologist defines the situation—would strip the symbols of their sacredness, pointing only to their instrumental value.

chapter, 6, is about age-sets and contains a systematic summary of the book's argument. In sum, from Chapter 3 onward *The Nuer* provides a functional analysis that demonstrates the consistency (albeit imperfect) of Nuer institutions.

Is Evans-Pritchard, in these chapters, describing a social system that is designed and created by the Nuer, and is therefore not a natural system? To answer this, one has to be clear about what *function* denotes. Radcliffe-Brown anchors the word in a biological metaphor, but somewhat cautiously. "The concept of function as here defined thus involves the notion of *structure* consisting of a *set of relations* among *unit entities*, the *continuity* of the structure being maintained by a *life-process* made up of the *activities* of the constituent units" (1952 [1935], 180). That is how he unpacks the concept *function*, when used to analyze "animal organisms." But societies, he notes, unlike animals, can only be observed in their functioning, so that it is impossible to "make a morphology which is independent of physiology" (181). You can describe a dog's height and weight and color and smell; there is no equivalent description for a society, which is manifest only in the functioning of its institutions. Societies, furthermore, seldom die in the same way that organisms die; they change their structure, whereas "a pig does not become a hippopotamus." Yet, despite this carefully marked distinction between a biological organism and a society, one is, nevertheless, left with a feeling that Radcliffe-Brown has in mind some kind of empirical reality, something that really is like an organism that is observed, not merely deduced. Consider the passage, already quoted, on functional unity: "a condition in which all parts of the social system work together with a sufficient degree of harmony or internal consistency, i.e. without producing persistent conflicts which can neither be resolved nor regulated." "Work together" and "harmony" suggest performance rather than just logical consistency. The word "conflict" here implies not simply contradictory principles or ideas, but potential or actual violence. The reader is invited to imagine a real world. Social harmony, in that discourse, is suggestively presented as a behavioral reality that can be directly observed, no less than can a well-adjusted organism.

A similar strain, at first sight, runs through *The Nuer*; we appear to be viewing actualities. "By social structure," Evans-Pritchard writes (1940, 262–63), "we mean relations between groups which have a high degree of consistency and constancy. The groups remain the same irrespective of their specific content of individuals at any particular moment, so that generation after generation of people pass through them." This must be read with care. The "constancy and consistency" pertain not to groups of people interacting with one another but to a conceptual framework, a set of principles for allocating people to territory and laying down the appropriate conduct between them, prescribing rights and duties, according to who is a friend, who is an enemy, in what situations, and so forth. These are not descriptions of how the Nuer actually do any of those things, but of ideas in Nuer heads, how they conceptualize their political system (or, at a further remove, how Evans-Pritchard believes they conceptualize their political system). *Function* in this context (the term is not used but is implied in the phrase "high degree of consistency") is closer to its more abstract mathematical sense: $x$ is a function of $y$, which means that the arrangement of elements in $x$ corresponds in some way to the arrangement in $y$. That meaning is quite clear in the following passage: "[S]tructural distance in the lineage systems of the dominant clans is a function of structural distance in the tribal [territorial] systems" (261–62).

In short, in *The Nuer* there are distinct signs that the natural science model that rests on a biological analogy stays mostly in the background. The metaphor of the organic unity of the body, the mutual dependency of the various organs, and ideas of social pathology, have been replaced by something intellectual: a pattern of ideas that hang logically together.

## The Road to Interpretivism

It was customary in Oxford, as in most universities at that time, for the newly appointed holders of chairs to deliver an inaugural lecture, informing the university at large of the state of their discipline, as they saw it, and of the intellectual goals that they intended to pursue. I attended the inaugural lecture given by Evans-Pritchard in 1948.

It lasted, as I recall, about thirty-five or forty minutes, considerably less than the norm, and it printed out in only fifteen uncrowded pages (1948). It was delivered, as were all his lectures, flatly. (His formal lectures were enjoyed only by those who could get past the monotone to perceive, in the well-constructed prose, the elegance of his thinking.) The content conformed to the occasion: tributes to his predecessors; a bow to practitioners in other universities; an account of the contribution he saw the discipline making to the university, to the world of scholarship, and to social needs. "The problems of social anthropology have been in one form or another problems of philosophic inquiry from the earliest times that there has been speculation about the origins of institutions and the purposes of association" (3). "What, in fact, we are trying to do today, and what I think we succeed in doing, is to show what light is shed by intensive studies of primitive societies on general sociological problems. . . . Our main purpose in studying primitive societies is to seek to understand the nature of human society" (13). Distinguishing the discipline from "a cluster of cognate subjects," he remarked, "Our closest relationship is with ethnology, [which is] the study of the history of primitive peoples and cultures. It contrasts in these respects with social anthropology, which studies societies rather than peoples and cultures and uses the methods of natural, besides those of the historical, sciences, seeking to formulate sociological laws of a general kind and not only to trace particular sequences" (4–5). Remarking on the change that had come over the discipline in "the last fifty years," he said: "It has now become generally accepted by social anthropologists that it is necessary for the student, if he is to speak with any authority, not only to have had a university training in it but also to have carried out at least one, and preferably two, intensive studies of different societies through the native languages" (7). Intensive fieldwork had shifted the discipline's central focus. It was no longer speculation about the origin of institutions, which led to "at best pseudo-history." Anthropologists instead should "use the empirical methods of the natural sciences and accept the limitations of these methods" [and] "base their theories on observed phenomena alone and seek to make significant generalizations about societies. . . . Use of the methods of the natural sciences implies that societies must be conceived of as systems analogous to the systems postulated by the natural sciences, and that the explanation of an institution or a custom must be in terms of its function in the maintenance of the whole system of which it forms a part" (8–9).

That lecture was delivered in 1948, and its philosophy, outlined above, appears to be structural functionalist and close to that of the previous holder of the Oxford chair, Radcliffe-Brown. Two years later, in 1950, Evans-Pritchard was invited to give the first Marett Memorial Lecture (1962, 13–28). What he said was a mile away from the inaugural lecture. The lecture itself was, if one may put it that way, animated; its content was combative. He said: "There is a division of opinion . . . among anthropologists . . . between those who regard the subject as a natural science and those who, like myself, regard it as one of the humanities" (13). Still condemning the previous century's "pseudo-history," he now found its error to lie in the very method ("use the empirical methods of the natural sciences") that two years earlier he seemed to favor: "The cause of confusion [lies] in the assumption . . . inherited from the Enlightenment that societies are natural systems or organisms which have a necessary course of development that can be reduced to general principles or laws" (17). Functionalism "assumes . . . that in the given circumstances no part of social life can be other than

it is and every custom has a social value, thus adding to a naive determinism a crude teleology and pragmatism. It is easy to define the aim
of social anthropology to be the establishment of sociological laws, but
nothing even remotely resembling a law of the natural sciences has
ever been adduced. What general statements have been made are for
the most part speculative . . . too general to be of value . . . mere tau-
tologies or even platitudes. . . . [I]n its extreme form functional determinism leads to absolute relativism and makes nonsense not only of
the theory itself but of all thought" (20).

If social anthropology is not a natural science, then what does an
anthropologist do? "He translates from one culture to another. . . .
But even in a single ethnographic study the anthropologist seeks to do
more than understand the thought and values of a primitive people
and translate them into his own culture. He seeks also to discover the
structural order of the society, the patterns of which, once established,
enable him to see it as a whole, as a set of inter-related abstractions"
(22). Continuing, "This structure cannot be seen. It is a set of abstractions, each of which, though derived, it is true, from the analysis of
observed behavior, is fundamentally an *imaginative construct of the anthropologist himself*. By relating these abstractions to one another logically so that they present a pattern, he can see the society in its
essentials and as a single whole" (23, italics added). Such analysis, he
adds, resembles "phonological and grammatical" analyses of a language that uncover structural patterns, which may be unknown to the
speakers of the language, and which make possible comparison with
the structures of other languages.

The contrast between the 1948 inaugural address and the Marett
lecture suggests that Evans-Pritchard might have had a "born-again"
experience during those two years; but this is not the case. In his early
ethnographic writings (as distinct from such programmatic occasions
as the introduction to *African Political Systems* or the inaugural lecture)
natural-systems modeling, although present, does not dominate. If
there ever was a conversion, it must have taken place before 1950. He
chose that year to come out of the closet, so to speak, by openly defying the still controlling trend in social anthropology, which gave obei-
sance to hard-science models.[8] The brief analysis of *The Nuer*, given
above, demonstrates clearly that his intellectual inclinations lay in the
direction of the humanities.[9] *The Nuer*, it is true, contains survivals of

8. This was part of the intellectual landscape at the time. When the British government, shortly after the end of the Second World War, set up a Social Science Research
Council to foster and give financial support to research in the social sciences, it appointed, as its first administrative head, a physicist.
9. An earlier book on the Azande people (1937) concerned their modes of reasoning.

past intellectual forms, including some quaint nineteenth-century-style pen and ink drawings of items of Nuer material culture. Nor does it have any polemic directly rejecting the natural science model of a social system. The book, nevertheless, is a study of the structure of Nuer thought, not a functional analysis of Nuer society modeled as a social organism.

For whatever reason, most likely a delicacy of feeling about using an inaugural lecture to openly and conclusively discard the creed of his predecessor,[10] Evans-Pritchard postponed, for two years, a public and explicit rejection of what he had advocated in the inaugural lecture—that anthropologists should "use the empirical methods of the natural sciences and accept the limitations of these methods." He insists, in the Marett lecture, that social anthropology instead should be considered a branch of history. "The thesis I have put before you, that social anthropology is a kind of historiography, and therefore ultimately of philosophy or art, implies that it studies societies as moral systems and not as natural systems, that it is interested in design rather than in process, and that it, therefore, seeks patterns and not scientific laws, and interprets rather than explains." Practiced in that way, the discipline would be "given the opportunity, though it may seem paradoxical to say so, to be really empirical and, in the true sense of the word, scientific."[11] He explains: "This will always happen if . . . the conclusions of each study are clearly formulated in such a way that they not only test the conclusions reached by previous studies but advance new hypotheses which can be broken down into fieldwork problems" (26–27). The "conclusions," presumably, do not concern particular historic or ethnographic facts, but rather patterns revealed in (or imaginatively constructed from) those facts.

What exactly has been discarded? In 1952, in the correspondence column of the journal *Man*, Radcliffe-Brown, commenting on a series of broadcast lectures that Evans-Pritchard had given, suggested that the difference between a *law* and a *pattern* was insignificant. A law is "a statement of regularities among phenomena for which there is empirical evidence," and that definition applies equally well to a pattern as to a sociological law. On the contrary, Evans-Pritchard had insisted in the Marett lecture, "These are conceptual, and not merely verbal,

10. In a letter published in 1970 in the journal *Man*, Evans-Pritchard states that he had been asked by Radcliffe-Brown, his predecessor in the Oxford chair, to "present to the University the same viewpoint" that Radcliffe-Brown had presented in his inaugural lecture. Radcliffe-Brown died in 1955. The story is briefly told in Kuper 1983, 130–33.

11. The "true sense" presumably is the now virtually displaced wider meaning of *science* that signifies any branch of systematized knowledge. In his inaugural lecture, he had made the distinction between the natural sciences and the historical sciences.

differences" (26). Not so, according to Radcliffe-Brown, "This does really seem to be fundamentally a matter of the choice of words."

But the choice of words does have significance. If we note only that both patterns and laws are generalizations about the connectedness of things, then the dispute is semantic. But that is not all that is implied in the two words; both terms can be unpacked and then the difference—the theme that pervades this book—emerges. Evans-Pritchard himself lays it out plainly: "Social anthropologists, dominated consciously or unconsciously, from the beginnings of their subject, by positivist philosophy, have aimed, explicitly or implicitly, and for the most part still aim—for this is what it comes to—at proving man is an automaton and at discovering sociological laws in terms of which his actions, ideas and beliefs can be explained and in the light of which they can be planned and controlled." *Pattern*, presumably, has no such sinister implications.

Both the "pattern" and the "law" types of inquiry are scientific in that they put forward hypotheses about what connects with what, and test their conclusions empirically. The "automaton" issue, however, makes a basic distinction between the two models. One investigates society as a moral system; the other as a natural system. The questions they ask are different. First, the moral inquiry is descriptive and analytic, asking: What kind of social structure is this? The natural-systems inquiry is not only descriptive but also asks: What causes this particular pattern of behavior? What are its consequences? Second, moral models ask about the meanings that people attach to events and actions; natural-systems models, in their strong form, are not concerned with meanings at all, but only with actions and events. (Choice-theoretic models, of the kind favored by Douglass North, sit uneasily between the two extremes.) *The Nuer*, once again, is a descriptive analysis of how the Nuer construe those parts of their experience that can be framed as a pattern of logically consistent ideas. (That the Nuer have other experiences that cannot be caught in this conceptual scheme is a problem; I will come to it in the next chapter.)

At first sight, Evans-Pritchard's moral-systems model might appear to be paradoxical because it eschews moral judgments, exactly as is supposed to be done in scientific modeling. There is, however, no contradiction. Recall the phrase quoted above: "in the light of which [actions, beliefs, and ideas] can be planned and controlled." The implication is that, although anthropologists study moral judgments, they have no business making them. Indeed, his contempt for positivism is fired by the fact that in practice positivism turns out to be normative, presuming to lay down how society should be, rather than only aiming to understand what it is.[12] In the Marett lecture (1962, 27) he writes, "This normative element in anthropology is, as we have seen, like the concepts of natural law and progress from which it derives, part of its philosophical heritage."

Evans-Pritchard displayed a vehement distrust of what then was called "applied anthropology," which, of necessity, requires moral decisions about what is desirable in social arrangements. In the inaugural lecture he remarks, cautiously, that the discipline has "some utility for colonial administrations." But "it is with more general theoretical problems, problems of our own society, as well as problems of primitive societies, that social anthropology is chiefly concerned." Then, roundly: "Knowledge of man and of society is an end in itself and its pursuit a moral exercise that gains nothing and loses nothing by any practical use to which it can, or may, be put" (1948, 14–15). Referring, in the Marett lecture, to those who "have made far-reaching claims for the immediate application of anthropological knowledge in social planning" and to anyone who "justified anthropology by an appeal to utility," he says this: "Needless to say I do not share their enthusiasm and regard the attitude that gives rise to it as naive. . . . [A]s the history of anthropology shows, positivism leads very easily to a misguided ethics, anaemic scientific humanism or—Saint-Simon and Comte are cases in point—ersatz religion" (1962, 27). This trenchant statement— Lord Robbins might have commended the style while deploring the sentiment—is itself, of course, a moral judgment and clearly stiffened by religious sentiments.[13]

The firm rejection of the natural science model, which had been endorsed, both in the introduction to *African Political Systems* and in Radcliffe-Brown's preface, as the proper tool for social anthropology, signals a major methodological shift. Function, if the word is retained at all, now refers to logic; the proper goal of investigation is structure. By the mid-1960s the fashion in anthropology had, for the most part, turned away from the natural-systems model and gone down the interpretive road to a place where it was not done to "sit with statisticians" or "commit a social science."[14] It went that way despite some severe and very obvious limitations to Evans-Pritchard's intellectualist model of social interaction. Those limitations are the subject of the following chapter.

12. Friedman, I argued in Chapter 3, did exactly this: he attempted to conceal a normative program behind a positivist mask. More on this in Chapter 6.

13. Evans-Pritchard was a convert to Roman Catholicism.

14. "Thou shalt not sit / With statisticians nor commit / A social science" (W. H. Auden, "Victor").

*Chapter 5*
# Imaginative Constructs and Social Reality

*The poet's eye, in a fine frenzy rolling,*
*Doth glance from heaven to earth, from earth to heaven;*
*And, as imagination bodies forth*
*The forms of things unknown, the poet's pen*
*Turns them into shapes, and gives to airy nothing*
*A local habitation and a name.*

—*Shakespeare*, A Midsummer Night's Dream

## Structure in *The Nuer*

One cannot but admire the elegance of *The Nuer*. Herbert Simon's word echoes again in the mind; if any monograph in social anthropology deserves to be called beautiful, it is *The Nuer*. As one reads it, one grasps, so it seems, the very essence of Nuer society, and knows it completely. Evans-Pritchard himself, perhaps, had in 1940 already quietly accomplished what, ten years later, he laid down programmatically as the goal of the anthropologist: "to discover the structural order of the society, the patterns of which, once established, enable him to see it as a whole, as a set of inter-related abstractions" (1962, 22).

It is easy, however, to forget that all models, being abstractions from a more complex reality, have limited applications. Neoclassical economists—this complaint ran through the first part of this book—create models that are too much removed from the complex reality of everyday experience; the more elegant they are, the further they are removed. At the same time, since most economists still want theirs to be a positive science, one that applies to the real world, they choose not to hear when Coase claims that they create imaginary worlds to fit their models. Evans-Pritchard is perfectly straightforward about the issue. Here he is again, describing *structure*: "[It] cannot be seen. It is a set of abstractions, each of which, though derived, it is true, from the analysis of observed behavior, is fundamentally an imaginative construct of the anthropologist himself. By relating these abstractions to one another logically so that they present a pattern, he can see the society in its essentials and as a single whole" (1962, 23). That sentence requires commentary, especially when set beside his other claim (quoted earlier) that, if this procedure is adopted, social anthropology will be "released from [the] essentially philosophical dogmas [of positivism] and given the opportunity, though it may seem paradoxical to say so, to be really empirical and, in the true sense of the word, scientific."

To be released from "philosophical dogmas" is not to see things as they are (that is impossible, because it would imply that one could perceive something without first having a model of what it is), but to see them in a way that is not possible when still bound by positivist dogma. The anthropologist, instead of paying attention only to what fits with the model of positive science, and inventing, say, a Nuer world to accommodate Radcliffe-Brown's vision of a natural science of society, would be "really empirical" and submit the model of Nuer conduct to the evidence of what Nuer do and say, and therefore would be scientific "in the true sense of the word."

From the point of view of scientific method, to say that Evans-Pritchard's *structure* is "an imaginative construct" is not at all paradoxical. An imaginative construct is only what others, less dogmatically antipositivist, would call an assumption or general proposition or presupposition that can be used to make sense of observed data. *Social structure, functional unity, expected utility, general equilibrium, natural selection,* and so forth are all imaginative constructs. Nor should the word *imaginative* be too comprehensively applied: it does not mean that Evans-Pritchard used nothing but his imagination to construct (that is, invent) Nuer ideas about space and time or descent and territory, and that, consequently, his depiction of the Nuer is a fantasy like *The Wind in the Willows* or *The Hobbit. The Nuer* clearly is anchored to some kind of reality. The issue is *what* reality and, in particular, what other realities have *not* been accommodated in the model, and do the omissions matter? *The Nuer* is an elegant book. Elegance is achieved by abstraction, abstraction entails omission, and omission must have an opportunity cost.

## Essence and Wholes

Omission also, if Evans-Pritchard is right, has a benefit: "by relating these abstractions to one another logically so that they present a pattern," the anthropologist "can see the society in its essentials and as a single whole." How is one to interpret the claim that a model, which entails abstraction, also captures the essence of Nuer society, portraying it as a single whole?

*Essence* is a slippery concept. It may be applied to whatever quality or qualities make a thing what it is: water can be hot or cold, clean or dirty, fresh or brackish, but if it were not wet, it would not be water. Sometimes essence is said to be "the thing in itself," which is the thing somehow envisaged apart from its attributes (possible, perhaps, when the thing is a creature or an object, something visible, audible, or tangible, but not possible when the thing is an abstraction like a social structure). The problem is that identifying an essence is a matter for argument: it is something—to use John Barth's word—that is *assigned*, not unambiguously given by Nature or by the Creator. An essence is itself an imaginative construct, and what Evans-Pritchard sees as the essence of Nuer society might seem to others to be nothing more than a set of secondary attributes, or perhaps even a total figment of his imagination. Nuer egalitarianism, we have already seen, becomes less of the essence when one thinks about the "bulls," who, if one accepts Evans-Pritchard's model of what is essentially Nuer, would be quintessentially non-Nuer. (The very word *quintessential*—the purest of the pure—indicates that the concept can be construed as a variable, some essences being more essential than others.) We have to conclude that there are a multiplicity of Nuer essences, each depending on who is making the claim or in what context it is being made. This is in fact a very simple matter: reality can be modeled in alternative ways. There are different ways to perceive the world.

A claim to have found *the* essence of Nuer society is not empirically testable, if there is no prior agreement about the criteria for identifying *the* essence. Whether or not Nuer society does have *particular* attributes can be ascertained, providing one has first agreed on what behavioral indicators will stand for those attributes and what frequency of manifestation is necessary to show that the Nuer really do think—for instance—of time and space and lineage and territory in the way that Evans-Pritchard claims they do. But *The Nuer* is not that kind of book; it contains no tables or frequencies; the evidence is either anecdotal or in the form of general statements.

In any case, those attributes (Nuer thought-patterns about time, space, descent, territory, age, productive resources, and so forth) are not themselves the structure that enables the anthropologist to see the society "as a whole." The structure is the pattern in which those ideas are related "to one another logically." It is not offered for empirical testing, for there is nowhere to test it. Evans-Pritchard does not claim that the structure that he describes is part of Nuer culture; it is his own "imaginative construct," and it stands or falls by its logic, not by any correspondence with an external reality. Whether or not the Nuer do distinguish between agnates and kin connected through women, for example, as Evans-Pritchard claims they do, could, in principle, be empirically verified by watching what Nuer do and say. But there is no empirical test for the structure itself. The parts, so to speak, hang together logically, and that is what makes the structure "true." "The essentials of Nuer society," therefore, are not objective features in a real world but a subjective logical construct. The imaginative construct, as in the case of Friedman's hypotheses, is valid or invalid quite independently of its applicability.

In what sense does a structure of this kind allow one to see the society "as a single whole"? The word *whole*, taken together with *society*, can easily be misconstrued. *Whole* has many meanings. Some of them are tangential to the present issue, but not entirely irrelevant to certain larger questions and the rhetoric associated with them. One such meaning is wholesome or complete or undamaged, all of which suggest that there is an intrinsic value in a model that allows one to see things as a whole, or even that "whole" societies are "healthy" societies. The confusion that is of concern at the moment is the difference between *whole society* understood as a comprehensive totality, an entirety that comprises all the people and all their actions and experiences (clearly an impossibility), and *society modeled as a whole*, meaning a selective logical arrangement that has no missing parts—in other words, a structure.

It is this latter meaning that Evans-Pritchard has in mind when he claims that a structural approach enables one to see the society as a whole. The clause "relating these abstractions to one another logically so that they present a pattern" explains what *structure* means; it is a definition, nothing more than that (except, of course, it is also a clear message that this is the appropriate model for anyone wary of "misguided ethics, anaemic scientific humanism or . . . *ersatz* religion"). A structure, therefore, is not a comprehensive and all-including entirety. Quite the reverse, it is an exclusionary selection of what is considered important. Evans-Pritchard is quite explicit in pointing out that there are various kinds of externalities that his structure does not encompass. One of them is what people actually do: "By political values we mean the common feeling and acknowledgment of members of local communities that they are an exclusive group distinct from, and opposed to, other communities of the same order, and that they ought to act together in certain circumstances and observe certain conventions among themselves. *It does not follow that behavior always accords with values and it may often be found to be in conflict with them, but it always tends to conform to them"* (1940, 263–64, italics added). That final exculpatory clause about frequency is not backed by numerical evidence, nor is the apparent contradiction between "often in conflict" and "always tends to conform" explained. Another acknowledged exclusion from the structure of Nuer society, as Evans-Pritchard imagines it, is one of the main abstractions—the age-set system. There is a structural consistency between the descent system and the territorial system, but "We are unable to show a similar interdependence between the age-set system and the political system" (1940, 264). This straightforward admission that the model has limitations should have disarmed critics, but, as you will see, it did not.

In short, *The Nuer* was not written to do the impossible, which is to present everything that could possibly be known about Nuer society, but simply to provide what is important, what the observer needs to know to understand that society. That returns us to the basic question behind any scientific endeavor: What is the guiding question?

At first sight the answer is obvious. The problem that gives rise to *The Nuer* is one that has been, as Evans-Pritchard put it in his inaugural lecture, a subject "of philosophic inquiry from the earliest times": What makes a society orderly? The Nuer live in "ordered anarchy": they have no rulers, no officials, no courts, no police, no government. They are warlike, quick to take offense, violent toward each other; they feud, they raid their neighbors, they fight about cattle and about women; and yet this anarchy is "ordered"—they do not fall into chaos and wipe each other out. How do they do it? The answer is that the Nuer have internalized certain beliefs and values concerning territory and descent that constrain their behavior, allow them to anticipate the behavior of others, and enable them to live their lives without experiencing "persistent conflicts which can neither be resolved nor regulated."

There is a commanding plausibility about this proposition. It seems to be the truth, even if not the whole truth. A Nuer fighting with a neighbor may endeavor to beat his head in with a club, but he may not use a spear—that would violate Nuer ethics. The book describes many other ethical constraints, less bizarre than that one, that make Nuer life relatively predictable because the Nuer, like everyone else, some of the time do what is right and proper. Of course Nuer, as I pointed out earlier, do calculate advantage. Having "divergent interests," it is inevitable that they should do so. No doubt they also are motivated either directly or by enlightened self-interest to behave themselves properly.

That kind of commentary, however, seems slightly off target. To foreground calculation of advantage, and even to foreground conscience as an explanation for conduct that leads to ordered anarchy instead of chaos, would be to falsify the spirit of *The Nuer*, and to insert into the whole book a focus on causality that is confined, almost exclusively, to the first two chapters. Of course, Evans-Pritchard would surely not have disputed the proposition that Nuer life is orderly (to the extent that it is) because the Nuer hold certain values (he also describes values that make them disorderly, such as their extravagant self-esteem), but I think he would have thought it a crass misunderstanding to conclude that such crude causality—addressing a positivist "why" question—represents the principal contribution to knowledge that his book makes. There would have been no need to visit Nuerland to find out that ethical restraint contributes to social order. The glory, so to speak, is not in what Nuer values do for Nuer society, but in what the values are. It is the discovery of a pattern, a structure, that is the target, not what its consequences are; its consequences are obvious. *The Nuer*, to say it again, construes social anthropology to be what Keynes maintained economic science is: "a branch of logic," "a way of thinking," "a moral science and not a natural science." *The Nuer* is descriptive and analytic; it is a grammar of Nuer ideas, "a set of abstractions, each of which, though derived, it is true, from the analysis of observed behaviour, is fundamentally an imaginative construct of the anthropologist himself."

## Structure and Environment

The benefits of this analytic procedure are easily stated, and they belong to the intellectual world of Friedman and Knight. Models produced to this design are elegant and intellectually satisfying; they can be "beautiful." It is true that such models in social anthropology are minimally tractable, if at all, because they do not deal in quantities. But if one is not concerned much with prediction and, anyway, contemptuous of positivism and its search for laws, that is not a drawback.[1]

At the time when *The Nuer* appeared and in the years of commentary that followed, it was not easy (as it is in present-day anthropology) to separate one's models from "observed behavior." Evans-Pritchard stole a march on the discipline's history when he made behavioral

1. There are other more practical benefits, too. Evans-Pritchard, in the manner of anthropologists of his day, was eager to undo the common notion, prevalent also among scholars of an earlier generation, that the mentality of the "primitive" was, in a fundamental way, different from and inferior to that of the "civilized" person. *The Nuer* can be read as an apologia designed to make its readers respect the Nuer people, and at least to understand their way of life, even if they cannot admire it. Models that are elegant and internally coherent are more convincing than those that leave loose ends, and therefore they are useful for putting across a message.

evidence a secondary matter. That he saw things this way is conveyed, perhaps, in the slightly apologetic note in the phrase "derived, it is true, from the analysis of observed behavior." The data seem to be used as a starter, and used selectively, so that conduct that defies the pattern (the "bulls" again) is externalized as an exception that must not be taken to test the rule. The purported rule is in fact a "pattern" and patterns, if they exist only in the eye of the beholder, have nothing to do with prediction.

There were other exclusions too. Evans-Pritchard's model, like those used in neoclassical economics, has a narrow range of applicability. There is vastly more information in *The Nuer* than can be accommodated in its structural model. He was, as I said earlier, well aware that this was the case. The age-set system hangs loose. Conduct often does not conform with the purported structural patterns. There are actors on the stage who have no part in Evans-Pritchard's play—missionaries, Arab traders, colonial administrators, and, among the Nuer themselves, charismatic leaders ("prophets"), who "had been the foci of opposition to the government" and who were, at the time of his research "under restraint or in hiding" (1940, 185). None of these people are encompassed within the Nuer social structure, as Evans-Pritchard presents it. They are treated as externalities, but, at the same time, they are surely relevant, if one thinks it important to know how the social structure works out in action, or, to put it another way, if one wants to test the model's applicability (as distinct from its validity). The issue would be precisely that raised by Coase (inventing a world to fit the model) except that, in the last resort, for Evans-Pritchard, as for Frank Knight, Friedman, and paradoxically (given the huge effect his ideas had on policy), Keynes, the model is an end in itself, and its limited use in understanding events in the world is a secondary matter.

Reading the book, one has the impression that Evans-Pritchard sometimes found it difficult to maintain this simon-pure idealism. There are frequent departures from plain description and analysis of the structure in order to describe the setting in which the structure is placed, and so, up to a point, to explain why the structure takes that particular form. In effect, social structure is not his only conceptual framework; he also uses causality. A structure (or anything that has to be explained) can be understood as the product of causal elements in its environment. This causal model pervades the two opening chapters. The environment—what he calls "oecology"—makes necessary a mixed economy (cattle products, fish, and garden produce), requires transhumance (movement to and fro as the seasons change), and limits the size of settlements. "Scarcity of food, a low technology, and absence of trade . . . and the pursuit of a pastoral life in difficult circum-stances [produce] indirect interdependence between persons living in much larger areas [than the small local groups] and [compel] their ac-ceptance of conventions of a political order" (1940, 93). Out of these conventions Evans-Pritchard builds his "imaginative construct." The conventions, which are a function of the Nuer environment, are for the most part stable. "Oecological relations appear to be in a state of equilibrium" (1940, 92), with one exception, in which change makes quite explicit the causal framework. Rinderpest reduced the herds. Scarcity of cattle raised their value and modified bridewealth by "low-ering the number of cattle which have to be paid" (1940, 69).

The concept *environment*, in causal models of this kind, extends be-yond ecology to include any variable that might have an effect on the structure, for instance (in the case of the Nuer) the missionaries, the Arab traders, the colonial administrators, and the like. It is evident from the book that relations with these particular environments were by no means "in a state of equilibrium." One result was the rise of the prophets. These were men possessed by "one of the sky-spirits. . . . Nuer have great respect for these spirits and fear, and readily follow, those whom they possess" (1940, 185). Prophets appeared "about the time when Arab intrusion into Nuerland was at its height and . . . after the reconquest of the Sudan [1898] they were more respected and had more influence than any other persons in Nuerland" (1940, 187). He continues: "Certain structural changes were taking place in response to changed conditions; the development of functions that were more purely political than any exercised by individuals before . . . As Sky-gods passed at the death of prophets into their sons, we are further justified in suggesting growth of hereditary political leadership which, with the strong tendency towards federation between adjacent tribes, we attribute to the new Arab-European menace" (1940, 189).

At the time Evans-Pritchard did his research in Nuerland, the "new Arab-European menace" was already more than a third of a century old. There were mission stations; airplanes were conducting punitive raids on Nuer villages; a pyramid "sixty feet high with large elephant tusks planted at the base and round the summit," constructed by a prophet who died in 1906, was dynamited by government forces in 1928;[2] prophets were political prisoners, were killed in fighting the

2. Lienhardt writes that Evans-Pritchard "was really gratified that the pyramid of the prophet Deng Kur (killed, and his pyramid partly blown up, by a punitive force) could still be clearly seen across the plain from Akobo to Malakal, outlasting the administra-tion which had tried to destroy it" (1974, 303). Deng Kur was the son of the prophet who built the pyramid.

government, or changed sides and became government chiefs. Evidently the imaginative construct that eventually emerged as the "political institutions" of the Nuer, and which encompassed not one of
these dramatic developments, was the outcome of a quite draconian
process of selection from "observed behavior."[3]

Highly abstract models—the "beautiful" theories that come to be
valued for their own sake and are evidence-resistant—did not sit easily
in an intellectual world still dominated by positivist philosophy, where,
as Evans-Pritchard put it in his Marett lecture, there was "a feeling
that any discipline that does not aim at formulating laws and hence
predicting and planning is not worth the labor of a lifetime" (1962,
27). Some of his critics could accept neither the idea that models could
be of value without being applicable nor the notion that an equilibrium model was an intellectual construct rather than an enacted social
reality.

The avowed ideational nature of the concept *structure*, as Evans-
Pritchard used it, sometimes went unnoticed, and critics complained
that equilibrium models gave a quite false impression that the societies
themselves were in reality stable. There was a line of critical commentary that ran like this: Nuer social structure, as Evans-Pritchard describes it, is obviously out of date. Once upon a time, before the
colonial administration and the Arab slavers and all the other disturbing elements came on the scene, the "balanced opposition between
conflicting tendencies" model might have been both valid and applicable, but it was irrelevant in the Nuer society that Evans-Pritchard
encountered.

Evans-Pritchard was aware that the structure he described did not
perfectly accord with the society he encountered. He wrote, "Nuer are
unanimous in stating that these prophets are a recent development."
That implies that the structure he presented once was closer to reality
than it was in the 1930s. But he nowhere explicitly claims that his
structure ever was a fit with any positivist reality, whether historical or
contemporary. Indeed, it would have been quite foreign to his general
scheme of things to have done so, because a structure is, as he said, an
"imaginative construct." The critics, it seems, were not complaining
that he gave the wrong answer to the questions he asked about Nuer

---

3. Prophets, however, are intellectually domesticated in Evans-Pritchard's analysis of
Nuer religious ideas. See 1956, 303–10. Outside that frame of reference, they perfectly
exemplified the old Adam: "The ascetic and abnormal element in the prophetic personality would seem to have been mixed up with personal ambition, a striving after
renown, power, and riches, a combination which made the prophets outstanding figures in Nuerland" (1956, 307).

ideas of time and space and descent and territory, but rather that he did not ask the question they wanted asked, which would have been about how the Nuer made sense of change.

There was also a more fundamental criticism. Positivism continued to be influential, and not all those who used equilibrium models believed, as Evans-Pritchard did, that their imaginative constructs should be so readily divorced from reality, probably because most of them were not as averse as he was to the notion that social anthropology might have practical uses. I do not think that any of them were naive enough to believe, as their colleague and critic Edmund Leach accused them of doing, that the societies they wrote about "are as they are, now and forever." If they appeared to write that way, it was because of the particular question they chose to guide them: "What are the continuities and how are they maintained?" To ask that question is not, necessarily, also to say that there is no change. To work out how deviance is controlled or how the crises of succession and inheritance are managed leaves open the possibility that the controls may fail and what began, for instance, as a rebellion may turn into a revolution. The question is there for the asking and is not denied legitimacy. But most structural-functional writers of the time left it to others to point out that deviants defined by those in power may, from a different point of view, be reformers. The relativity of such matters is made all too clear in the assertion, often heard at the present day, that *rebel* or *terrorist* are words that totalitarian regimes use for freedom fighters.

Leach's attack on the writings of the elders of his generation was delivered with characteristic exuberance; it was also somewhat off-target. He wrote: "[S]ocial anthropologists . . . are strongly prejudiced in favour of societies which show symptoms of 'functional integration,' 'social solidarity,' 'cultural uniformity,' 'structural equilibrium.' Such societies, which might well be regarded as moribund by historians or political scientists, are commonly looked upon by social anthropologists as healthy and ideally fortunate. Societies which display symptoms of faction and internal conflict leading to rapid social change are on the other hand suspected of 'anomie' and pathological decay" (1954, 7). This point of view, Leach suggests, is derived conceptually from Durkheim and experientially from a characteristic of the primitive societies where field research was done: they had no written history. "In the result we get studies of . . . 'Nuer society,' not . . . 'Nuer society in 1935.' When anthropological studies are lifted out of time and space in this way the interpretation that is given to the material is necessarily an equilibrium analysis, for if it were not so, it would certainly appear to the reader that the analysis was incomplete." He concludes that the "confusion between the concepts of equilibrium and stability is so deep-rooted in anthropological literature that any use of either of these terms is liable to lead to ambiguity."

Leach put the blame for this confusion on one-visit field research in societies that had no historical record, coupled with a preference for Durkheim as the guiding theoretician rather than Weber or Pareto (no mention of Marx). The one-visit notion is not convincing. It would not have required a longitudinal study to establish that life in Nuerland was being changed by contact with Islam and with the colonial administration. Evans-Pritchard was certainly influenced by the Durkheimian sentiments that Leach attributes to structural functionalists in general—a focus on social solidarity, functional unity, and the like. But Evans-Pritchard surely was aware of the difference between equilibrium analyses and stable societies. His goal was to describe an imagined entity, a structure, which was timeless in the sense that any logical statement is timeless. If told that two and two make four, one does not ask "Is that *still* the case?" (It is an irony, as you will see, that Leach himself put into practice an elaborated version of what, if I have correctly described the book, Evans-Pritchard had already done in *The Nuer.*)

## A Plurality of Structures

A decade later, toward the end of the 1950s, the winds of intellectual fashion shifted and brought faction, conflict, and social change to the foreground. An indicator and an early facilitator of this conceptual shift was a book by Edmund Leach, *Political Systems of Highland Burma,* which appeared in 1954. This book, too, has become a classic and is still in print (albeit from several different publishers and therefore lacking the majestic constancy of *The Nuer*).

The people of the Kachin hills, which lie along the frontier between China and Burma, organize their political interactions in three different ways: Shan, *gumsa*, and *gumlao*. Shans live in the valleys, where the ground is level enough to grow rice in irrigated fields, which support relatively dense populations. Their political structure is centralized: the people are divided between small kingdoms and ranked as lord and subject. In the hills, where it is more difficult to find level ground, crops are grown by shifting cultivation. A patch of jungle is cleared, the trees and brush are burned, and the thin soil is fertilized by the ash. Such a field produces for about two years and then is abandoned. The yields are low and the technique cannot support dense populations. The political structure in these regions is *gumlao*, which I will gloss as acephalous. Roughly speaking, it is the inverse of the Shan style and, with respect to the notion that no one is a lord and everyone is equal, resembles the structure that Evans-Pritchard creates for the Nuer. The third structure, also found in the upland regions, is *gumsa*; it is neither Shan nor *gumlao*, but somewhere in between, sitting on a fence, so to speak, between hierarchy and equality.

Recall again, from the 1950 Marett Memorial Lecture, Evans-Pritchard's description of structure. A structure is "a set of abstractions, each of which, though derived, it is true, from the analysis of observed behavior, is fundamentally an imaginative construct of the anthropologist himself." With this declaration Leach must agree (he does not mention it), for he too states: "The structures which the anthropologist describes are models which exist only as logical constructions in his own mind" (1954, 5). Elsewhere he talks of "scientific fictions" and "*as if* descriptions." Nevertheless, he also writes, with apparent disapproval: "The beautiful lucidity of Evans-Pritchard's own writing is only possible because he limits himself to the description of certain unreal types of situation—namely the structure of equilibrium systems"(1954, 283). Evans-Pritchard, he insists, is "one of the most staunch upholders of equilibrium theory in British social anthropology." Yet Leach himself uses the same technique, arguing—correctly—that it is indispensable: "In practical fieldwork situations the anthropologist must always treat the material of observation *as if* it were part of an overall equilibrium, otherwise description becomes almost impossible" (1954, 285).

So what is the argument about? For sure, Evans-Pritchard did not believe that his structure portrayed an actual stability, that Nuer society was unchanging. The linking of Nuer ideas of territory, descent, time, space, and the like into a structure is an imaginative construct, necessarily timeless. Evans-Pritchard's statement about imaginative constructs, however, also contains the sentence that I analyzed earlier: "By relating these abstractions to one another logically so that they present a pattern, [the anthropologist] can see the society in its essentials and as a single whole." That is the claim which Leach in effect disputes: the complaint is not that Evans-Pritchard uses equilibrium models, but that his model is too abstract—it omits too much. To model a social system as in stable equilibrium and as a single whole is to model it so narrowly that the model is applicable virtually nowhere, because such a model cannot account for change, and all societies are, to a greater or lesser degree, in a process of change. Evans-Pritchard, Leach might have said in the manner of Coase, has invented a society to fit his model. Of course Evans-Pritchard did nothing of the sort; he modeled the logic of acephalous political systems, making a general statement that is both abstract and timeless.

How far that model is applicable to Nuer society in 1935—or, indeed, anywhere at any time—is a different question.

But if one does want to make sense of a present-day reality, it is a real question. "What is much more difficult," Leach wrote (1954, 5), "is to relate such abstractions to the data of empirical fieldwork. How can we really be sure that one particular formal model fits the facts better than any other possible model?" Certainly the model of stable equilibrium that allowed one to "see the society in its essentials and as a single whole" did not fit the facts that caught Leach's attention in the Kachin hills. Those facts required three models: Shan, *gumlao*, and *gumsa*.

The three structures vary along the dimension of centrality: *gumlao* is acephalous and Nuer-like, and Shan, at the opposite extreme, resembles, in this respect, the kingdoms described in *African Political Systems*. The distinction between acephalous and centralized political systems, which is a main theme in *African Political Systems*, also gives shape to Leach's book. His three societies, however, are not separate in the sense that the eight geographically scattered societies described in *African Political Systems* are separate. Nor is it simply the case that his three happen to be neighbors in the Kachin uplands. His claim is different, and is a radical departure from the *African Political Systems* paradigm. He maintains that the people of the Kachin Hills must be seen as a single society that makes use of three different and mutually inconsistent structures. This is not a difficult idea, once one realizes that a model is an abstract from a more complex reality. Nor is it novel, for the experience of everyday life clearly shows that one and the same time-and-place situation may be construed in a variety of ways. People argue about what is right and proper and, as part of the same argument, about what constitutes reality. To say it again: terrorists here are elsewhere called freedom fighters. The idea is even present in *The Nuer*, but it is marginalized as an issue that is not immediately relevant. Recall the statement: "Certain structural changes were taking place in response to changed conditions; the development of functions that were more purely political than any exercised by individuals before . . . As Sky-gods passed at the death of prophets into their sons, we are further justified in suggesting growth of hereditary political leadership which, with the strong tendency towards federation between adjacent tribes, we attribute to the new Arab-European menace." In other words, the Nuer, when Evans-Pritchard lived among them in the mid-1930s, behaved toward the prophets in ways that, in addition to ordered anarchy, also suggested a political structure nearer to the Shan than to the acephalous model. The bulls too represent a shift in that direction.

There are two features in Leach's book that are departures from *The Nuer*, and a third feature that is not. *The Nuer* made it clear, as it had not always been in the past, that an anthropological study of a society, while it focuses initially on the relatively hard external data of what people do and say, ultimately is concerned with what they think, how they make sense of their lives. This is an outcome of Evans-Pritchard's antipositivism; anthropology must be interpretive: it is the study of values and beliefs, not, as in a natural system, a study only of actions and events and their interconnections, causes and consequences. In *The Nuer* Evans-Pritchard follows this procedure but does not foreground it as protocol; he more or less takes it for granted. That is perhaps why Leach, in following the same path, acknowledges no debt. On the contrary, his offhand dismissal of Evans-Pritchard as "one of the most staunch upholders of equilibrium theory" leaves the impression that he (Evans-Pritchard) could not distinguish between equilibrium (a feature of a model) and stability (a feature of an actual society). This was certainly not the case.

The first departure in Leach's work, a significant one, was to recognize complexity—a plurality of often disputed structures—as a problem and an opportunity. When a model turns out to have extremely limited application, the range of understanding can be increased by using other models. A second model (and a third, and fourth, and so on) is introduced to take notice of data that previously were externalized, and then, at a higher level of abstraction, a master model is constructed (if that is possible) in an attempt to encompass lower-level models. Leach did this by logically relating Shan, *gumsa*, and *gumlao* along the dimension of equality/inequality. Evans-Pritchard did not advance to that level. In the case of the bulls, he downplayed, somewhat ambiguously, features that contradicted the model of Nuer egalitarianism. The prophets he simply described, assuming that his readers would have in mind some standard model of charismatic leadership, and made no attempt at a higher-level theoretical integration between it and the model of ordered anarchy.

The second departure, also significant, will lead us eventually away from the spare elegance of structural models toward a real world and the confusion of particulars that becomes apparent when one takes into account action by individuals. One reads *The Nuer* and from its cool, detached prose derives an immediate and extraordinarily vivid awareness of the everyday realities of Nuer life (at least of those that Evans-Pritchard chose to bring into the light): the harsh landscape; fixation on cattle; lean, athletic, wound-scarred bodies; bellicose temperaments; and the like. But, in a way, this all is a magician's trick. The point of the book is not what Leach calls "the social reality" but the model of ordered anarchy that Evans-Pritchard constructs out of that reality. Nor is he much interested in the fit between the model and the observed reality, readily pointing out that behavior does not always accord with values. The model's limitations are noticed, but there is no subsequent effort to transcend them. Reality, as I have several times said, plays second fiddle in *The Nuer*.

In Leach's book, reality has a stronger presence. Anthropologists, he writes, describe "only a model of the social reality . . . [the model is] a coherent whole—it is a system in equilibrium. But this does not imply that the social reality forms a coherent whole; on the contrary it is in most cases full of inconsistencies; and it is precisely these inconsistencies which can provide us with an understanding of the processes of social change" (1954, 8). Let us see what this means, and then ask about its implications.

Shan, *gumlao*, and *gumsa* are inconsistent with one another: no one can base interactions with another person simultaneously on more than one of these structures, for it is impossible to treat another person, at one and the same time, both as an equal and as an inferior (or superior). Moreover, it takes two (or more) to make a relationship, and if the persons concerned (the agents) do not agree on what is proper, that makes the logical inconsistency a practical issue. This is still simple stuff; all it means is that people can construe their relationship differently. They model it in different ways, and they contest it. That may end the relationship, or one actor may prevail and so change or confirm the existing relationship. If enough people opt for change, then, for example, a community basing its behavior on the *gumlao* model of equality may shift into *gumsa* (some degree of leadership), or even into the full-blown ranking of the Shan pattern.

What is here that was not in *The Nuer*? First, Leach makes an explicit claim that "scientific fictions," "*as if* descriptions," or "ideal models," as he variously calls them, besides being "models which exist only as logical constructions [as distinct from physical realities] in [the anthropologist's] own mind" (1954, 5), also are actors' models: "[M]y claim is that Kachins and Shans actually think of their own society in this sort of way" (1954, 285). The Kachin also have "scientific fictions" or "ideal models" or "logical constructions" about the working of their own society, and their models, like the anthropologist's own constructions, are distanced from reality.

Second, not only do they have the models in their minds, they also "recognize that these differences are not absolute—individuals may change from one category to another" (1954, 285–86). Agents have a choice about which model they want to use. In this framework one could find a place beside Nuer egalitarianism for Nuer bulls and prophets, and so make analytical sense of them, which cannot be done when, as in *The Nuer*, they are merely described and treated as exceptions, external to the acephalous model.

Third, the choices are modeled in the form of expected utility: "I consider it necessary and justifiable," Leach wrote, " to assume that a conscious or unconscious wish to gain power is a very general motive in human affairs. . . . I assume that individuals faced with a choice of action will commonly use such choice so as to gain power . . ." (1954, 10). Again: ". . . every individual of a society, each in his own interest, endeavours to exploit the situation as he perceives it and in so doing the collectivity of individuals alters the structure of the society itself . . ." (1954, 8). These statements are the equivalent of the "divergent interests" mentioned in *African Political Systems* and they constitute a straightforward acknowledgment of expected-utility thinking.

What is the evidence that the Kachin have these "ideal models," which are their own "scientific fictions"? It can be inferred from what they do and say, particularly from their myths and rituals. "Ritual and myth 'represents' an ideal version of the social structure. It is a model of how people suppose their society to be organized. . . . It is a simplified version of what is, not a fantasy of what might be" (1954, 286). That is to say, even when a myth appears to be a fantasy about gods or demons or ancestors, it also carries within it "a symbolic statement about the social order" (1954, 14). Ritual, likewise, is "a symbolic statement which 'says' something about the individuals involved in the action" (1954, 13).[4]

If indigenous structural models (such as *gumsa*, *gumlao*, and Shan) are the folk equivalent of "scientific fictions," they are certainly not deployed by the Kachin (or, mutatis mutandis, by anyone else) with what is supposed to be the scientific attitude. They do not concern truth—they concern power. "Myth and ritual is a language of signs in terms of which claims to rights and status are expressed, but it is a language of argument, not a chorus of harmony" (1954, 278). He adds: "[T]he question of whether a particular community is *gumlao*, or *gumsa*, or Shan is not necessarily ascertainable in the realm of empirical facts; it is a question, in part at any rate, of the attitudes and ideas of particular individuals at a particular time" (1954, 286). This is not as clear as it might be, because "ideas and attitudes" are themselves "empirical

---

4. Leach presents these ideas with the air of one shattering illusions, but they are familiar enough, and surely less challenging than is his unbounded extension of the term *ritual*, usually reserved for sacred or mystical matters, to cover all forms of prestation.

*Prestation*, briefly mentioned earlier, is a form of giving or exchanging in which the thing given counts for less than the message about relative status conveyed by the giving. I will return in Part III to prestations and to their opposite, *transactions*, which are exchanges not involved with status.

facts"—it is or is not the case that Kachin have them. What the observer sees and hears are claims. In that respect, Kachin are not so different from Leach, Evans-Pritchard, Fortes, Friedman, Coase, North, and the rest of us, who likewise try to impose on one another (or at least to make intersubjective) our own ways of modeling "reality." Leach's "data of empirical fieldwork," then, turn out to be discourse (including in that term what is said through actions)—"ideal models," claims, lies, pretenses, threats, maneuvers—all made manifest in both cooperative and adversarial encounters, in which the agents try to impose on one another their own definitions of what reality is and what it should be.

This is a marked departure from the significance of ritual identified in *African Political Systems*. Recall, "Members of an African society feel their unity and perceive their common interests in symbols, and it is their attachment to these symbols which more than anything else gives their society cohesion and persistence. . . . Myths, dogmas, ritual beliefs and activities make his social system intellectually tangible and coherent to an African and enable him to think and feel about it." To this was added: "Furthermore, these sacred symbols, which reflect the social system, endow it with mystical values which evoke acceptance of the social order that goes far beyond the obedience exacted by the secular sanction of force. The social system is, as it were, removed to a mystical plane, where it figures as a system of sacred values beyond criticism and revision" (Fortes and Evans-Pritchard 1940, 17). These sentences seem to exclude expected-utility thinking. Ritual focuses the mind on the public good and away from private interest. Leach, however, moves the discussion nearer to reality. No doubt the people of the Kachin hills would say that they are in favor of "fertility, health, prosperity, peace, justice—[of] everything, in short, which gives life and happiness to a people." But the issue is *how* bliss is to be achieved. Through freedom (*gumlao*) or through order (*gumsa* or Shan)? Ritual is then modeled not as oil that quiets troubled waters, but as fuel that feeds the fires of conflict.

We have also come a long way from the structural model as a device that allows one to "see the society in its essentials and as a single whole." Only at the furthest level of abstraction—Coase's invented world—can a society be presented as a single logically coherent (and by implication undisputed) whole. Nearer to reality, one encounters a plurality of structures that exist not as factual descriptions of things as they really are but as claims, strategically deployed, about what should be or about what is. Social structures, in this model, have their existence in claims.

Earlier, asking how Evans-Pritchard's imaginative construct was applicable to Nuer society in 1935, I quoted Leach: "How can we really be sure that one particular formal model fits the facts better than any other possible model?" The problem was difficult, he said, and gave no answer, perhaps because the question, apparently so simple, hides a crippling complexity: what "the facts" are depends on the model used to construct them.

It is time to shift attention from the truth-value—the actuality—of models to the process of competition between them, and to do so in the case both of folk models (like *gumsa*, *gumlao*, and Shan) and of models championed in intellectual arenas. Structures then are imagined not as virtual empirical facts, not as truths, but as the claims people make. The question of their actuality in any other form than as claims then withdraws behind a series of strategic and processual questions about the ways in which claims to define the situation—to define "reality"—are made: What are the ways in which people promote one structure rather than another? Why do they do it? What are the forms of persuasion used?[5]

I will take up those topics again in Part III. Meanwhile, in the following chapter, which concludes Part II, I will review certain political agendas allegedly underlying both expected-utility and structural-functional models.

---

5. Leach, in a later book, predicated structure *also* as a "by-product of the sum of many individual actions, of which the participants are neither wholly conscious nor wholly unaware" and "a social fact in the same sense as a suicide rate is a social fact" (1961, 300). In other words, the choices that people make between alternative structures can, at least in theory, be summarized as a statistical norm in a natural-system model. Logically that must be the case. But when actors justify what they do by appealing to such a norm ("Everyone does it!" or "We should do what we always do!") the norm that they invoke has the form of a statistical actuality but in fact is a saving lie presented as a claim. Leach is saying that under the saving lies there is an objective "reality." I agree; but, to the extent that it is unknown to the actors, it cannot influence the strategic choices that they make. I will come back to this question later; see "Conceptualizing Structure" in Chapter 8 and Part III, note 2.

# Chapter 6

# A Piece of the Action

*Most people sell their souls, and live with a good conscience on the proceeds.*
—*Logan Pearsall Smith,* Afterthoughts

## The Unexamined Life

Why does the expected-utility model continue to be so widely deployed when it has manifest limitations? One obvious answer would be expected-utility's own: a model stays in business because enough people, if they ever think about changing it, see no net advantage in doing so.

Conservatism of that kind comes partly out of inertia, which protects established paradigms. For more than a century the expected-utility model has been the economists' intellectual tool of choice, and for many centuries the individual-centered view of human society (that people are by nature selfish) has had axiomatic status (along with its contrary) both among philosophers and in the thinking of ordinary people. To be a received idea is already to carry a defensive shield. Once found and given approval (and sufficient mystification), an idea is not easily dislodged, even by experiences that deny it; still less is it likely to be shifted by argumentation alone. The expected-utility model, in short, has a presumption of approval, which constitutes its first line of defense.

This inertia, in part, is the product of a necessary and prudent laziness that protects not only expected utility and other positivist models but also any kind of model. If we questioned every model and every structure that we encountered, nothing would ever be done, we would neither produce nor reproduce, and that would be the end. Alternatively, the inertia is an aspect of our bounded rationality; we have neither the knowledge nor the computational capacity to think every-thing through. On the positive side, it makes good sense to use the tools that we have, until they clearly fail to do the job. A frivolous change is a waste of skills already learned.

The inertia also rests on a more basic human need to find order in things, to find a pattern that will defy life's uncertainties. A scientific model does exactly that: it provides the image of an orderly universe, an order in nature. Such a notion has a powerful appeal not only to model makers in the social sciences but also to everyone in everyday life. We see order as a necessity, and ourselves as dependent on pre-diction, planning, and foresight. Every normal person to some extent thinks along those lines, and, when in that mood, we can perhaps understand why economists are impatient with talk about duty, con-science, or morality: it puts the usefulness of their calculations in doubt.

No less threatening are remarks that draw attention to human falli-bility and our transparent incapacity to keep the world in order; they are reminders of how small is the domain controlled by our rational-ity. Intellectual chaos among the economists and, beyond them, chaos in the economy itself is the specter, I suppose, that Coase's 1937 essay might have raised through its intellectual adventuring in the direction of institutions—a transparent irony (outside neoclassical economics), given that institutions are themselves makers of order and coopera-tion. Apprehension of iconoclasm (fronting as constructive innova-tion) would explain why "The Nature of the Firm" was not instantly welcomed into eager debate;[1] and why Lionel Robbins should, a few years earlier, have indulged himself in extravagant invective in sup-port of the neoclassical position; and why Milton Friedman made strenuous efforts to conceal the absence of reality in his calculations.

The climate of the times, certainly over the past century, has given a bonus to any model that presents itself convincingly in the garb of natural science. Propositions in that idiom are proofed against com-monsense objections, partly because they are inaccessible to those whose language is common sense, and partly because it can reason-ably be claimed that translation from a technical language into every-day language may fundamentally distort scientific propositions. Science, moreover, has a good popular press (except from a varying but always-present band of intellectual romantics, most recently manifest-ing themselves as "postmodernist," who scorn what they consider the

1. Of course there are other considerations. Coase, as I explained in Chapter 2, had at that time no established reputation. The same essay, if it had come from Robbins or Hayek, would surely have upset the applecart.

faux certainties of a Cartesian world).[2] In everyday speech, *scientific* sometimes comes close to meaning both *true* and *effective*. This is surely also the case among those who direct affairs and are anxious to be reassured of the rationality of their intuitive decisions. Now that oracles are out of fashion (except in the case of Hitler and of President Reagan's household) statisticians have come into their own, being able to provide plausible "objective" support for the politician's decision, whatever horse he picks to win.[3] History shows up their mistakes and yet the experts stay in business. Why they do so is another version of the question I have been asking about the expected-utility model and its recensions.

Inertia and other psychological motivations for using intellectual tools that are patently inadequate can be concealed by ad hominem arguments that make an immediate connection between the validity of a model and the person deploying it. Distrust the person? Then reject the idea! These arguments, being high on outrage, tend to be crass. They focus on the wickedness of people, sometimes because tracking down faults in a system is harder work and less emotionally rewarding than fingering a villain. Nevertheless, although tedious and often offensive, this kind of commentary is part of our world and is not always wasteful. I am, in short, at the conclusion of Part II, taking time off from the main inquiry to consider arguments that arise from Cicero's would-be truth-uncovering question: *Cui bono?* Who benefits? Who has a piece of the action?

## Political Agendas: Neoclassical Economics

When models are articulated—expressed in words or other signifiers—and held up for critical consideration, it is always with the expectation that a better model is waiting round the corner. This, in theory, is the

---

2. They get a full critical hearing in Rosenau 1992.

3. Ely Devons, sometime professor of applied economics in the University of Manchester, was a senior statistician in the Ministry of Aircraft Production in Britain during the Second World War. He wrote about this experience as a civil servant in a book that is a convincing demonstration of how the most determinedly rational of planners cannot avoid venturing beyond the limits of rationality. Monthly production targets were derived from a large range of virtually unpredictable variables; therefore the statisticians psyched out what their formidable minister (Lord Beaverbrook) would think plausible and adjusted the figures accordingly. Devons said this about statistics: "The passion for figures did not merely result from the help which they gave in deciding issues of policy, but also because figures gave the processes by which decisions were reached, an apparent air of scientific rationality. A document which contained statistics was nearly always considered superior to one which was mere words. . . . Further evidence of this attitude to the use of statistics is provided by the practice prevalent among some officials of writing memoranda with gaps left for the figures, and then presenting them to the statistics division for the gaps to be filled" (Devons 1950, 156–57).

way science proceeds so as to expand the range of our understanding. The practice, however, is not so straightforward. Everything so far said about expected-utility models and structural-functional models makes it clear that those who present and defend one or the other do in fact leave a lot of information in the domain of the tacit. Conscience and duty stay on the sidelines when neoclassical economists are on the field. Missionaries and Arab slave-traders make an appearance on Evans-Pritchard's stage, but have no part in his play. One rarely sees a "warts and all" presentation. There are exceptions, and North's book on institutions and economics is refreshing because it parades the expected-utility model's limitations. But in other instances—and probably more often—we are treated to the opposite spectacle: a tendentious defense of the indefensible. Friedman, as I will shortly show, did exactly that. The preceding chapters on expected utility and on structural functionalism time and again revealed professed rational inquirers irrationally disregarding evidence or failing to confront a "simplicity" by asking "what complexities are subsumed beneath it."[4]

Why do they do it? That splendid exhibition of academic billingsgate that Lord Robbins used to stigmatize those who doubted the perfect catholicity of expected-utility theorizing and saw a need to factor institutions into economic models—"incredible banalities," "spineless platitudes," "tedious discussions," "amateur technology," "thoroughly unscientific and question-begging," "trite generalizations," "insufferable dreariness and mediocrity"—makes one wonder why the theory should be so vigorously defended, when it has obvious limitations. There must be a hidden agenda.

In fact there are several. Darwin's hatchet man T. H. Huxley spoke of "the great tragedy of Science—the slaying of a beautiful hypothesis by an ugly fact." Earlier I quoted Herbert Simon's eloquently sympathetic description of economists reluctant to "accept facts in the real world that seem to fly in the face of that beautiful theory." Aesthetic gratification, of course, is not officially deployed in defense of expected-utility models because doing so would flatly contradict the foundational canon that economic science is a positive science, which deals always and only, as a matter of principle, with propositions that are open to empirical testing, which is not the case with ethical or aesthetic statements. Virtue and beauty are matters of opinion, not fact. That principle—sooner or later you must come down to reality—is a

4. Notice again the equivocating possibilities of the word *rational*. From one point of view, defying or ignoring evidence is irrational. But if the person has a vested interest in maintaining a defective model, a refusal to recognize its failings is, in the economist's definition, perfectly rational. The goal determines what is rational.

restriction on the freedom of the ivory tower, which is the scholar's privilege to let his imagination wander creatively in search of new knowledge, whether or not it will also be useful knowledge, and, at the same time—the word is not misplaced—in search of beauty. Huxley used the term, contrapuntally linked with "ugly," to amuse his readers; Simon, I think, intended a less playful interpretation. It is an irony that *tractable*, the word Coase used to mark a required feature in an economic theory, a word that at first seems so practical, even banausic, should lead to aesthetics, to logical and intellectual forms that, being beautiful, are intrinsically valued even when they are of no instrumental use.

The joy of patterning is a reward that economists mostly keep to themselves. Sometimes it comes out. J. M. Keynes said it, indirectly but unambiguously, when he asserted that economics was "a way of thinking," or "a branch of logic," not a "pseudo-natural science." So did Knight, comparing economics with "elementary mathematics." But mostly economists do not discuss the aesthetics of their discipline with outsiders, because the outsiders are not equipped to appreciate that kind of beauty, and because the political identity of economists, both in the scholars' world and even more in the world of government and business, rests on a reputation for hard-headed, unsentimental, face-the-world-as-it-really-is practicality. The discipline wears a mask that is severely instrumental, entirely dispassionate, not in the least expressive of emotion. Its practitioners do not (on stage) celebrate the beauties of neoclassical reasoning; instead they seek both to explain how the economy works and to make it work the way they believe it should.

Given the limitations of expected-utility theorizing, that task is difficult. The regnant model is positivist and adapted to answering the scientific part of the task, which is to explain how the economy works. To explain how it *should* work requires a venture beyond the world of fact into the world of opinion. The consequent difficulties give rise to some strange defensive arguments, which will lead us to another kind of explanation for the tenacity with which economists defend indefensible propositions.

Friedman, in "The Methodology of Positive Economics," begins his essay by separating *positive* economics from *normative* economics and from the *art* of economics. Positive economics concern what goes on in the world. Art consists of rules for applying the findings of positive economics to problems in the world (in other words, deciding which assumptions are realistic). Normative economics, which today have an extensive and somewhat tumultuous existence, lay down what *should* go on in the world. Following Robbins, normative economics are epis-

temologically excluded from positive economics, which is a science
and therefore concerned with means and not with ends, with how
things work and not with how they should work. Nevertheless, the
three kinds of economics are connected. Friedman says, persuasively,
that neither normative economics nor economic art make sense unless
based on sound positive economics; for example, one cannot *rationally*
plan to attain what one would like, if positive studies have shown it to
be unattainable.

But in fact people cannot be rational in all their decisions, because
there is no rational way to decide between goals which are ends in
themselves, intrinsically valued. A rational act is one that selects between means to achieve some given end. Rationality deals in facts, and
ultimate goals are norms, not facts. To make a rational selection between norms would require their prior conversion into means and the
selection of some further transcendent norm. Decisions about norms
therefore are beyond the reach of positive economics. Friedman,
somewhat hesitantly, argues that in practice this is not a problem. He
makes a most unconvincing suggestion to the effect that economic
goals are not, in themselves, matters of dispute; the issue most often,
he claims, is what will work. Normative economics are therefore
mostly steered by positive economics, even encompassed by them, and
therefore need not be factored into the model as an independent variable. That is itself a normative statement and a pious hope, and certainly far adrift from psychological reality. If that were positively true,
Martin Luther King Jr. would have been without his dream and, so
long as we stayed within the proven truths of the dismal science, the
rest of us would never experience disappointment.

The suggestion is carefully hedged: "I venture the judgment, however, that currently in the western world, and especially in the United
States, differences in economic policy among disinterested citizens
[*sic!* the question is being begged] derive predominantly from different predictions about the economic consequences of taking action—
differences that can in principle be eliminated by the progress of
positive economics—rather than from fundamental differences in basic values, differences about which men can ultimately only fight" (5).
Everyone agrees, he writes, that the minimum wage should be enough
to live on. The real issue is a positivist one: Will raising the minimum
discourage entrepreneurs and so lessen available jobs? That issue is
still around today. The economic logic of the situation is sound and
simple: other things being equal, a minimum wage above the market
level will create job shortages. But other things are not equal and
economic logic doesn't address the politics of the situation. Has there
ever been an indisputable answer as to whether the market or the

government should determine the minimum wage? Economic depressions are bad, everyone agrees. Has positive economic science conclusively decided how or to what extent governments should intervene? Has positive economics finally put to rest the debate between socialism and free-market liberalism? To claim that such differences "in principle can be eliminated by the progress of positive economics" is to retreat into an imaginary world in which the principles of positive economics are always valid and everywhere applicable. In particular it cordons off a space for *utility*, one of the pillars of neoclassical economics; preferences are unidimensional and sufficiently homogeneous to ensure that all important debates are about means and none are about ends. That is not true anywhere, because people are not that homogenized, rational, or disinterested, not even people in the United States in 1953, the year that Friedman published his essay and the year in which the anything-but-disinterested Senator Joseph McCarthy became chairman of the Permanent Subcommittee on Investigations.

Second, the manner in which Friedman gives the discipline the status of an applied science is distinctly Byzantine. Normative economics have been quietly subordinated to positive economics, as just described. In the United States, Friedman's claim implies, economists do not (and by implication no economist should, anywhere) set normative goals, to be achieved through positive economics. The system will itself, the suggestion is, determine what goals are realistic. But that proposition is itself quietly transformed into a normative statement. "Positive" economics, in the Friedman pattern, do not in fact describe how the economic system works, but how it would work in an imaginary world, which is surreptitiously transformed into how it *should* work in the real world, if people had the sense to arrange matters so that it could work that way. What pretends to be a description has in fact become a prescription. This is a step in the direction of what Evans-Pritchard, with Comte and Saint-Simon in mind, labeled "ersatz religion."

Thus a norm is set. Let the system work in the "natural" way; and if it does not, then authorities should act like zookeepers and rearrange the environment so that nature can function as nearly as possible in the natural way. This allows those who are in fact controlling the system (and, if North is right, benefiting from it) to claim that they are merely doing what is inevitable in the nature of things, which is the practical version of saying that positive economics determine (or should be allowed to determine) norms. In short, a feature concealed in the simplicity of the god-term *positive economics* is its inability to take account of equity and justice. The neoclassical economic paradigm provides a useful rhetoric of inevitability for those in control, enabling them to protect privileged economic positions, conceal their incapacity to manage the economy, and at the same time escape responsibility for its periodical failures.

The market-equilibrium model can be used as a pseudoscience to support laws that disadvantage trade unions on the grounds that they interfere with the free movement of labor and therefore with the efficient "clearing of the market." It is also used to justify the removal of regulations intended to control market-inspired excesses. The fact that the value-free posture (being on no one's side) is not sustained in practice and is at the same time a central defining feature of the neoclassical paradigm suggests that there will be rhetorical devices to conceal the discipline's involvement with setting values. In particular, one would expect a rhetoric that puts the appropriate spin on power and its distribution. The power that has to be domesticated to the model and kept off the agenda, moreover, is not an impersonal natural force, but *discretionary* power, the power that distinguishes a human being from a machine. Straightforwardly put, what has to be hidden is the evidence that some people can manipulate the economic system to benefit themselves at the expense of others, and at the expense of efficiency. This can be done if the economic system is convincingly presented as a *natural* system, which means a system that both works autonomously and is without moral significance.

Economists, like other people, are caught in the deceptions and ambiguities that the word *natural* carries in our language. Natural is what goes on in nature, and what goes on there is not susceptible to moral judgment; a natural disaster is no one's fault. But unnatural conduct is reprehensible. If one then reflects that the definition of *unnatural* varies from one society to another, and from one age to another, it is clear that the term *natural* (indeed a god-term, in both its negative and positive forms) has covertly crossed the line from the natural world of things to the social world of people. An act in defiance of nature is conceptually a most complex thing. In the strict logic of a natural system it is impossible, because defiance implies will or discretionary power, which is absent from a natural system. In a less stringent version of nature's "laws," such actions are foolish and doomed to fail. Finally, against the background of an eighteenth-century deistic version of natural law, to act against nature is unnatural—defying God's design for an harmonious world—and therefore morally wrong. The secular version of that last position makes possible a populist rendition of neoclassical economics that gives free enterprise and market equilibrium the virtual status of intrinsic values that require no further justification. Once that premise is accepted, laws that hamper trade unions or allow pollution or permit the wasteful destruction of resources are rational because they preserve an intrinsic value, which is market freedom. More generally, from that point of view, economics are not so much embedded as they are the very foundation on which other institutions must base themselves—indeed, an ersatz religion.

The interaction between that vulgarization of the neoclassical paradigm and its purer versions is marked, in academe, by ambivalence. On the one side the discipline is considered by its practitioners to be hegemonic. Neoclassical economists can be eager proselytizers, enthusiasts who sell the optimizing paradigm and its market framework as an intellectual and practical cure-all. Their way of viewing the world is not simply the best way—it is the only rational way. The move into the study of organizations and institutions, described earlier, is one manifestation of this. Another is the presently fashionable policy-level push to let the market handle any and every problem of production or distribution (cases that range from parking in universities, to running schools, jails, and hospitals as profit-making private enterprises, to selling off various public utilities in the United Kingdom, to sending out spare professors from Harvard to redesign Poland and the former Soviet Union and from Friedman's Chicago to make the gravy trains run on time in Pinochet's Chile). A bold penetration of neoclassical reasoning into the virgin territory of duty and morality and irrationality is a book by a recently en-Nobeled economist who wrote (as an economist) *A Treatise on the Family* (Becker 1981).[5] On the other hand, with each incursion into the realm of practical politics, it becomes that much more difficult to keep out of sight the moral evasiveness that neoclassical economics requires from its practitioners.

Laying down theory, as Friedman was doing in "The Methodology of Positive Economics," is a world away from practicing the "art" of economics. When it came to practice, he, and before him Keynes, did not assume that the free market was a natural system moved by the law of self-interest, the analogue of a solar system moved by the law of gravity. What they envisaged was a constructed cybernetic system. Their goal was to so manipulate contexts that market behavior could approximate the fictitious ideal. A free market did not emerge spontaneously; it had to be cultivated and from time to time its excesses had to be pruned. There was no disagreement about that. How specifically to do the job, how best to intervene, what tools were likely to be most efficient—those were the points at issue. What, then, is the heart of

5. Not all economists manifested this sense of their own effortless superiority. "If economists could get themselves thought of as humble, competent people, on a level with dentists, that would be splendid!" That is the closing sentence of a book by the most distinguished of all modern economists, John Maynard Keynes (1932, 373).

the matter? If the market is known to require constant corrective action, why should anyone maintain the myth of market *freedom*?

At the center of the discourse, but often concealed, is the issue of
power. A free market, so long as reality is ignored and only the ideal
envisaged, logically produces "an 'utter dispersion of power,' creating
a state of true equality for all."[6] Everyone has equal access (not true);
therefore everyone has equal power (a non sequitur); therefore (a tru-
ism) no one has power. Moreover, when economies are imaged as
natural systems, the parts move, as do the planets, according to "natural laws." It again follows, first, that no one has power, the system
works in its own way, it is autonomous; second, since no one is in
charge, no one can direct the system to their own advantage, therefore—
another non sequitur—it must work to everyone's advantage. (It
could just as well work to everyone's disadvantage.) The system that
balances itself benefits everyone: at the point of equilibrium the market clears itself, and both buyer and seller are content. With propositions of that kind, the pure neoclassical theory has propelled itself out
of economic science and into politically loaded poetics, or, if one
chooses not to be cynical, into theology, into a religion that, although
in fact ersatz, its followers consider "truth." The supposed science has
become a ritualized exercise in the celebration of a paradigm which,
purporting to define the nature and purpose of economic activities, in
fact justifies particular distributions of power.

Despite these shortcomings, the technician aspect of their calling is
not a feature that economists conceal. On the contrary, it is written
into the constitutions of profit-making advisory institutions and appears daily in the op-ed pages of the newspapers, where econosages
tell their readers what sense to make of trade deals, market shifts, and
government actions. The unadvertised part of this agenda is not the
public role of neoclassical economists—they pervade the news media
in all its forms—but the particular political interests that they choose
to support. Whether the theory shapes the politics, or the politics
shape the theory, is sometimes hard to say, and the balance clearly
varies according to the regime in power. The period and the place of
the three economists I chose to discuss—the United States since the
Second World War—features marketplace capitalism, and, more recently, the demise of the command economies in the Communist
world. The virtues of the free market are on the open agenda; its systematic weaknesses and limitations are less often paraded. One feature in particular is kept off the public agenda, despite having almost
the status of received wisdom in common folklore: although the market

6. Nelson (1991, 6) quoting Stigler.

manages production relatively well, the distribution of wealth under market capitalism is governed by the principle of might is right. The rich and powerful get what they want first; others take their chance on what is left.

In other words, expected-utility theorizing is vigorously defended because it suits those in power to have it defended. It is not, of course, defended on those grounds. The main argument, as I described earlier, is inevitability: the economy is a natural system and to interfere with it is unwise and ultimately self-destructive, as the cases of the USSR, India, North Korea, or Maoist China are supposed to demonstrate. Of course governments in capitalist countries in fact do interfere continuously to "correct the market" and perform various other maneuvers that in fundamentalist neoclassical theory are unmentionable.[7]

The insistence that these sallies to control the market are merely occasional "corrections" applied to a system that is otherwise autonomous conceals the use and extent of state and corporate power. *Free* in *free market* has a narrow technical reference to action that is unfettered by any consideration other than maximizing utility. But in common speech the term is associated with liberty and the right of the individual to do as he or she wishes, which in turn puts a favorable spin on the activities of those who are behaving like wolves. The inexorability of nature is applied to social systems, and natural selection is left to dispose of the weak and unfit. Those who are strong and survive incur no blame for what they do, because they could not do otherwise. On the other hand a natural system is one in which order is spontaneous, not the product of regulation and constraint, and therefore it promotes freedom to do all that one wishes. Freedom is the negation of tyranny. The wonderfully hypocritical contradiction in all this is made apparent, from time to time, by captains of industry, courageous and outspoken defenders of the free market, who go cap in hand to the government to help them out whenever the market threatens to trash them.

Is all that I have written about the deceit and hypocrisy that prevails in free-market discourse in fact true? Certainly it is a fact that when Chrysler's ox was being gored by free-market competition, Lee Ia-

----

7. The fairy-tale quality of the supposedly positive model is sometimes openly stated: "But in modern economics the market is seen as a complex and imperfect system which has to be carefully looked after by the government: property rights have to be defined and protected, contracts have to be enforced, 'market failures' have to be corrected and income has to be redistributed to ensure social justice . . . the theory of competitive equilibrium is not usually taken seriously at the practical as opposed to the theoretical level . . . it provides a framework for thought" (Sugden 1986, 2). Keynes, as I said, agreed. This produces an agreeable contradiction: markets are only "free" when they are regulated; the invisible hand falls down on the job.

cocca and the firm were saved by a government intervention that removed the market's freedom to put Chrysler out of business. It also is the case that when free-market deregulation made it possible for the owners and operators of savings and loan institutions to embezzle huge sums from the public, public money was used to stop the market from reaching an equilibrium position that would have been socially and politically disastrous. There are also countless cases, in the United States and elsewhere and throughout history, in which public money was used to enrich private entrepreneurs—as cynics say, privatize the gains and socialize the losses. This at least can be said: the myth that market freedom is ultimately for the good of us all, to paraphrase Keynes again, makes it easier for the nastiest of men, acting from the nastiest of motives, to benefit themselves.

But it does not follow from any of these instances of entrepreneurial nastiness that when an economist deploys the expected-utility model and reaches a conclusion about employment statistics, or production figures, or anything else that an economist attends to, the only test of the model's validity and applicability is what material payoffs accrue to him or her from coming to that particular conclusion. Even when it is the case that the economist has been hired by someone with an axe to grind to come up with conclusions that the economist himself believes are false, it still is possible, and desirable, to disinterestedly test those conclusions.

This, of course, is a somewhat purist stance; the principle of prudent laziness, mentioned earlier, indicates that not much is to be gained by giving that same economist the benefit of the doubt a fourth or a fifth time. Distrust the person, distrust the argument; in the end it will come to that. In principle, of course, facts are facts, whoever produces them. Nevertheless, we conduct much of our lives on other principles—necessary laziness or bounded rationality—and allow a person's reputation, whether good or bad, to decide whether or not we should accept his or her opinions as facts. So, even if it is from a precise point of view a bad thing, we do frequently decide what is true on the basis of who is saying it. It is a human thing to do, and in fact that rule of thumb is an important element in making sense of stratagems that are used to define situations.

## Political Agendas: Structural Functionalism

An accusatory cui bono discourse was also visited on structural-functionalist anthropologists. It began in the late 1960s and the fag end of it is still around today. For the most part social anthropologists in the middle years of the century were, like Evans-Pritchard, ambivalent about applied anthropology; they did not often thrust their expertise at those in power, as the economists did.[8] Their arena, moreover, was much smaller than that of neoclassical economics and the victims of scholars said to have sold out truth for their own advantage were people half a world away. We ourselves and those around us are the victims of academics who clear the field for the "nastiest of men" (the phrase Keynes used to describe profit-obsessed businessmen). Nonetheless, if the wrong was done on a smaller scale and to people in another country and by no more than a handful of practitioners, the accusations were no less vehement.

Recall Leach's attack on colleagues who had done research in Africa. They wrote, he said, as if the societies they studied were not only homogeneous—they could be subsumed within a single structure—but also entirely stable: their structure appeared never to change. There is, as I said, plenty of evidence in *The Nuer* that Nuer society was changing and that Evans-Pritchard not only noticed this fact, but also wrote it down in the descriptive parts of his book. He did not build it into his analysis, I suggested, because that was not his concern. His intention was to model an acephalous political structure, to make sense of ordered anarchy.

There are, however, other ways to see the situation. I will begin by asking why anthropologists at that time chose to make order, stability, and continuity their central problem, rather than conflict and change. Why did Evans-Pritchard decide to understand the Nuer through a model that directed attention at the containment of conflict and the maintenance of the status quo, and therefore away from radical social change? Why, for example, were the prophets virtually externalized?

All eight essays in *African Political Systems* are about peoples subjected to colonial rule. The writers, however, focus on "the indigenous political system" and either do not discuss the effects of colonial rule at all, or review them at the end of the essay under such headings as "The period of European rule" or "Post-European changes." They wrote as if their goal was to reconstruct a past reality, leaving the colonial present for another occasion or for another investigator. "Twenty-five years ago there was no one who had authority over all the Tallensi; no one who could exact tax, tribute or service from all," wrote one of the editors, Meyer Fortes, who lived in Taleland in the mid-1930s.[9] The question, however, still remains: Why did he not

8. There were some exceptions. Malinowski saw anthropology as inevitably (and as a moral obligation) involved in the colonial encounter, particularly in Africa. More on him later. Applied anthropology had a better innings in the United States around that time. Today, through consultancy, it is beginning to find a foothold in the corporate world.

9. I am not suggesting that was not the case in Taleland in 1911; I am suggesting that

choose to take the colonial administration into account and derive his imaginative construct from the society he saw around him in the 1930s?

There are, as I said, several answers. All models are selective, and all thinking requires abstractions, and in the case of the Tallensi, a model that externalizes the colonial rulers gives better access to the principles that underlie "ordered anarchy," assuming that is the goal of the inquiry. Alternatively, the goal might in fact be to write an account of Tale society as it was before the colonial period. Third—what now is dismally called "salvage anthropology"—we should learn all we can about these social structures before they become extinct. Fourth, the precolonial structure would still be part of the contemporary mind-set. Evans-Pritchard's model of Nuer social structure would be at least partially applicable to the Nuer situation in the 1930s (always assuming that the Nuer did in fact construe their political system according to Evans-Pritchard's grammar). It would still influence the way they tried to make sense of what was happening around them.

All these reasons can be argued one way or the other. There is, however, another genre of explanation for the bias toward indigenous political systems; it is aimed, as in the case of the expected-utility theorists, ad hominem, at the writers. It began to appear about thirty years after *The Nuer* and *African Political Systems* were published, when the colonial regimes in most of sub-Saharan Africa (except South Africa) were either out or clearly on their way out. The message was simple: All structural-functionalist writing in colonial situations is tainted because it was intended to serve the interests of the colonial powers. The writing, therefore, gave no scientific understanding of the social systems which it purported to describe and analyze, but only revealed (after the appropriate deconstruction) the colonial mind-set of the writers themselves. Put simply and at its worst, anthropologists sold out their intellectual integrity. More generously, they were creatures of the time, and, like everyone else, perceived truth where they had been socially conditioned to see it. I earlier wrote of *res tegendae* in neoclassical economics, things to be kept under cover, agendas constructed with power and influence in mind, rather than truth. Now the same inquisitorial light is turned on social anthropology. In this kind of critique the primary assumption, as I said, is that one can sufficiently evaluate what is written simply by knowing who wrote it. There is no point in seriously testing the applicability or validity of a model,

---

Fortes, like Evans-Pritchard, was not primarily engaged in historiography, as that sentence might imply, but rather in modeling Tallensi political structure as an imaginative construct that externalized colonial rule, a procedure that is theoretically no different from what is done in various versions of the expected-utility model or any other model.

because the model is entirely a function of the motives and mentality of whoever produces or uses it.

That claim has no immediate merit whatsoever; it is an unwarranted shortcut in the investigative procedure and an error born out of sloth, a cavalier disregard for the available evidence, and an indication of the bigotry and intergenerational malice that normally goes along with a shift in intellectual fashions. A model is valid/invalid, applicable/not applicable absolutely, in and of itself, whoever has constructed it, whoever is applying it, whatever their motives. At least that is the case within the framework of the saving lie that, for the moment, guides my argument.

On the other hand, a model is also constructed to deal with a particular problem or answer a particular kind of question. Quite independently of the validity of the answer, one can legitimately ask, as a separate inquiry, why that particular question was chosen. Structural-functional models focused on continuity and were designed to find out what maintained social structures in their existing forms despite forces that might otherwise have changed them. The alternative question is this: What are the forces that overcome structural inertia and lead to social change? It seems fair to ask why anthropologists at that time did not focus on Leach's "faction and internal conflict leading to rapid social change" or, for that matter, on the changes generated externally by the colonial regimes. Certainly there was enough change going in the first half of the century in virtually all the societies then being studied by anthropologists, including the eight that feature in *African Political Systems*. All of them, to repeat, were under colonial administration.[10]

One answer, which I gave earlier, is simply that the anthropologists were interested in how systems maintained themselves, and, in the case of the Nuer or the Tallensi, in the principles that underlay ordered anarchy. That, so to speak, was the topic du jour in social anthropology. If it is then said that in most of Africa, ordered anarchy, for instance, no longer had much to do with the way people lived, and therefore to engage in such studies was to retreat into an ivory tower, there is always Evans-Pritchard's principled answer, quoted earlier: "Knowledge of man and of society is an end in itself and its pursuit a moral exercise that gains nothing and loses nothing by any practical use to which it can, or may, be put." But the question has not gone away: Why was *that* the favored topic in *that* particular context? Why were those anthropologists apparently not interested in change?

10. *African Political Systems* was published in 1940 just after the outbreak of the Second World War. All the contributors had conducted their field research in the 1930s, when it was still not so clear (as it was by 1945, when the war ended) that the writing was on the wall for colonial regimes.

The cynical answer is inescapable. An expected-utility model suggests that the anthropologists made that particular choice because they had calculated its costs and benefits to themselves—that is, the material, not the intellectual, costs and benefits. They needed at least the permission, if not the support, of the colonial administration. Colonial regimes strongly favored order and stability (as governments do anywhere); they generally were uneasy about change, and they abhorred insurgency. Anthropologists therefore concentrated on stability, on the sources of order, on ways in which unruly behavior was—or could be—inhibited. An understanding of the principles that underlay obedience and compliance would lead to enlightened and inexpensive government. In short, they concentrated their attention on the maintenance of order and on stability because the colonial governments wanted them to do so.

Certainly the suggestion that anthropologists working in a colonial setting consistently and consciously (if quietly) steered a course that would bring them into favor with the colonial administration is not implausible. Most of them were funded by agencies which did not look kindly on colonial insurrection, and known Marxists had difficulty getting support for research in colonial territories. Their very presence in a colonial territory was by grace and favor of the local administration. But the further conclusion that their conscious purpose was to preserve colonial rule is a long way off the mark. Some of them—Gluckman is an example—were well to the left of the political spectrum on issues of colonial independence. In the late 1920s and through the '30s there was an edgy and sometimes acrimonious public debate in the journal *Africa* and occasionally in the London press between Malinowski and various colonial officials about the proper role of anthropology in colonial territories.[11] Moreover, I can think of no more than a handful of those I knew who worked in Africa who were not, at some time in their career, at odds with the local administrators and vehemently on the side of "the natives."[12] My guess is that in most

11. In the early 1930s, Malinowski, a dominant figure in British anthropology, began a vigorous campaign to focus field research, especially in Africa, on the colonial situation. See the essay "The Anthropologist as Reluctant Imperialist" by Wendy James. It is in *Anthropology and the Colonial Encounter* (Asad 1973), a book of essays which range from the evidential and scholarly to near-mindless polemic. It, along with a symposium published in *Current Anthropology* (vol. 9, 1968) are useful starters for anyone interested in "the role of anthropology in creating, preserving, and implementing ideologies of oppression" (Faris 1973).

An essay on Gluckman by Richard Brown (1979) describes, judiciously and with exemplary clarity, the moral and political difficulties that beset anthropologists working in colonial situations. See also Brown 1973, Kuper 1983 (Chapter 4), Frankenberg 1989, 165–93, and *Anthropological Forum* 9 (2).

12. Evans-Pritchard was surely in this category. A chance encounter in the street with

cases in the 1930s it never occurred to the anthropologists that general equilibrium theory, which they used to direct their research and their analyses, could be a scripture written to glorify and preserve colonial domination. They saw the model as "scientific," whether in the broad or the narrow sense of that word, designed to expand our store of knowledge about social systems by gathering objective information, which might possibly be useful to colonial administrators but had nothing whatsoever to do with legitimizing the colonial presence. Leach provides the last word:

> It seems to me now, as it seemed to me then, that the principal task of academic anthropologists in the field is to pursue research which may lead to advances in sociological generalizations and that the anthropologist, as such, is not *professionally* concerned with whether administration is efficient or inefficient, just or unjust. On the other hand I also still believe, as I believed then, that administrators working in backwoods areas of modern states, whether they be labelled as colonialists, nationalists, communists, or anything else, are likely to be better administrators if they know something about the sociology of the people they are supposed to be administering.
>
> This by no means precludes the possibility that, in my private opinion, the world would be a better place if no such administration existed at all. (1977, 60–61, italics added)[13]

## Change the Question

An expected-utility model assumes that people do not act in accordance with the dictates of conscience or to perform a duty, but only to maximize utility (narrow meaning). Moral models make a contrary assumption: people do what they have been taught is right and proper, whether it pays off or not. The residue unconsidered by the expected-utility model is our humanity, which is certainly part of our experience. The moral model, by mapping only what is considered right and proper, has no place for change, and change is also part of our experience.

---

the bursar of the Oxford college to which we both belonged, and a noticeably frosty exchange of greetings, provoked this reminiscence. The bursar had been Evans-Pritchard's commanding officer in a Military Government unit in Cyrenaica. Two Arabs had been arrested for shooting a man. "Feud," Evans-Pritchard explained to me (he had a staccato spoken narrative style), "Was going to hang them. Feud. Couldn't make him understand feud. Broke into his office that night. Took all the evidence. Burned it. Couldn't hang them. No evidence." See also Chapter 5, notes 1 and 2.

13. This passage occurs in a collection of eight essays published in *Anthropological Forum* under the title "Anthropological Research in British Colonies: Some Personal Accounts." The essays, in particular those by Firth, Leach, Morris, and Lewis make it very clear that those who insist that all anthropology done in a colonial setting is of necessity morally and intellectually compromised hugely simplify a complex and varying situation—an instance, perhaps, of Foucault's "tyranny of globalizing discourses."

Expected-utility and moral models are complementary: each addresses a question that the other ignores. If economists were trained in moral inquiry, and if moralists were taught to see the beauty of neoclassical general equilibrium theory, and if both used both models to solve problems, would the job be done? For sure it would produce better solutions to *practical* problems. Administrators do that all the time, combining in practice what cannot be combined in theory. So do politicians, although, as I said earlier, they are also likely to rely on their political "instincts" or employ an astrologer and have someone find a suitably rational justification later.[14]

Practical problems may be solved in this reach-me-down way, but no unified theory emerges. Moral models and scientific models are contraries and, since intellectual endeavors are ruled by the tyranny of logic, intellectuals, at least in their intellectualism, find it difficult to live with two incompatible "true beliefs," even when the logic of their own argument tells them that there is no alternative (as in the agent/principal regression that ends only when morality is invoked). They make the issue truth, instead of usefulness; they elevate one belief and push the other into the background, or ignore it, or sometimes deride it. Coase, having opened the door to moral considerations, closed it again when notions of honesty and fair dealing were about to invade "incomplete contracting." Nor are the economists alone in this reluctance to treat tools as tools and not as ontological realities. Data in *The Nuer* and the introduction to *African Political Systems* ("divergent interests") show a clear need for a rational-choice model, but the behavior described is left unanalyzed. Leach himself, having boldly declared power to be a utility (although not using that word), stops short of developing a rational-choice model.

The lesson seems clear. A unified model that simultaneously presupposes self-regarding (rational) and other-regarding (moral) motivations is a logical impossibility: those assumptions remain as contraries and there can be no logical synthesis. The sensible course is to be thankful for both tools, admit each does a limited job, not claim they do what they cannot do, and, for practical purposes, work both sides of the street.

It is time to change the question and ask not how near or far these particular models are from the truth, but how models of any kind are deployed. What strategies do people use, and with what effect, when they attempt to define situations for one another?

14. The reference is to Ely Devons and the Ministry of Aircraft Production. See note 3 above.

# Part III
# Agency and Rhetoric

*For Art and Science cannot exist but in minutely organized Particulars*
*And not in generalizing Demonstrations of the Rational Power.*

—*William Blake,* Jerusalem

*"Freedom is the thing examined. Inevitability is what examines. Freedom is the content. Inevitability is the form.*
  *Only by separating the two sources of cognition, related to one another as form and content, do we get the mutually exclusive and separately comprehensible conceptions of freedom and inevitability.*
  *Only by uniting them do we get a clear conception of man's life."*

—*Tolstoy,* War and Peace

This book runs at two levels. One is abstract theory—Blake's "generalizing Demonstrations" or Tolstoy's "form"—which are ideas conveyed discursively in propositions about social systems. Ideas of that kind occupy its first two parts. The third part, which is about agency, attends to "minutely organized Particulars" and to Tolstoy's "content." It draws on the ethnography of everyday life, in which ideas are presented not only as theories to be judged true or not true, but also as weapons. In other words, they are put to use, and that requires not only propositional knowledge but also know-how.

Agency models presume alternative structures and therefore are choice-theoretic and goal-directed. In them the simple bottom-line neoclassical scheme, in which *utility* has its narrow meaning, dissolves into a complexity of motives, calculations, messaging, and self-presentation, some of it devious. Players are modeled as doing what they think will "pay" them; but what they think will pay them, and how they play their hands, are complexified not only by morality and bounded rationality, which are a trouble for rational-choice theorists, but also by the use of irony, hyperbole, humor, hypocrisy, equivocation, plain deception, and various other forms of tactical indirection, which most social theorists do not place at the top of their agenda.

There are two complementary ways to construct a choice-theoretic model: (1) through psychological or cognitive frameworks that focus on the *chooser*, or (2) through agency models that describe (a) a *range of structures* and (b) the *strategies* used to make one or another structure prevail. Psychological and cognitive models derive from theories about the emotions we feel (psychology) and about the mental procedures that we use (cognitive studies) in coping with our experiences. Although my focus is on the choices, not the choosers, some basic presuppositions about the human psyche—our need for meaning and order, for example, or our disposition to seek advantage—are required to construct an agency model. All three models—psychological, cognitive, and agency—have their uses, and they are complementary rather than contradictory.

This third part of the book moves away from the use of logic, which is correct reasoning from given premises, in the direction of rhetoric, which is persuasive "reasoning" intended to make a premise or a point of view—a presupposition—acceptable. I will use a simple interactionist and intentionalist[1] model of the part rhetoric plays in social systems. The model is constructed out of three elements: one is a repertoire of alternative ideas (structures) both about how a system should work (a morality) and about how it actually works (a presumed reality); the second is a cast of performers; and the third is a set of techniques used by performers to foist ideas on one another and so define the situations in which they interact. The model connects agents (the performers) with structures (the ideas) by describing the persuasive techniques (rhetoric) they use either simply to prevail over one another, which I will call the *palaestral* application of the model, or (sometimes) also to promote a structure they prefer, which is its *instrumental* (or *consequential* or *constitutive*) version.

Both versions (the paleastral and the consequential) presuppose the saving lie: no structure and, more generally, no idea (including, of course, the model itself) could be an eternal verity. In varying degrees all structures and all theories are fallible when put to use, not because they fall apart when confronted by "absolute truth," but because they are liable to be displaced by another structure, which the performers hope will better suit their purposes. Truth, in this model, is only something to be argued about, and the sole eternal verity is that there are no eternal verities.[2] This fallibility of ideas, the absence of Truth, gives agency, and therefore rhetoric, a part to play in social life.

In communicative encounters a situation is defined by imposing on it a structure. To structure something is to give it an identity (a name) and impart to it, *imaginatively*, a stillness, a concreteness, a wholeness, and an exclusivity that are not the reality. I will begin by showing (Chapter 7) that presuppositions of structure and permanence per-

1. *Intentionalist* means that the model concerns purposive action; it does not further assume that what comes to pass is explained entirely by what the agent intended.

2. Pyrrhonic assertions of this kind, I have discovered, whether or not explicitly linked with pluralism and its uncertainties, may cause unease or even give offense, so let me change the words and say that of course there is an eternal verity, which is reality, or, more down to earth, which is Leach's "by-product of the sum of many individual actions." But all that we can know of this Truth is one or other of its many versions. Reality, in other words, is itself an imagined construct that comes to us most readily when a version of it gives an unexpected result.

vade our everyday life. Then I will describe the rhetorical strategies people use to affirm a particular structure as a basis for action—how, in other words, they define situations. Chapter 8 deals with indirect and therefore more complicated manifestations of the same activity.

To state Leach's foundation again, structures are (1) in the category of the mental, (2) modeled as not only in the mind of the observer but also in the minds of the people observed, for whom the structures are their designs for living,[3] and (3) modeled in the plural.

3. Obviously I am not suggesting a perfect correspondence between the two. Observers may identify tacit models, structures that the actors cannot articulate. Actors likewise may be reflexively aware of models that observers have missed.

# Chapter 7

# Affirming Structure: The Amen Category

*What we call the beginning is often the end*
*And to make an end is to make a beginning.*
*The end is where we started from.*

—*T. S. Eliot, "Little Gidding"*

## Somewhere to Stand

Recall how the book began: we use ideas both as tools to make sense of our experiences and as weapons to control people by persuading them to model the world as we want them to model it, which presupposes different ways to see the same world and makes room for choice and debate. Second, standing outside the debaters and the various models they uphold, there is a reality against which models can be tested, but only up to a point. That limitation exists because, although there are conclusive tests for some propositions—hands warmed *in* the fire is my boilerplate example—for most propositions about social interaction the test and its results are less immediate and more open to debate.

I also said that no one model can be the sole conveyer of truth. Truth is not the issue; usefulness is, and where one model's usefulness fails, another may do what is needed. It is surely good to preserve that spirit of pragmatic, open-minded inquiry: there are different ways to see the world. To put it unrelentingly into practice, however, turns out to be not just difficult, but impossible. Some things must be taken for granted. The unexamined life, Socrates said, is not worth living. That may be the case; if you are reading this book, you probably believe it, even if sometimes you wish it were not so. But for sure you leave much of your life unexamined. You could not do otherwise: incessant critical examination, questioning everything, having no presuppositions, taking nothing for granted, would mean a life not only without rest, but also without action (other than asking questions). Some things must be made to stand still, assumed to be true, taken on faith. "Give me somewhere to stand and I will move the world," said Archimedes. Everyone needs a place to stand.

One place to stand is that ubiquitous attendant on human interactions that I have variously labeled conscience, duty, morality, community, collectivity, society, or structure, all of them matters that rest on faith, not on reason. These words suggest an entity that commands not only faith but also obedience. For this feature there is a convenient word, *numen*, which translates variously from the Latin texts (in an order of increasing majesty) as nod, assent, command, authority, supreme authority, divinity, divine will. I will use the word (and its adjective *numinous*) to encompass whatever terms (*conscience, duty, morality, the community, the collectivity, public opinion*, and the like) are antonyms to the utility set, which includes *the old Adam, expected utility, expediency, rational choice, economic man, individualism*, and so on. Reason and calculation shape the utility set; numen foregrounds faith and uncalculating obedience.

Numen always attends encounters between social beings. There are no unmonitored encounters, except the *homo homini lupus* kind, which, by definition, take place in a state of nature, not in the framework of a society. Numen is the quality of being sacred, and I choose the word to draw attention to the part of our social life which we do not think to question or are reluctant to question. (People do not use *sacred* for conduct that has become second nature, but if the conduct is brought into the open and questioned, they are likely to exhibit surprise, even shock, and perhaps to say that the questioner is unbalanced or evil-minded.)

Numen is not itself any particular structure. Rather it is a quality that structures require: they demand faith; they are promoted at least as presuppositional. If structures are not taken on faith, there can be no way to comprehend, in any communicable way, what goes on in social systems. Structures have no firmer existence than as saving lies, but they make social life possible because they make it understandable; if everything is modeled as in flux, nothing has meaning.

To oppose structure and nonstructure is also to oppose structural time, which repeats itself, to linear or historical time, which does not. Structural time is timeless—it is time that does not pass. The idea permeates our daily life and our culture. There is a passage in Ecclesiastes (3:1–8) which no one can read—or, better, no one can hear—without being moved by the beautiful cadencing of the words and also, perhaps, by their message, which is exactly about structural time.

To every thing there is a season, and a time to every purpose under the
heaven:
A time to be born and a time to die; a time to plant, and a time to pluck up
that which is planted;
A time to kill, and a time to heal; a time to break down, and a time to build up;
A time to weep, and a time to laugh; a time to mourn, and a time to dance;
A time to caste away stones, and a time to gather stones together;
A time to embrace, and a time to refrain from embracing;
A time to get, and a time to lose; a time to keep, and a time to cast away;
A time to rend, and a time to sew; a time to keep silence, and a time to speak;
A time to love, and a time to hate; a time of war, and a time of peace.


Notice how each second clause cancels out the first. The journey ends
back where it began, everything goes in a circle, and the forward
movement of history is denied; all change is denied. Time, being
made to go round and round, or to move to and fro like a pendulum,
is itself denied. The passage is a perfect representation of structure.
Earlier (Ecclesiastes 1:8) it was plainly and summarily said: "The thing
that hath been, is that which shall be; and that which is done is that
which shall be done; and there is no new thing under the sun."

Why do those words resonate so strongly in our minds? One would
expect them not to; we have a developed linear sense of history, of a
past and a future, and of time passing and gone for ever, which is the
very opposite of "to every thing there is a season." Literacy helps the
linear image; unlike the Nuer in the 1930s we have records of the distant past. So does the idea of progress: the present is different from
the past, and the future will be different yet again (and better). We
further believe (a saving lie, for sure) that, whatever is said about
natural selection, at least to some extent we can control our future. We
also have tools that seem to give us control over time; we manage it by
objectifying it, making it the same for everyone, and the same in every
context; we factor it into years, months, weeks, days, minutes, seconds—
the time that belongs to a clock, something that exists outside ourselves and is given its own reality.

But we do not always experience time in that way. Time can be
highly subjective. When you are a child you do not sense time as you
do when you are older. In childhood, time does not threaten. How
slowly the years move! How they pick up speed with each passing
decade! Time, also, is conditioned by activity and emotion. A time of
contentment is a time that speeds by unnoticed. Boredom makes an
eternity. A moment of terror likewise is an eternity.

We have a strong sense of past and future but we also seem to have a
no less strong emotional need to deny linear time, to convince ourselves

that it is not a reality. We convert it into structural time, in which same-ness comes round and round, and there is "no new thing under the sun." The passage of time in our civilization is pervasively marked by pessimism, fear, and regret. Time gets easily out of control. "Where did the time go?" we ask, contemplating tasks that we should already have done. Time is like money—it is slippery—and Ben Franklin doubled the discomfort by reminding his young tradesman that time is money. Time can also dehumanize us; time-and-motion studies, piecework, and the apparatus of Taylorism and Fordism make the worker an ap-pendage to a machine—they robotize him.

The same pessimistic theme is found in our literature. Virgil: *Sed fugit interea, fugit inreparabile tempus* (Time flies by and cannot be re-stored). It is a regret for things done and things left undone. Herrick: "Gather ye rosebuds while ye may / Old Time is still a-flying / And this same flower that smiles to-day / To-morrow will be dying. Ovid: *Tempus edax rerum* (Time is the devourer of things). Time is a destroyer. Time is the reaper, a scythe, death. We resent time passing because it denies our immortality.

Then we resort to a saving lie. Think of the attributes of God. God is immortal; his truths are eternal verities; they defy time. Think of the *Gloria* in the King James version of The *Book of Common Prayer*:

> Glory be to the Father, and to the Son, and to the Holy Ghost.
> As it was in the beginning, is now and ever shall be: world without end.
> Amen.

Amen means *Let it be so! Make it so!* Eternity is affirmed. Even death is denied. The burial service in the King James version first picks up the pendulum theme—"earth to earth, ashes to ashes, and dust to dust"—and then, immediately and triumphantly, caps it with "in sure and cer-tain hope of the Resurrection to eternal life." It is a saving lie that we hold for our comfort.

But there is more to structural time than spiritual consolation. Structural time affirms order and meaning. We need to make things stand still, because we cannot make sense of them if we cannot identify them. To identify something is to fix it under a name and give it the il-lusion of stability, and therefore of existence. We cannot think about anything until we place it in a category, and to categorize something is to take it out of time. Whatever is entirely particular, whatever is unique, is beyond comprehension. We comprehend it when we take away its uniqueness and put it into a category, and so provide it with a context, mark it with an essence, and give it meaning.

To be timeless is to be fixed. A structure must have that attribute.

Recall Leach: we have no choice but to model things *as if* they were standing still. Structures are fixed for the same reason that meanings are not infinitely flexible. Water is wet; it is a matter of definition. To talk of "dry water" is to go beyond an oxymoron into meaninglessness. Phrases like "flexible structure" or "fluid structure" or "structure in motion" are misleading; when unfolded to discover what they mean, they reveal two or more structures, each modeled as fixed. We slide easily into the idea of movement without fixity. "Everything flows and nothing remains," is the usual translation of what Heraclitus said. The verb translated as "flow" (*chorein*) more nearly means "to make way for another," and the corresponding noun (*chora*—in Latin, *locus*) indicates "the space in which a thing is." Those meanings quite change the notion of "flux" that usually goes with the dictum. Heraclitus was speaking not of flux but of one *thing* replacing another *thing* in a space conceived as fixed. That is how *structure* is here envisaged. The world fictionized as standing still yields to description; it becomes a world that is comprehensible (albeit always disputable).

## Defining the Situation: Exchanges

Besides being able to describe structures directly, people also live them—act them out—and their conduct constitutes another kind of evidence for the existence of structures and their presence, if not always in the forefront of people's minds or on their tongues, at least in what they do. People can enact structures without being able to describe them or to give them a lexical identity.

The phrase *define the situation* presupposes a plurality of structures in competition with one another and assumes an adversarial encounter in which one person tries to foist his or her definition onto another and so stabilize their relationship. *Foist* suggests the nature of the encounter: it is not simple *homo homini lupus*. Its mode of persuasion is somewhat less than naked force; ego and alter already have enough in common to let them communicate; so there is at least a modicum of civility. But neither is the encounter necessarily sweet reason; *foist* retains a sufficient whiff of nastiness to make clear that defining a situation is not an occasion when both parties want only the "truth" (even if they say they do); they have axes to grind. When someone successfully "defines the situation" for me, I agree, like it or not, whether I believe what has been said or not, to behave in accordance with whatever conventions the definition stipulates. That agreement structures the situation. By closing an argument it puts an end (for the time being) to uncertainty and so opens the way to cooperation (even if reluctant).

In his *Table Talk* Coleridge has this apothegm: "In the Trinity there is, 1. Ipseity; 2. Alterity; 3. Community." The Trinity might be glossed as "me, you, and the rest of us"; more formally as "self, other, and society." Those three elements are the building blocks of exchange theory, which analyzes the process of placing or displacing structures. *Ipse* and *alter* interact, and out of their interaction comes *community*. Or, to put it in plain style, an exchange arena—it is hard to avoid combative metaphors—is one in which people, who begin as wolves, may get to know their adversaries and learn how to make civilized exchanges. In that process, conduct modeled as expected utility is replaced by conduct modeled as the outcome of ethical norms. The exchangers need not become fond of one another, or even respect one another; but they do learn to respect their community's rules for interaction and thus they cooperate. An exchange of that kind is a *prestation*.

The word *exchange* can be marked—given a more specific meaning—in a surprisingly large number of ways. One can exchange gifts, greetings, pleasantries, stories, gossip, threats, insults, blows, badinage, kisses, help, or marriage vows. Exchanges can be fair, or they can be one-sided, an uncertainty that is caught in an apotropaic saying of my childhood uttered when swapping something—"exchange is no robbery." There are stock exchanges and telephone exchanges and, if you are on a diet, food exchanges. The idea of exchange remains a constituent in a variety of other words: *substitute, swap, transact, trade, deal, oblige, reciprocate, retaliate, pay back*, and many more.

The central components in most of these instances is a pair of persons or parties and things passing between them in both directions. In a few of them, for example *food exchange* or the verb *substitute*, the center of attention has to be the thing, because only one person is involved. That, however, can also be the case when there is more than one person. *Stock exchange, transact, buy and sell, trade,* and *market* all attach the idea of impersonality to the deal, highlighting the object exchanged, although by definition persons are involved. The thing, whether a commodity or a service, is fronted and the status of the people involved is backstaged and thus downgraded as unimportant. These exchanges are, as I noted earlier, *transactions*. Salespersons in a department store are not valued in and for themselves, but only as facilitators; they are instruments, like the store itself or a credit card; they are impersonal devices that have no moral standing. Customers, likewise, are valued not in themselves, but for their money, and when they have no money, no one rolls out the red carpet. Transactions are the exchanges on which neoclassical economists concentrate their attention. Or, more precisely, they model all exchanges as transactions.

Prestations invoke a social matrix, which, ipso facto, activates moral considerations. A prestation is an exchange which enacts—makes a claim to (*pretends to* in archaic English)—a particular kind of relationship. It is a message about where ego and alter stand (or where ego would like them to stand) in the array of structural possibilities that their society makes available to them. It highlights the relative status of the giver and the receiver. "It's the thought that counts," we say, making excuses for a paltry gift and wishing to preserve the relationship. The object doesn't matter; the fact that they remembered the anniversary (or whatever was the occasion) indicates that they value us and the relationship they have with us.

Established prestations deal in structures that are transmitted down a series of encounters. Mauss entitled his essay about exchanges *The Gift*. The gift he had in mind is an Indian gift; it requires something in return.[4] That balancing gift, in its turn, calls for a counter-gift. The gift and the return gift and its return gift (and so on) constitute a series that enacts a relationship, enabling people to live out and so declare their feelings for each other. Thus a prestation, unlike a transaction, carries with it a message of continuity; it presumes a series. By contrast, paying money for a purchase is a one-time event; a newspaper bought in an airport or (the extreme example) coffee bought from a vending machine establishes no personal relationship between buyer and seller and does not bind the two parties to future interaction. Prestations, however, do exactly that. *Do ut des* (I give in order that you may give). Recipients, once they accept the gift, place themselves under an obligation to make a suitable return; they affirm a relationship, a definition of the situation, and they anticipate continuity. Prestations, when reciprocated, belong more to the unexamined part of our life that is taken for granted than to the mode of self-awareness. They discourage critical scrutiny.

Certain other features separate them analytically from transactions, and also serve as indicators to the people concerned. Timing is sometimes, but not always, an identifier. Transactions are marked by a simultaneous exchange, even when the simultaneity is feigned by a credit note. The word *transact* connotes completion, something accomplished, and there are sometimes small rituals that signal the end of a negotiation, such as the fall of the auctioneer's hammer. Transactions are in the perfect tense; prestations, because they presume a structure, have no tense; they are continuing; they bundle past, present, and future all into one. They exist across time, serially, the reciprocal

---

4. That expression has been miserably perverted. "Indian giving" now expresses contempt—an irony, since reciprocity, which is the mutual exchange of gifts, is the harbinger of civilized society.

offering coming after a customary interval. The right interval constitutes an indicator of trust. A return too long delayed puts the proffered relationship in jeopardy; a deliberate pause before returning a
greeting may carry the message that it was not entirely welcome. Con-
versely, reciprocity that is more rapid than convention allows signals
an absence of trust, a dissatisfaction with the present form of the relationship, and perhaps a desire to convert it into a transactional arrangement or end it altogether.

Much of our social life runs on automatic pilot. Fixity (the unthinking
assumption of continuity, which is the mark of structure) is maintained by putting calculation and curiosity on hold. The world of
prestations is a noninquiring world. A culturally ambiguous network
of Sindhi families of my acquaintance distributed, on the occasion of a
marriage and in a wholly non-Hindu fashion, silver-colored boxes
decorated with wedding bells, and supposedly containing pieces of wedding cake. There was never a wedding cake at their wedding feasts
(and no wedding bells at the ceremonies), and the boxes, presumably
put into circulation by some novelty-prone person in the past, had become a kind of heirloom, passed unopened from family to family and
from one generation to another, the contents long since mildewed
away. (I heard this from a woman in one family, more deracinated
than the others, who had the temerity to break with prestational etiquette and open a box that, she noticed, had already passed through
her hands before.)

Reciprocated prestations are (by definition in the model I am constructing) conservative things. Even when they are occasions for wariness, as in the archetypal example of the Kwakiutl potlatch, I see them
as claiming positions in a structure and not as threatening the structure itself.[5] In that context, *prestation* signals cooperation and trust, an

5. The word *prestation* is taken from the French, in which one of its meanings is *dues* or
*allowances* owed to a particular status (for example the family allowance paid for children). The equivalent Latin verb means to predetermine, or to fix in advance. In ordinary English the word refers to payments that are required by law or by custom, such as
the dues owed to a feudal lord. The word in anthropology has a wider meaning, referring to exchanges that have the attributes described in these paragraphs—and some
other connected attributes, which will be considered shortly.

*Prestation*, although found in anthropological discourse in the nineteenth century, is generally associated with Marcel Mauss, who used it in *The Gift*. I need the word and will use it
despite the risks involved. *The Gift* has the peculiar quality of any classic text that is open to
diverse interpretations: it inclines commentators, who see themselves as one of the few in
step with master, to be righteously affronted by the egregious misrepresentations of less insightful persons, purveyors of " 'received wisdom' in anthropology" as Bloch (1990, 169)
scornfully labels them. For other lively examples see Parry 1986 or Laidlaw 2000, or catch
the tone of the Douglas introduction to Mauss 1990. How closely I am in step with Mauss
in the selection of features that I attach to *prestation* is not a first concern.

On the potlatch see Mauss 1990, 33–46.

acceptance of structures as they are. In fact, as you will see later, enacted exchanges that are notionally prestations may show signs of competition and mistrust, which means they are becoming transactions, or that they are about to be terminated and the situation given a different definition. There can be, recalling Mauss's play with the word *gift* in the Germanic languages, poison in the gift.[6] Short of that point, however, people do not constantly struggle over, or endlessly renegotiate, their designs for everyday living, many of which are below the threshold of awareness; nor are articulated designs ipso facto contested. The portrait of human society as being always on the road and never reaching the inn does not fit its most salient feature—a necessary part of its definition—which is orderliness, fixity, and predictability.

Prestations are a vehicle for this stability. They become habitual, and the status of the giver and his or her relationship with the receiver are taken for granted. Greeting a neighbor or a colleague, acknowledging the company when one enters a room, even buying presents for a friend or a relative are none of them occasions for radical from-the-ground-up calculation about the recipient's or the giver's self-image. A prestation series becomes in time virtually second nature.[7] If pressed and asked why they reciprocate, givers might offer a rational, economistic, explanation that involves a payoff, perhaps saying, "If we don't send them a present, they'll call us skinflints and gossip about us." But they are just as likely to say "We go back a long way together," or "She's our cousin," or "That's the way it's done." Such behavior, if pulled out of the mainstream of what is taken for granted and held up for examination, is most often explained as fueled by conscience or a sense of duty, not by calculations of interest. Prestations are supposed to come from the heart, the seat of feeling, not from the head, and if you start to calculate the cost-benefit ratio of an exchange, you diminish its status as a prestation, push it in the direction of a transation, and thus destabilize it. Prestations, in short, are the currency of structure.

An established relationship, based on prestations, deals with information in a way that is consistent with the taken-for-granted uninquisitive quality of structured relationships. The knowledge that shapes them is largely unarticulated. At least it need not be spelled out in full; the code for its communication is restricted.[8] Information is transmitted by hints, allusively and indirectly, through signals that are simple

6. 1990, 62–63 and Chapter 3, note 122.

7. The process in which the need for contractual enforcement diminishes and is replaced by trust, suggested at the end of Chapter 3, is exactly the passage from transaction to prestation.

8. The contrast of elaborated/restricted codes was put into circulation by Basil Bernstein (1964). Bernstein was interested in the disqualifying effect of a restricted code. In

in themselves but may carry a large semantic load, and at the same time are incomprehensible to those outside the prestation circle. A captain of industry in Britain in the sixties (I think it was Lord Chandos), interviewed on the radio about the old-boy network and appointments, said, "For example, if someone phones and asks about giving so-and-so a job, I might say that so-and-so is a worthy chap . . . and the caller says, 'Thanks; I did wonder. I'll look elsewhere.' "[9]

Second, the stock of information is by convention treated as stable. There is no probing beyond the boundaries to expand it, no criticism or evaluation, no effort to search through it and discard what is outdated or what might not be accurate. The caller does not ask the captain of industry exactly what his words means, or on what evidence it is based, or if it is up to date. The information is there, solid and unshiftable and undisputed, like scripture. It is a whole thing, not to be taken apart, not to be analyzed, just accepted and acted on—good for minds that want their information in ready-made authentic chunks. In other words, to say it again, what is claimed in a prestation is structure, and to question and dissect and ask for evidence would be to weaken the foundation on which prestations rest, which is trust.

The prestation style assumes boundaries and is a marker of them, and boundaries are bringers of order and stability. The captain of industry was able to communicate in such a concise fashion because he was working within his own prestation circle, navigating in familiar seas. Boundaries exist because only those who understand the highly nuanced signals are able to receive the messages. Sometimes this exclusion is intended, but, even when it is not, the boundaries are still present in the guise of a custom-bound, unthinking acceptance of a fence that separates insiders from outsiders.

All these features—boundaries, stability, the trust and familiarity that are suggested in unspoken or half-spoken messaging, things taken for granted—are captured in the notion of structure as an amen category that affirms continuity and foregrounds ideas of duty, community, a moral order, and the public interest.

---

the present instance I see it more as an exclusionary device in the manner of a thieves' argot, a way to control a situation, a source of power.

9. Sometimes words themselves become superfluous:

> Nor do they trust their tongue alone,
> But speak a language of their own;
> Can read a nod, a shrug, a look,
> Far better than a printed book;
> Convey a libel in a frown,
> And wink a reputation down.
> —Jonathan Swift, "The Journal of a Modern Lady," 1.188.

But our experiences, when we offer prestations to make our world stable, agreed upon, and predictable, include communications that fail, because alter does not know what ego is talking about or will not accept the proffered structure. The encounter may then lose its informational format and become an overt attempt to dominate, in which structures (moralities) are deployed as weapons.

## Morality as a Weapon

When I was new to India, I traveled on a train from Bombay to Baroda. While the train was still in the station, I had a confrontation with a beggar. It was very one-sided, or at least I endeavored to make it so. I was sitting beside an open window; he was down beside the track. He was tall, dark-skinned, with a strong-boned face and a full mustache, robust; had it not been for the ragged turban and shirt and the thin, high-pitched voice, he might have been a soldier. He carried himself that way, not cringing, not, as beggars in India sometimes did, exhibiting some grotesque deformity; he looked healthy enough. "Sturdy" was the adjective that came fleetingly to mind out of some dimly recollected eighteenth-century condemnations of able-bodied vagabonds prone to violence.

I reacted in the standard English petty bourgeois fashion: I ignored him. That seemed to be the rational thing to do. Begging, in my culture, is a nonproductive parasitical activity and, for the good of society, it should not be encouraged. Nor did I want beggars to get into the habit of pestering me (a perfectly irrational application of rationality, since this was a railway station and the train was about to leave, thus giving me near-absolute anonymity).

To be more accurate, I tried to ignore him. I looked over his head, which did not reach the level of the window; I looked past him; I looked around the compartment. At first I took care not to meet his eye, then I tried to meet it and look through him. I did not want to acknowledge him as a fellow human being, not even by telling him to go away. He persisted. He didn't raise his voice, but he seemed to make his presence more and more insistent. I began to feel embarrassed. Other passengers in the compartment were amused by my inability to deal with him. I (*ipse*) wanted no dealings with *alter* (the beggar); the onlookers—a "community"—somehow made the relationship a reality, despite my refusing it.[10]

10. The term *community* will be used here in two senses, one social and the other cultural. The social sense is defined by interaction, the cultural sense by the possession of common values. The people in the compartment, including myself, were a community

Wanting to conceal my confusion I began to fill my pipe, hiding behind the fiddling that goes with pipe smoking—fishing in the pouch,
rubbing the tobacco between my palms, tamping it down in the bowl
of the pipe, drawing a lighted match several times across it, making
out as if I were doing something that required total concentration. I
threw the spent match out of the window. The beggar—I am sure he
was enjoying what I later realized was a virtuoso performance—picked
up the match and placed it sideways between his teeth, grimacing at
me. Then the train began to move, and the man sitting opposite me
tossed an appreciative coin out of the window, and I was left wonder-
ing what the beggar's final gesture signified.

What was the message? It might have been, "I am so hungry, I will
eat even a spent match." I think not. His focus was not on his own
condition, but on his would-be relationship with me. He was marking
us as unequal, me the superior, him the inferior, my dependent, the
person who had a rightful claim on my benevolence. There is, in fact,
a particular Hindu spin on the gesture, which meant nothing to me at
the time. He was taking up my waste (analogous to food left on a
plate) and putting it in his own mouth. He was taking on my pollution, thus marking himself as my total inferior and at the same time as
my benefactor.

The man across from me, as people did on trains in India, drew me
into conversation and in the gentlest way instructed me on how to
handle situations like that. The cost of throwing out a few coins, he
said, was trivial. Of course, he was right; a fraction of a penny spent to
avoid the irritation and to demonstrate to people around that I was
not an asocial oddity would have been rationally spent. Besides, he
added, a small ironic smile crossing his face, gifts to the poor earned
spiritual merit. It was, he concluded, the normal way for a well-to-do
person to deal with the poverty of others. Evidently there were ways
of defining the situation that had not occurred to me.

Some comment is required on the motivations of the three main actors in this scene (the beggar, myself, and the man who gave me advice). The beggar's motivations and mine are obviously instrumental.
He was initially energized, expected-utility fashion, by the coin he
wanted me to give him. In exchange, by humbling himself he offered
me the symbols of high status. As I steadfastly ignored him, or tried to,
he made himself more and more aggressively humble, and at some
point, I suspect, the coin became secondary, the mercenary motivation
was displaced, and what he wanted was a moral victory that would

in the cultural sense, sharing a knowledge of English and some middle-class values, and
were moved to become an interactive community when one of them decided I was in
need of guidance.

demonstrate to the audience my unfitness for the high status that he had offered me.[11]

My own behavior falls into a similar (but not identical) pattern of movement between morality and expected utility. I did not want to be pestered by beggars, and, given that goal, I did what seemed rational at the time: I ignored him. I was looking to my own comfort. There must have been, it is true, some trace of Puritan morality in the background; giving money to sturdy beggars is wrong because it supports a style of life that is without virtue. But that motivation was more or less dormant. I did not think of it and then act. I acted first and only thought of it later when reflecting on what my mentor had told me about the proper way to deal with beggars in India. In the end, the encounter dragged me out of a moral mainstream that I did not realize was carrying me along. (I am sure the beggar did not have a similar epiphany of relativism; he probably saw me as nothing but the meanest of the mean, a Bania tricked out as a *bara saheb*.)[12]

What motivated the mentor, the kindly middle-aged man who so amiably set me right? One could make a case for some reached-for utility, but it seems thin. Perhaps he wanted someone to talk to. Perhaps he liked the sense of power that goes with mentoring. Perhaps he enjoyed civilizing a member of the one-time ruling race (the encounter took place five years after Indians gained their independence from Britain). Most likely he just wanted to help. At the same time he was on a high moral ground; he made clear to me what was the right thing to do and, retroactively, structured the situation that should have existed between the beggar and me.

If I had given a coin to the beggar, I perhaps could be said, by virtue of agreeing on a definition of the situation, to have formed a community with him, albeit of the most evanescent kind. Alternatively, if I had wanted to, I could have ignored them all, the beggar, the other passengers, even the mentor. We all were transient, and the price of privacy would have been small—I was never likely to meet them again. Instead I spent several contented hours conversing with the mentor,

11. If he had been concerned only about money he would have not wasted so much time on me but would have moved on to another window. I suppose it could be argued that halfway through the encounter he abandoned the selfish goal and instead wanted to make the world a better place by making me a better person. But that reaching out to find public spirit is not persuasive. As I said, he wanted a moral victory in order to humiliate me, which is not the same as wanting to uphold morality.

12. *Bara saheb* (lit. great master) was still at that time a term (sometimes slightly derisory) for a European in a position of authority, as most Europeans had been a few years earlier. *Bania* is a generic term for a variety of castes traditionally engaged in commerce, banking, and money-lending. They were proverbially tight-fisted. (The mentor, who taught me the value of generosity, gave me his business card. His name identified him as a Bania.)

and, for a brief time, he and I and the others in the railway carriage did constitute a community. As a social community—based on interaction—it was of short duration, having neither a past nor a future. From a cultural perspective, of course, we were part of a community that transcended both the actors and the incident in the same way that a language transcends any particular speakers of it. We were enacting the definition that we shared of how to conduct brief encounters between middle-class, ethnically varied speakers of English.[13]

In that moral community my membership was marginal because, as my conduct toward the beggar had demonstrated, my values were not in line with those of my fellow passengers. The beggar won his moral victory exactly because, without intending it, he made me aware that there were things I did not know. He also made it clear to everyone else in the carriage that I was less than properly domesticated. That was why the amusement of my fellow passengers embarrassed me. Obviously they knew the proper thing to do, and, obviously again, I was not doing it. I felt marginalized, like an outsider. Yet from a commonsense point of view it seems absurd that I should suddenly become embarrassed by my alien status. I had been that way all along; I was in fact an outsider, British, white, and not a Hindu, as I suppose most of them were. But those are cool, detached, analytic statements. In the railway compartment my outsiderness was enacted, hot and immediate.

I am indulging in this mild diversionary analysis of my psyche, as it was half a century ago, because reflection on that incident brought home to me the adversarial use of morality in confrontations. The beggar began by offering me homage, making me a high person by demeaning himself. In the first stage of the confrontation he used a tone of voice and a body language that I suspect is universal: a soft, partly whining, partly caressing voice, hands held out in supplication, eye-catching but to convey adoration, not a threat. When this failed, he became more explicit—he put the spent match between his teeth. The gesture failed with me, because I did not know what it meant; others in the compartment must have been aware of its significance. It was the ultimate act of subservience, putting my waste into his mouth

13. My encounter with the beggar did have a past and a future, if one uses a wider, cultural definition of *community*. Ethnicity and the recently ended colonial history were part of the context, very much at the margins of my understanding of the situation, though possibly more salient in the case of the mentor. The incident also extended into the future insofar as I learned how to behave toward beggars in India and, more generally, eventually to adopt the passively tolerant attitude toward poverty that seemed to prevail there at that time. But those are distant perspectives; they lack the commanding presence of a past and future that shapes encounters in communities—for example villages or families—that exist in the sustained contacts of everyday life.

and thus, by that act of self-pollution, bringing into the arena the notion of *dharma*, which is God's design for the world and for the ordering of high and low in human society.[14] In doing so he transformed what I wanted to define as a simple transaction (in this case a *non*-transaction) into a moral confrontation that was not about a couple of *paisa* but about fundamental social and religious values. At the same time he shifted the confrontation from just the two of us to an arena that encompassed the mentor and the other people in the carriage. In other words, when he invoked the collectivity and its values, he took control of the moral high ground by demonstrating to me and to the other people in the compartment that I was an outsider. He won the confrontation. He defined the moral high ground, held on to it, and excluded me. I kept my money but was out of countenance. I felt I had been out-witted and somehow demeaned; I felt—in both senses of the phrase—put out.

## Inclusion and Exclusion

There is an ambiguous English proverb, "Every man's neighbor is his looking glass." It could mean that you are what your neighbor thinks you are—you exist only in your reputation. Alternatively, the proverb bespeaks conformity, similarity, standardization. To see what you are like, look at your neighbors because they are your image. It therefore indicates an intolerance of difference. Both interpretations make sense: identities are made of reputations, and identities, if not clone-like, should at least conform to accepted standards. Mere difference is redefined as nonconformity, and nonconformity edges on subversion. That xenophobic spirit emerges when we come upon customs that are different from our own. Even the blandest variance, such as English/American spellings, can excite reactions which mix amusement with a touch of outrage. "Tyre?" I have been asked, "T-y-r-e! You *really* spell it that way? How odd!" It is as if we are offended by the thought that anyone could be different from ourselves, and are taken aback to see in our neighbor what we do not see in the mirror.

The same unthinking condemnation of difference also exists in domains where critical scrutiny is supposed to be the rule. Recall the epigraph to Chapter 1: "Economists are very reluctant to recognize and accept facts in the real world that seem to fly in the face of [their] beautiful theory, or undermine its basic assumptions." The phrase

---

14. *Dharma* has the same wide coverage that we give to *nature*. It is the dharma of the rich to give alms to the poor; it is also the dharma of water to flow downhill; and, as one of my teachers, an elderly Brahmin lady, explained, po-faced, "It is the dharma of the penis to seek a hairy cleft."

*expected utility* has a numinous, quasi-sacred quality, as does any successful saving lie. It has authority; it demands uncritical acceptance not as a presupposition but as *the* truth. Neoclassical economists (the few renegades apart) would of course deny the concept's scriptural overtones, and if asked why it has such a robust existence in their episteme—remember that neither Coase nor North ventured far outside the congregation of true believers—they would surely insist that the beautiful theory survives not because of its beauty but because it mostly works; it meets the standards of a positive science. The difficulty, I argued earlier, is that it often does not.

There is abundant evidence in earlier chapters that inclusion and exclusion, marked by adherence to a faith (and with it membership in a community of the faithful) is a feature of academic discourse and is used as a weapon to impose definitions on a situation. Scholars see themselves as antagonists in combat with others who define situations differently. Radcliffe-Brown: "The task of social anthropology, as a natural science of society, is the systematic investigation of the nature of social institutions. . . . The progressive achievement of knowledge of this kind must be the aim of all who believe that a veritable science of human society is possible and desirable." Notice the hectoring tone; notice the word *must* and that tendentious adjective *veritable*. Read the editors of *African Political Systems*: "We speak for all social anthropologists when we say that a scientific study of political institutions must be inductive and comparative . . ." *Must* is there again and all that is lacking is the adjective *veritable* (or *true* or *genuine* or *authentic*) between *all* and *social anthropologists*. Readers are left in no doubt that they must agree with these presuppositions if they do not want to be exiled to the land of the intellectually unwashed. The abusive and quite violent language (by the standards of academia) that Lord Robbins applied to colleagues who thought that institutions should be factored into economic analysis carries the same message: this is the only way to understand the world, and if you do not see it that way, you are an outsider, unworthy of respect. There seems always to be a need to skewer those who differ, perhaps because against their failings our own excellence will stand bright and clear. In that spirit Evans-Pritchard denounced the positivists (and by implication his mentor, Radcliffe-Brown). Friedman, less impassioned and more the gamesman, is nevertheless vehement in castigating those who think that unrealistic assumptions lead to theorizing about an imaginary world. Always the message, direct or implicit, is an imperative: "Join us! Or be evil—or, if not evil, be a mere nothing!"

As is to be expected in this mode of persuasive discourse, there is no attempt to spell out analytically the benefits that accrue to true believers, and to do so might diminish the moral authority of the message. But, although unspoken, the benefits are obvious enough. To live inside the walls of a true belief, to be recognized by others as having the right to do so, and to profit from the connection are powerful inducements to endorse its scriptures. Economists are reluctant to recognize imperfections and limitations in the beautiful theory because in several ways (mentioned in Chapter 6) it pays them not to do so. They would not have the same clout in government and business (nor their differential pay scales in academia), if they did not own a scripture and were, as Keynes suggested they should be, equated with dentists and considered skilled technicians with no special access to divine mysteries. They enjoy distinction (as does any such group) to the extent that people believe (and they themselves believe) they are privy to knowledge that is not available to outsiders; in that respect they are superior persons. They can reach out for resources inaccessible to the *profani*, the uninitiated who do not understand the mysteries.[15]

But more is involved than material rewards. Such people enjoy what some economists, hiding the hole in expected-utility, call "psychic utility." Even when there is no material profit, to belong in any company of academic true believers—structural functionalists, neoclassical economists, Marxists, Freudians, phenomenologists, feminists, postmodernists, each having their own "myths, dogmas, and rituals"— is emotionally rewarding. Membership provides not only an identity but also a sense of effortless superiority; it is the equivalent of the church which is *spes una salutis* (the one hope of salvation).[16] There is no place for doubt. Doubt makes a member marginal, and marginality is not merely cerebral, a matter of intellect; it can also be unnerving.

A scripture that holds such congregations together cannot be *seen* to be fundamentally in question. Questioning is next door to disbelief, and its neighbor is mockery, which puts an end to the mystery, breaks down the fence that protects the initiated, and so diminishes their power. Leach, an enthusiastic iconoclast, desanctified the positivist version of anthropology that is found in Radcliffe-Brown's programmatic writings (and in parts of *African Political Systems*) and—though not Leach alone—brought about the anomie that presently reigns in social anthropology.

But, it may be said, it is the case that inside any academic enclave

15. *Procul, O procul este, profani* (Keep well away, you who are not initiated!)—Virgil, *Aeneid* vi.
16. St. Augustine: *Salus extra ecclesiam non est* (Outside the church there is no salvation).

questioning goes on endlessly, and the result is not always the destruction of its episteme. If scripture cannot survive questioning, why is it that in all the sciences, both natural and social, the experts are constantly fighting to show that they are right and other experts are wrong? How does a scripture survive that strain? More precisely, how does its standing as scripture remain undamaged?

There are four answers. First, as in the case of neoclassical economics, there may be a central core of received "truth" exempted from the skirmishing that goes on; the core is left intact and held to be an eternal verity. Or, if it shifts, the shift is said to be just a small adjustment, a perfecting, not a substitution. Neither North nor Coase were ready to abandon the expected-utility frame.[17] Second, since the debates are conducted in the priestly language, knowledge of their existence, let alone their content, need not much leak out. What matters is not that those inside the temple should all get along, but that those outside should take it for granted that inside the temple all is well enough. Third, as I said earlier, no one can do without a scripture. No one can live by rationality alone; no one survives without verities that are held to be eternal (even if only for the time being). Disputing about which verities are eternal does not remove the need for a place to stand, any more than arguing about cuisines removes the need to eat.

The fourth answer points to our habitude: we have a disposition to conserve and to be apprehensive about change. Scriptural metaphors and phrases like "true belief" perhaps too much suggest zealotry and therefore activism, a world of academic crusaders, nonstop fighters for the one and only truth. Certainly *zealotry* fits the exuberance of Robbins or Friedman hunting down infidels or McCloskey skewering

17. No such core survived from positivist social anthropology. In the last third of the twentieth century, the discipline abandoned the central redoubt of "the social system" seen as a set of ideas that constituted an objective reality, which had enough order in it to be definitively known. Nothing took its place; everything is "contested" (a word much favored in the titles of academic publications). The result is that we social anthropologists exist as peripheries, spun off from a center that is now defunct, and most of our politics are the politics of identity. It makes life exhilarating, and perhaps it is the way a discipline renews itself, but it surely also is one reason why social anthropology does not command from other academics the respectful curiosity that it did around midcentury. The *profani* were let in to view the disarray inside the temple.

The model of the discipline as an arena, pure and simple, exactly matches the model that is nowadays used to make sense of society: a field of contest between ethnic groups, between the genders, between the generations, and whatever else, each asserting its right to be the only kid that matters on the block. It also matches the model that I have used to put this book together: the academic world is a world of claims about one's own virtues, concealment of one's shortcomings, attention to the shortcomings of others (when others are attended to at all), and all of this coupled with a marked lack of interest in shelving partisan commitment and asking how things work, what patterns they reveal, and what principles organize them, and so finding a place to stand.

true-believing economic orthodoxy, but numen (or "received opinion" or "the ruling paradigm") owes as much for its continuing existence to inertia as to fanaticism. There are not many McCloskeys in the field. The default mode requires least effort. When there is a dilemma, for example a contested choice between doing what is right and doing what is smart, the resolution is often to "do what we normally do," which shelves both morality and expediency by absorbing them into the domain of habitude. Placing the decision there gives it the default status of being beyond question, until some eager person revives the issue and brings it again into contention by asserting that "what we normally do" has normally proved disastrous. That objection would surely have to be strongly argued, for a precedent carries with it its own authority, as its use in law, that great stabilizer, testifies.

Letting matters be decided default-fashion in the mode of "normal choice" looks like a form of laziness. It's easier to let things be, even when you know they could be better done, if only someone would make the effort. Most of the time we are not maximizers; we are not even satisficers; we just get along by doing "what we normally do." But it is a providential and necessary laziness. To question everything, as I said earlier, is to invite chaos, the "formless void" that denies order.

Of the four answers to the question why scriptures survive, the first two concern the mechanics of the process. The third and fourth address the essence, which is the quality of numen, sacredness, of being impervious to questions and criticism and analysis. This quality is found only in the context of a community. To hold the moral high ground is, first, to be identified with a community, whether of interaction, of belief, or of both. For the beggar it was Hinduism and the dharma; for neoclassical economists it is "general equilibrium theory, with utility-maximization as a driving mechanism." Second, having defined a situation by enacting one's association with a numen and so gained the upper hand, it is necessary to dissociate adversaries by demonstrating that they do not belong in that community of believers. In that process the numen is affirmed. Believers can exist only in the context of nonbelievers.

A numen is effectively conveyed by an emotive word or phrase (brotherhood, utility, "meet a payroll," and the like) or a symbolic act (the match between the beggar's teeth), which draws on taken-for-granted presuppositions about what is right and good, what is "natural." These presuppositions are powerful to the extent that they are collective, a word which, in this context, conveys more than simply being shared; it suggests an entity, a force, something that has a capacity to direct, command, and incorporate, in a rather literal sense, those who belong to it. One of the Star Trek series had in it a malevolent and formidable entity—not quite a character—called the Borg.[18] The Borg was a collectivity made up of many apparently identical entities which had more or less the form of a human beings (with some exterior plumbing and wiring) but were programmed through a single brain. In our model of persuasion, numen is imagined as operating like the Borg; it centralizes, homogenizes, and therefore eliminates individuality; it is authority personified; it is Hobbes's Leviathan. It is also, of course, an imagined entity that gives the strategy of inclusion and exclusion its persuasive force.[19]

Structures are fixed by anchoring them to a collectivity and its associated scripture, thus bestowing on them the privilege of being held on faith.[20] In this way they acquire default status and are not easily dislodged. In the end, experience should have the last word, but the end can be quite distant. Any spectacularly negative payoff ought to be a clincher (hands warmed *in* the fire) but, to say it again, negative and positive are to some degree matters of opinion, and what seems to be disastrously negative may be seen as positive by true believers; Jonestown or the Heaven's Gate affair are two of several examples that come to mind. Structures apparently invalidated by experience can be saved by "secondary elaborations of belief."[21]

How can structures held on faith be unfixed? North writes of changes that are done rationally in small steps: "incremental change comes from the perception of the entrepreneurs in political and economic organizations that they could do better by altering the existing institutional framework at some margin" (1990, 8). A change is incremental, I assume, if it is not seen to alter any basic principle. But that scenario is too simple: what is basic is a matter of opinion. There is also a *pars*

18. I assume the name comes from cyborg, a "cyb(ernetic) org(anism)," which (in the *OED*) is "an integrated man–machine system."

19. Fantasies of this kind lie just under the surface in discourses that use such terms as *collective representations*, *collective consciousness*, or *collective mind*. The three phrases are from Durkheim's *The Rules of Sociological Method*; they refer to actors' models and to the fact that these models are shared between individuals. *Collective unconscious*, an evolutionary concept used by the psychologist Jung, signifying that the experiences of past generations have been built into the brain's inherited structure, has similar connotations.

20. *The Kingdom of Individuals*, a book that strays further than this one into the psychological domain, describes some of the strategies that organizations use to fix and unfix ideas and attitudes. See Bailey 1993.

21. "If in such a closed system of thought a belief is contradicted by a particular experience this merely shows that the experience was mistaken, or inadequate, or the contradiction is accounted for by secondary elaborations of belief which provide satisfactory explanations of the apparent inconsistency." This was Evans-Pritchard's equivalent of the nineteenth-century "disturbing cause" or the late-twentieth-century "spin-doctoring" (1951, 99).

*pro toto* issue: small tokens evoke whole structures. Matters that from an analytic standpoint appear to be trivial or peripheral may, in enactment, raise issues that are not trivial: the occasion for the Indian Mutiny in 1857 was the use of animal fat to grease cartridges, the sepoys being required to crimp them with their teeth and so pollute themselves. North's account brackets away the entrenched quality of structures, which, to the extent that they are held on faith, anchored in emotion, and therefore intrinsically valued, cannot be priced, and may not yield automatically to rational arguments about utility. His model, therefore, does not address the struggle that usually goes on when institutions are altered (even, sometimes, "at some margin"— animal fat and cartridges) and therefore does not consider the strategies used to manage the nonrational factor in contests over change.[22]

Now we will boldly go where Star Trek did not go and suggest not only a plurality of Borgs but also strategies that can be used to de-Borg a Borg and put another in its place, or simply, as an end in itself, to get the better of an opponent in a contest to define a situation. To do either of these things one has to redefine the situation by removing one structure and installing another. This can in theory be done through logical argument: find a premise that the other people accept and then demonstrate that their definition of the situation does not follow from their own premise, but yours does. That is the way of reason, the analytic way. It is also the long way round and frequently ineffective, because no common ground can be found, or because the debaters cannot subdue their desire to prevail long enough to hear what is being said. Enactment proceeds differently: it preempts logic by establishing or overthrowing the premises which necessarily precede a reasoned discourse. That is, it deals directly with saving lies, and, perhaps appropriately, as the next chapter will demonstrate, it may do so in quite devious ways.

---

22. The very word *incremental* hints at a rhetorical strategy; it has an apotropaic quality about it, a denial that anything radical is being done or contemplated.

*Chapter 8*
# Contested Structures

*World is crazier and more of it than we think,*
*Incorrigibly plural. I peel and portion*
*A tangerine and spit the pips and feel*
*The drunkenness of things being various.*

—Louis MacNeice, "Snow"

### The Lintel

In the late sixties in Losa, a community of about eight hundred inhabitants in the Maritime Alps of northern Italy, I heard a brief and apparently simple tale—an anecdote—about a lintel. I will repeat it and
use it to model Losa both as a moral community and as an arena in
which incompatible structures coexist, are contested, and change. The
techniques of contestation, as you will see, are anything but simple
and straightforward.

   The storyteller was Roberto, a wealthy corporate executive who
drove down from his office in Milan to spend weekends in his substantial house in the center of Losa. He came in his chauffeured car.
Roberto was an eager collector of local memorabilia. Hiking in the
mountains, when he was passing a *baita* (a shack built in the upland
pastures, occupied only when cattle were taken up the mountain to
graze—virtually every *baita*, including this one, was by then derelict)
he noticed that the stone lintel over the doorway had a date carved on
it, the numbers spaced across its length. He worked out that it came
from Losa's old *municipio* (town hall), which had been destroyed in the
Napoleonic wars, and he decided that he must have it for his collection. He knew which family owned the *baita* (everyone knew at least
the basics about everyone else in Losa and its environs) and the following weekend he sought out its head, offering both to buy the lintel

and to have it replaced with a concrete beam. The owner, identified in the municipal register as *contadino*, a peasant, refused. He did so respectfully, explaining with great politeness and some eloquence that for his part he would be happy to *give* the stone to the gentleman (*signore*), but unfortunately this could not be done because the *baita* was jointly owned with his three brothers. It would be wrong to give it away or sell it without first asking their permission. He would have been more than glad to do that, but it was impossible because one brother was in the Argentine, one was in the United States, and the third was in Nice, and he had been out of touch with all of them for many years. In the circumstances, the best he could do would be to cut off his portion of the stone, one fourth, and give it to the gentleman.

Roberto, telling the story, said the man was a fool for passing up the chance to make a bit of money without having to do anything to earn it. Some people were like that—perverse and a bit stupid. Then he added that he himself, Roberto, had not been very smart. "If I'd sent Vincenzo to ask for it as a favor—to prop up a gutter or something—he'd have got it without any fuss." (Roberto was a modern-day seigneur in Losa. Vincenzo, a construction crew foreman, was one of his henchmen.)

There are two obvious questions: (1) Why did the peasant refuse to sell? (2) Why did Roberto think that Vincenzo could have had the lintel for nothing? You can easily, and correctly, deduce the lintel owner's motives: he intended to cock a snook at Roberto. Nor—the second question—is it difficult to work out that, at least in Roberto's mind, the lintel owner had some kind of affinity with Vincenzo. You can also guess that both the refusal and the presumed link with Vincenzo had something to do with class. Roberto was a wealthy man and a *signore* (a gentleman) and the lintel owner was a peasant who worked with his hands, as did Vincenzo. The motives are clear enough, and so also—in broad outline—is the context of class antagonism. What is less clear is why the peasant chose to deliver his refusal in that elaborately rhetorical fashion. What could have been a plain "no" expanded into a parable about the various alternative and contradictory structures available to define morality in Losa.

Roberto, at the outset, clearly intended to define their situation on the principle of expected utility—of a market economy. He was a buyer, the peasant was a seller; they would negotiate and agree on a price. The lintel would be replaced with a concrete beam, the peasant would also get money, and Roberto's collection of memorabilia would be enriched. The interaction would be strictly a business transaction, each party acting, as neoclassical economists assume is the norm in every interaction, "rationally"—that is, each would act in what he believed to be his own best interests.

There is a marvelous univocality about the neoclassical economists' one-size-fits-all expected-utility definition of any exchange situation that interests them professionally: no status is relevant except that of the rational, self-interested, calculating, economic person. Expected utility is (purportedly) a universal language. It presumes common ground, is neutral, and is without cultural entanglements. Roberto belonged to the upper class and the lintel owner was a peasant; they both lived in the same community and therefore probably shared certain moral standards; they both spoke the three languages of the region (Italian, Piedmontese, and the local dialect, Niçois); and their families had lived there for generations and carried with them the baggage of a long history of past encounters. In the expected-utility frame, however, these facts were no more relevant to understanding the transaction than was—recalling Friedman—the length of their hair or the color of their eyes. In economic transactions all such contexts count for nothing.

It is tempting, if you have not been initiated into the mystery of neoclassical economics, to assume that this model, so demonstrably short of reality, deserves instant dismissal. In the present instance it does not. In a negotiation (or in the analysis of negotiations) some encounters may be persuasively contextualized within the very narrow limits recognized by neoclassical economists. When, in our (usually justifiable) suspicion of the "truths" that economic policymakers foist on the rest of us, we complain (as I have done) that the idea of "economic man," besides being demeaning, is empirically false—moral values also influence conduct—we are using a language that may be appropriate for intellectual inquiry about the applicability of propositions but is not necessarily so for understanding the *enactment* of ideas. When an idea (a structure) is deployed in a competition to define a situation, its effectiveness, not its truth, makes the call.

In that light, Roberto's opening move—suggesting a deal—is a reasonable (and economic) way to initiate an interaction. It assumes a motivational structure in the other person that is uncomplicated because it transcends culture and is part of a universal human nature: whoever they are, all they want is a good bargain. That element of universality makes transactionalism, on the principle of least effort, a suitable opening gambit in an exchange when one hopes to keep the matter uncomplicated. Furthermore, the definition may hold: exchanges, including communicative ones that convey information, are as often transactions as they are prestations.

Roberto failed to impose a simple market definition on their encounter. The peasant (but without saying so directly) did not agree that the language of transactions, used to make the offer, was unencumbered. Rather it entailed, even if it did not voice, class antagonism; and, in addition, it thus offended a different morality, to which I will come shortly, that the peasant claimed—disingenuously—was his guide. Tacitly rejecting the definition of himself and of Roberto as one-dimensional profit-minded bargainers, he responded with a prestational claim that appears to be simple and unambiguous but is in fact a layered complexity composed of two structures, one concealed within the other and contradicting it.

On the surface, the peasant's redefinition of their encounter as a prestation is no less straightforward than Roberto's "economic man" transactional definition. The invocation of his brothers and their rights appears to be an unambiguous statement about the peasant himself and his moral community: he was the kind of person who is guided by the obligations of brotherhood. But there is also a hint in his words that Roberto, by offering him money as an inducement to betray brotherly obligations, was not behaving properly. In this there is a further implied assumption that he and Roberto shared—or should have shared—the same moral standards. They were *paesani*—people who belonged to the same moral community, who defined right and wrong in the same way, and who shared a relationship of solidarity and mutual consideration that had the same taken-for-granted quality as brotherhood itself. In conformity with this ethos the peasant spoke of his readiness to *give*, not sell, the lintel. The remark about brotherly obligation, therefore, could be construed as a reproach. It implied that poor people like himself upheld *paesano* morality and lived by its standards, while the rich used their money to get what they wanted, even when it meant subverting moral proprieties. None of this was openly stated; it was insinuated. The peasant's finely polite manner indicated that Roberto's crass market attitude, and his disregard for traditional family values, should cause him to feel a touch of shame.[1]

Roberto, telling the story, did not feel any shame that I could see. He recounted the peasant's sentiments about his obligations to his brothers without comment on the implied morality (other than a mildly sceptical grin). I think he took it for granted that his audience (myself and others) would realize that what the peasant said was not all that the peasant was talking about. No one bothered to remark on the discrepancy between the claim of a strongly felt obligation and

1. Am I stretching the evidence? Perhaps; I cannot know exactly what was in their minds. But discovering that is not my purpose. I want to know what, in that culture, *could have been* in their minds. See later remarks on the idiographic/nomothetic distinction.

admitting to having been out of touch for many years. The message, in other words, had nothing to do with his obligation to his three brothers; it meant something else.

Roberto did understand what was going on: he was being mocked. The peasant's elaborate protestations that he would dearly like to make a present of the lintel if only he were free to do so fell into the same category as his sermonizing about brotherly obligation: the words said one thing, they meant something different and contrary. That second meaning is coded in the shape-shifting noun, *signore* (gentleman), which the peasant used to refer to Roberto.

## Structures in Losa

In Losa at that time the word *signore* had three distinct meanings depending on the roles attributed to a *signore* and the structures in which they were said to operate. Two of these meanings provide a context for the story of the lintel. In the first, a *signore* was a person of wealth and standing who served the community, taking on the obligations of leadership, helping those less well off, and in return receiving the respect and admiration of ordinary people. Structured in this way, *signorilità* presupposed not only a stratified population—"The rich man in his castle / The poor man at his gate / God made them high and lowly / And ordered their estate"—but also a relatively closed community. This was indeed the case in Losa, even down to the beginning of the Second World War. Ordinary folk had little to do directly with the world beyond their village and their valley, and when they needed to deal with the higher levels of the administration or the Church—to get a place in hospital, to avoid or defer conscription, for example— they sought the help of the gentry, because the gentry had *le braccia lunghe*, long arms that could reach out into world of the Church and the State. When the occasion called for it, people in Losa in the sixties still treated that definition of *signorilità* as operative. Roberto, for example, had a considerable clientele of people obliged to him for the favors he had conferred on them using his wealth and his long arms.

The lintel owner's use of the word *signore* when rejecting Roberto's offer permits this notion of noblesse oblige to drift ironically into their encounter via the insinuation that Roberto was overlooking not only his obligations as a *paesano*, but also the special obligations that attached to those *paesani* who were also *signori*. The irony is there because a second and contradictory definition of *signore*, along with a correspondingly different social structure, is drawn into the situation. The peasant used this second definition to typecast Roberto and so to define their situation. Once again, however, the case was not made propositionally; it was implied.

The exemplar of this second type of *signore* was another man in the community whose status was slightly uncertain. He had useful outside connections (mainly with Church dignitaries and in the world of commerce) and he was fairly rich, but his identity in the municipal register was not at Roberto's level, *benestante* (independently wealthy), but *commerciante* (businessman). Several years earlier he had bought a stretch of rock-strewn mountainside from three peasant brothers, who, they themselves boasted, had exploited his ignorance by inflating the price of land that they knew was absolutely unfit for agriculture of any kind. (He had told them he wanted to use it to develop thorn stock on which to graft roses.) He held the land for a couple of years and then sold it, at a huge profit, to a cement company that needed to have access to the cliff behind it. He must have known all along of the company's plans. The three brothers felt themselves cheated. Word got about and he became the boilerplate case of the bad *signore*, the person who uses long arms not to benefit ordinary people but to do them down.[2]

The lintel owner made no direct reference to class conflict. His entire discourse was overtly framed in only one part of the traditional *paesano* morality (brotherhood). It was left to Roberto to fill in for himself not only the *signorilità* part of that morality but also to make explicit, in his remark that Vincenzo could have had the stone for free, the unvoiced class antagonism. Thus the peasant managed both to disoblige a rich man and at the same time to claim, implicitly, a moral high ground. That morality, however, was an instrument, not a directive; the values of *signorilità* and brotherly-cum-community solidarity were used to convey their precise negation.[3] By saying one thing the peasant insinuated its opposite.

2. In opposition both to noblesse oblige and to the *signore* as exploiter, a third and increasingly prevalent definition emerged out of the postwar prosperity that came to Italy—the so-called Italian miracle. Generalized prosperity and an eager consumerism produced the notion that *signorilità* was neither an estate nor a class but a style of living that was open to anyone who took the trouble; everyone could be a *signore* or a *signora*. This sentiment was realized—to use an anachronism—in a form of Yuppiedom, which generates a community of people who strive to be equal and not to fall behind the rest, who exhibit the greatest wariness in dealing with one another, and who are very much given to the kind of rhetorical one-upmanship that is revealed in the peasant's maneuvers around Roberto. I think this third meaning of *signore*, although it certainly could be used to let the wind out of self-important people, had at best a marginal significance in the encounter over the lintel. It was not directly invoked in the peasant's *paesano* rhetoric and the incident was not construed in that way by Roberto, who perceived only class antagonism.

3. The verb in that sentence—*convey*—suggests that the words *vehicle* (surface meaning—*paesano* values) and *tenor* (underlying meaning—class antagonism) would have been

That raises two questions. First, what motivated this indirectness? Discourse on the class struggle was certainly not without its own ample vocabulary to mark approval and disapproval. Second, how is it possible to do that? How does a message, which *surreptitiously* contains its own contradiction, invalidate itself and authenticate the contradicted meaning?

## Motives and Tactics

In the discussion of motivation and tactics that follows I am not suggesting that the peasant systematically rehearsed in his mind all the alternative ways in which he might score off Roberto. Identifying what is in another's mind is chancy. The peasant may have been reflexively aware of everything that he did in his encounter with Roberto, or he may not. If we wish, we can speak of "implicit theory," presumably of the kind that underlies the correct use of grammar by those who cannot say what the grammatical rules are. Or we can suppose, as I think Herzfeld does with reference to Greeks using irony (2001, 73), a "theoretical orientation" which the peasant, if suitably prompted as M. Jourdain was, could have set out discursively. We can leave the question moot. Sometimes it is convenient to write in an idiographic mode and speak to the particular capacities of an individual. My goal, however, is not to see the encounter only as a small event in Losa's history but rather to make nomothetic sense of it by identifying its general features. For that, it is necessary to survey whatever courses of rational action were available in that culture and in that particular context. To do that, one examines the costs and benefits both of what the peasant did and of various alternative responses that were culturally available to him when Roberto first asked to buy the lintel. Whether or not in fact he made these calculations is at present beside the point. (The distinction idiographic/nomothetic matches Tolstoy's content/form or Blake's particulars/generalizing demonstrations.)

It is conceivable (barely—I will say why in a moment) that the peasant was acting straightforwardly and from the best of possible motives as a true believer in *paesano* values and *signorilità*, that he was genuinely upset by the amorality implicit in the money offer, and was trying, so to speak, to save Roberto from his baser self. Roberto did not think so; neither do I. The notion is altogether too Panglossian. Mockery, not soul saving, was the motive. There are some oblique but quite

appropriate, if they had not already been so firmly attached to discourse on metaphor. The two structures are not metaphorically linked as source/target or vehicle/tenor; they are connected by irony, which requires them to be contraries. I will come to irony later.

unambiguous signs, to which I will come in a moment, that make the disrespect obvious.

When Roberto first made his bid to define their encounter as a transaction, the peasant might simply have accepted the offer. Or he might—Roberto would surely not have been surprised—have asked to be paid more. But to do that would be to accept Roberto's initial definition of their situation and to forego the chance to play the game of moral one-upmanship. That particular opportunity-cost was glancingly noticed by Roberto, when he said that the man was a fool for not accepting easy money.

The peasant might, third, have deliberately driven up the price to make Roberto balk. That would have provided a left-wing soapbox from which to deploy themes of capitalist greed and thus occupy a different kind of moral high ground. For that there might have been some costs.

First, at that time and in that place Marxist rhetoric associated with The Revolution had become something of a joke. One old man, who had been imprisoned in Mussolini's time as a Communist, used to drive a small flock of sheep past the elevated verandah where Roberto's aged mother sat in a wheelchair, sunning herself. He would stop and chat, looking up from the street, and on each occasion he would end the conversation with a warning *"Viene la rivoluzione . . .* Come the revolution and I will be sitting up there, Signora, and you will be driving the sheep to pasture." They saw it—everyone saw it—as an ironic joke between *paesani*, not merely mitigating but for the moment altogether eliding the difference in wealth and class between them. The lintel owner had no place for that kind of irony. He was not sharing a joke with Roberto. (He did introduce an element of farce, but in a different way and with a different effect. I will come to that shortly.)

Second, the idiom of straight rentier-bashing might have been rhetorically ineffective because it addressed a theme that was situationally ambiguous. In Losa at that time the left/right political division was complicated. Losa had no more than a handful of Communists. The dominant cleavage lay between Christian Democrats (slightly in the majority) and Socialists. The Socialists were led by Roberto and some other well-to-do people, whose ideological convictions had less to do with socialist dogma than with their wartime experience, when, in 1943, they fought in the Partisan wars against Mussolini's Fascists and the German occupying forces. To have openly invoked the idiom of class warfare against Roberto, the leader of the principal left-wing group in the village, might, given the ironic contradictions of the

situation, have been confusing. Effective rhetoric cannot rest on assertions that invite instant bewilderment.

Third, to have played the class-antagonism card directly and openly
would have deprived the lintel owner of the pleasure afforded by winning the indirectness game. More on the joy of rhetoric later.

*Paesano* values, in contrast, preserved that gratification. They also
had an immediate payoff, because they were a topos, a rhetorical commonplace that could be presented, in apparent innocence, as the one
and only and obviously "true" definition of their situation, one that
was instantly compelling on Roberto, who was himself a *signore* and a
*paesano*. The peasant deployed *paesano* values as if they were beyond
contention, normatively imperative, despite the fact that everyone
knew that, in practice, contradictory definitions of *signore* existed and
that not everyone who claimed the title behaved in accordance with its
traditional values. Family values in America have the same commonplace standing; there are dreadful families, and all families have problems, but to condemn the family roundly as an institution generally
meets with disapproval, even outrage. *Signorilità* and *paesano* values
had exactly that status. Roberto, having accepted them (by not contesting them), was thus logically constrained to accept the moral reasoning that supposedly prevented the peasant from handing over the
lintel. In that way the lintel owner both defined and occupied a moral
high ground.

That moral high ground, as I said, was an ironic fabrication. To use
irony with the intention of hurting or embarrassing a victim is to walk
the edge of a precipice, a fall being irony that goes unperceived and is
accepted as sincere. Certainly there are occasions on which ironists
prefer to entertain themselves and never let the victims know that
they are victims. The lintel encounter was not of that kind. Therefore
the peasant had to frame the message in such a way that it would be
difficult for Roberto not to realize that what the message ostensibly
conveyed was not the authentic message. In particular, he needed to
make clear that his deference was in fact mockery. Roberto said nothing about the peasant's demeanor, other than what is implied in the
elaborately polite words and phrases of the refusal. But even without a
confirming visual image of the peasant's self-presentation, the words
alone indicate the kind of gamesmanship that is played in Italian *complimenti*: praise is bestowed with such vigor and extravagance that the
victim is embarrassed and the complimenter's lack of sincerity is made
very obvious.[4] (In hayseed America there is a convenient, if rather
inadequate, response to such treatment: "Aw shucks!"—shucks being

4. See the entertaining account in Barzini 1966, Ch. 6.

corn husks, worthless things.) The mildly idiotic concern for the interests of long-absent brothers in a *baita* that was already derelict, the very respectful forms of address, the anxious protestations to be of service, and the use of *signore* as a term of reference all signal humbuggery. So, above all, does the peasant's absurd offer to have his one fourth of the stone cut off and given to "the gentleman."[5]

The offer was absurd because the stone's value to Roberto was the date carved along its length. It was also absurd because to cut the lintel would cause the doorway to collapse and thus deprive the other brothers of their share of the *baita*, which itself was absurd because the *baita* was already a wreck. There is a Monty Python quality about the scene that makes the peasant, if one were to assume that the offer was sincerely made, look like an idiot. I am sure the offer was made with a straight face; but it was hardly sincere.[6] It was ironic.

What else could one read into the suggestion except mockery? When Henry Ford told his customers they could have their new car in any color they wished so long as it was black, the irony is at their expense because the offer that appears to cater to their preferences instantly repudiates itself. The peasant's offer is in the same category, a form of disrespect paid from behind a posture of deference. But his performance is more complicated than that; it contained yet another level of mockery. The peasant was clowning, ironically self-disparaging, mimicking the Boeotian, half-witted creature that the gentry were supposed to see in a typical peasant. In this way he sent two messages. First, he caricatured himself in order to caricature Roberto by insinuating that this was how Roberto, being crass, saw peasants. Second— the counterpunch—by invoking, with apparent sincerity, the framework of *signorilità* and at the same time putting on an idiot mask he enacted the idea that only idiots take *signorilità* seriously.

There was little that was hit-or-miss about the peasant's performance; he neutralized "the aleatory characteristic of attributions of intent" (Herzfeld 2001, 67) in the use of irony.[7] Roberto, the victim, was left under no illusions about what was the intended message. The peasant, hyperbolizing his own imbecility, had effectively extracted

5. It might be suggested that direct rentier-bashing would be hazardous, because Roberto was rich and influential, and the peasant, being prudent, chose not to openly offend someone who, if angry, could make him suffer for it. The elaborate politeness of the refusal would lend itself to that interpretation, but not enough to make it convincing, especially when one considers the tomfoolery conveyed in the suggestion to cut off one fourth of the stone.

6. I like to imagine the peasant reinforcing his declaration about the obligations of brotherhood with what in Losa (and elsewhere) is taken to be the ultimate signal of heartfelt sincerity—the right hand placed across the heart.

7. There is an extensive literature on how difficult it is to know whether or not a

the substance of ambiguity from their encounter while leaving its outer form intact.

## Unfolding and Compressing

The enactment of that elaborate and complicated ironic doublespeak is made possible by a process of unfolding and compressing that occurs in the cognitive channels connecting *performance* (what the peasant said) with *contexts* (structures that are needed to make sense of what he said). Situations are defined by deciding which channels are open and which closed.[8]

The channels carry traffic in both directions. I begin with unfolding, which is the movement from a performance to one or another of the structures that are available to give it meaning. The tale required, for the telling, less than five hundred words, in no more than two paragraphs, one of them containing only three sentences. Yet the tale itself and certain keywords in it function as cues or commands that, when selected, download large blocks of information (offered as fact or as opinion) which animate—give meaning to—the words actually spoken. Think of the term *signore* which the peasant bestowed on Roberto: out of it cascades an immense, diverse, and internally contradictory flow of information about Losa's history, its economy, its place in the larger society, the structures available to describe these features, the codes required to enact the structures, and many other related matters. Recall also the peasant invoking his brothers and his moral obligations. The words do an immediate and direct job: they block Roberto's bid to define the encounter as a market transaction. But they also invoke, indirectly, the larger *paesano* morality, in which brotherhood is an implicate. In both examples, a fragment contained in the performance leads out to things larger than itself (the contexts). Think of the trope as an unfolding of meaning.[9]

speaker is deliberately being ironic. See, for example, Booth on "stable" irony and the "reconstruction" (deciphering) of ironic messages (1974, passim); Muecke on "covert" irony (1969, 56–59); or Hutcheon on "the unbearable slipperiness of irony" (1995, 115–24).

8. Goffman's *transformation rules* (1961, 76), which govern what is acceptable or not in a "focused encounter," are functionally equivalent to my *channels*. I have not used his terminology because, although our models are similar in form, they differ in the question that is being asked. His starting situation is a culturally established "congruence" about what should go on within the "membrane" that seals off a "focussed encounter" from "properties" that would put it into disarray if they were admitted. His players, by and large, seem more concerned with keeping the game and its rules intact than with winning. He speaks of the "euphoria" (1961, 66) that players feel when they find themselves "spontaneously" maintaining "the authorized transformation rules." My players are different; they are out to win a primary contest that will decide what the game and its rules (Goffman's "membrane") are going to be.

9. I could identify both unfolding (part to whole) and compressing (whole to part) as

Hirschman (1979) speaks of the "first step" in analysis as converting "the real into the rational or the contingent into the necessary." In other words, in analysis things that are experienced (Hirschman's "real," Shakespeare's "things unknown," Tolstoy's "content") are "given shape" by converting them into something thinkable, that is, into structures that explain, in the form of structural rules, what the things are and why they are like that and not different.[10] Placement of something enacted and experienced (an event, an action, or a word) in a category and then in a structure gives it meaning. To know the different structures (contexts) that can be invoked by the term *signore* is to know what meanings *signore* can have.

It may be asked (touching again both on the nomothetic/idiographic issue and the tacit knowledge implied by the notion of "implicit theory") where are the "folders" that store all that information about Losa. In this particular case I am sure that both Roberto and the peasant were familiar with the three structures folded into the term *signore* and, if asked, would have had the words to describe them propositionally. Without that propositional knowledge, Roberto could not have remarked that Vincenzo could have had the lintel for nothing. I am equally sure that the peasant knew exactly what his remarks implied. But even if neither of these things had been the case, the guiding model would still require me to look for "a repertoire of alternative ideas," that is, for a language, a *langue*, that gives meaning to the *parole* that is enacted in the story. To put it simply, if we are to understand the enactment of structures (ideas), we have to know what these structures are. Otherwise the enactment is not an enactment at all but remains a part of "things unknown" because they have not been "given shape."[11]

Now reverse the flow, moving from context to performance. From that perspective, context serves as a folder of alternative structures that are constraints and resources for some kind of algorithmic planning by a performer. People, in other words, use the knowledge available to them to size up situations and make their plans accordingly. The peasant, even if by what we loosely call "instinct," nevertheless

---

synecdoche or metonymy, but the function involved is wider than that contemplated in the formal rhetorical definition of those words (Burke 1969a, 503–17). Nor do they sufficiently connote agency.

10. Hirschman, using the words "contingent" and "necessary," is not referring to if/then propositions about cause and effect in the natural world but to syntactical forms, such as, for example, the convention that links *dogs* with *bones* by *chew* and not *chews*.

11. Saussure's *langue* and *parole* (or the *competence* and *performance* of the generative grammarians) are akin to my *context* and *performance* in that both involve a macroscopic/microscopic distinction. But they are not identical; context/performance addresses the substance of what is generated rather than content-free generative rules.

made a means-end (that is, rational) calculation of what could be done to make his definition of the situation prevail. In making that calculation he reversed the process in which meaning is *unfolded* and moved instead from context toward performance by *compressing* Losa's history, its class structure, its economy, and its place in the larger society, and so on, into the tale of himself and his brothers, or into the single word *signore*. The tale and the word function like parables to present one of the alternative moralities available to regulate community life in Losa.

To compress is to selectively omit context. We have already encountered a form of selection in the remarks made earlier about the neoclassical paradigm in economics and its presupposition that all exchange-situations are predefined as transactional. Discourse in economics is transactional (the thing exchanged being information and "truth") and therefore is always (purportedly) propositional and analytic, never rhetorical. When economists engage in analysis, they have agreed beforehand on the foundational expected-utility presuppositions that allow them to argue rationally. Issues that could only be settled by rhetoric have already been settled, and logic can regulate the debate so long as contexts that would undermine the expected-utility assumption continue to be bracketed away. The decision to use the expected-utility presupposition can only have been reached via rhetoric; it antecedes logic.[12] Note also the presence of authority (or of collusion); the situation is one of order and cooperation because the rules have been set. The question of how they came to be set is not asked, and, if raised, is likely to be dismissed as rule infringement; if you can't accept the presuppositions, stay away from the debate. Roberto's opening gambit, bidding for a transactional exchange, has exactly that flavor: it asserts, implicitly, that the rules of engagement are a commonplace and so obvious that they could not be otherwise. So also does the peasant's (hypocritical) presumption of *signorilità* and *paesano* morality.

Now consider how the peasant promoted his definition of the situation. He did not assert it; instead he manipulated Roberto into constructing it for himself. He compressed a structure (or rather a pair of mutually contradictory structures) into a parable and a keyword. To the extent that he was rhetorically adept, he left Roberto no choice

12. The uninitiated may be offered an anterior presupposition, from which expected utility can be logically derived. It takes the form of "self-evident" statements about human nature. Lionel Robbins, you will recall, in that feisty manifesto on the "nature and significance of economic science," described the neoclassical assumptions as "so much the stuff of our everyday experience that they have only to be stated to be recognized as obvious" (Robbins 1937, 79).

about how to define their encounter. Rhetorical skill is exactly being able to select the symbol (for particular persuadees) that will cause them to invoke the contexts that the persuader has chosen for them.

Where is the persuasion in this rhetorical device? Hirschman, in the same essay, robustly castigates a nomothetically inclined author who reached too eagerly for paradigms and disdained the particulars, having the "brash confidence" to instruct his readers, authoritatively, how to interpret the events described. Another author, who wrote like a historian, idiographically dwelling among the particulars, is praised for "allowing the readers to formulate" propositions for themselves. That is exactly what a well-chosen symbol does. The persuadees, building outwards from the symbol, come to believe that they have themselves constructed the definition of their situation, and, in a limited and distinctly ironic way, they have done just that.

The device—inducing people to accept an idea or a course of action by making them believe that the idea is their own by virtue not only of acceptance but also of creation—is widely and effectively used (with varying degrees of subtlety) by orators and politicians—indeed, by anyone who has a story to tell. An audience is kept attentive to the extent that it finds itself filling in the spaces that the writer has left open. The rhetorical skill, of course, lies in knowing what to leave out and in supplying the right clues and cues.[13]

Up to a point that is a plausible interpretation of the story of the lintel: Roberto was being manipulated into reaching, seemingly of his own accord, conclusions about the nature of their encounter that had in fact been preselected by the peasant. But it is also insufficient; it says nothing about the irony that is so patent in the peasant's manipulative scheme.

## Combative Irony

The peasant made his overt argument with apparent directness and simplicity—we are *paesani*. (Even that was not without indirectness; he talked only of his brothers.) But the real message was: "We are *not* paesani, because you are a rentier!" Ostensibly (and ironically) the peasant treats Roberto as an innocent who will accept the *paesano* message as authentic, at the same time expecting him to get the real message. The irony in this case is more than simple dissembling; it is dissembling in such a way that what is outwardly hidden from the victims is at the same time made obvious to them. This is an irony of

---

13. Is there a rhetorical term for this figure? If not, I suggest crossing *suppressio veri* with *suggestio falsi* in order to produce *suggestio veri*.

ridicule akin to Socratic irony but by no means identical; I will call it "combative."

There are many kinds of irony.[14] Combative irony is enacted and contrived for a purpose. It is not spectator irony, neither the mean-spirited judgmental variety of Hamlet's "For 'tis the sport to have the engineer hoist with his own petar," nor the gentler kind that would see irony in the wealthy Roberto's confident and well-intentioned ploy so promptly negated by an ungrateful, not-at-all-wealthy peasant. A fortiori this is not an instance of dramatic irony. No tragedy is involved; no inexorable fate, known to the audience but not to the players, strikes down their hopes and ambitions. The victim, Roberto, is not left unaware; he is made to be an audience for the spectacle of his own entrapment.[15] Irony that is merely observed is, for the observers, self-distancing; they are not engaged. Those who use combative irony are on the field, committed to action.

Combative irony differs, too, from Goffman's "subversive" irony, which also is enacted but is not combative. Subversive irony is collusive, deployed to protect a "focussed encounter" by taking the bite out of contexts (his "properties") that, if presented directly, would disturb the regnant definition of a situation (1961, 76). Rosa, an elderly woman (in another community in the Italian Alps) was terminally ill. A neighbor woman dropped by to see if Rosa needed anything from the shop. Rosa handed her a letter to post, giving her 100 *lire* to pay for the required 100-*lire* stamp, and saying, "With the change, buy yourself a coffee!" The coffee would have cost at least 150 *lire*. They both laughed and the woman went on her way. Rosa was making an ironic joke by indirectly voicing the idea (the opposite of what she hoped was the truth) that her friend might gossip about Rosa's failure to return favors. The irony was deployed to safeguard their friendship. That was not the peasant's irony; he used irony precisely to deny mutual regard.[16]

In the encounter with Roberto the peasant was not protecting a defined situation. There was no prior agreement about what might be allowed to penetrate the "membrane," because there was, as yet, no membrane. Goffman, as I noted earlier, is concerned less with how in-

14. Typologizing irony is a cottage industry. See Muecke 1969, Booth 1974, Hutcheon 1995, and their bibliographies.

15. Had the peasant been content, as ironists sometimes are, to leave his victim in the dark, he would not have been deploying combative irony, as I define it, but simply creating a situation of dramatic irony and thus, through inward laughter or the appreciation of spectators, ministering to his own sense of superiority.

16. In the same way, irony can be used to dismiss by mockery an acutely troubling matter, such as our mortality or, more generally, the possibility that a cherished and deeply reassuring saving lie may be, after all, a lie. Berlin calls it "flippant" irony (1980, 273).

choate situations get defined than with how those already defined are protected from contexts (alternative structures) that would put them in peril.

Combative irony, by definition, presupposes antagonism. Liddell and Scott gloss *eironeia* as "ignorance purposely affected to provoke or confound an antagonist" (a near enough description of the peasant's intentions) and add that it was a device used by Socrates against the Sophists. Socratic irony is a weapon; it is not the kind of constructive persuasive exchange envisaged in Gandhi's *satyagraha* (struggle to find truth) in which the debaters are imagined not as contestants but as partners in a cooperative endeavor to find *the* truth that is waiting there to be discovered.[17] Socratic irony is bare-knuckle stuff, rhetorical assault and battery, intended to wear opponents down, to exhaust their capacity for logical combat, to knock all ideas out of their heads and thus make space for an implantation of "the truth" that Socrates, all the time protesting his own perplexity (and patently dissembling), professes not to know. In these circumstances the verb *persuade,* with its etymology of sweetness, would, as when a handgun is called a "persuader," itself be an irony.[18]

Socratic irony pays lip service to the protocols of logic and is purportedly deployed in the service of truth. The victims are reduced to silence because they cannot show that their conclusions follow from the premises that they have been maneuvered into accepting. Combative irony is different; it is not a demonstration of correct logic but rather a preemptive (and duplicitous) assertion of the rightness of a premise—in the present case, *paesano* values. At the same time it is a demonstration of superiority—of superior cunning and superior agonistic skills: the peasant, from a posture of humility and self-disparaging half-wittedness, shows himself to be smarter than Roberto. Combative irony challenges the victims to look at what is being done to them and to acknowledge that they are helpless. It is the *complimenti* situation. To protest against *complimenti* with a feeble and embarrassed murmur of "Shucks!" is to throw in the towel. To challenge ironic mockery with anything but a counterirony is exactly that—an admission of defeat.

## Humor

Irony and humor are ways to deny another person the right to occupy a moral high ground. Whether barbed or friendly, humor fends off

17. That was Gandhi's hope. His interlocutors sometimes saw things differently. "Behind all his courteous interest, one has the impression that one is addressing a closed door," Nehru wrote (cited in Moraes 1973, 173).

18. It derives from the Latin *suavis*, meaning "sweet" or "agreeable."

claims to moral superiority. Sometimes it asserts there is no high ground to be occupied. The peasant was saying exactly that when he mocked *signorilità*, enacting its demise but never saying plainly that it was defunct. So too was Rosa, making a little joke about using the nonexistent change to buy a coffee.

Rosa's exchange with her friend was quite complex; it did contain an element of mockery. They were part of the same community, the same prestation circle, equal in status, and they were friends. Rosa made a joke of the idea that her friend might take advantage of Rosa's inability to return the favor. For sure there is an apotropaic element in her words, an irony that safeguarded their relationship. There is also a clear prestational offering of friendship; a joke shared is a friendship shared. That is not the case with ridicule, which feeds on hostility. There was a great deal of ridicule in the peasant's farcical maneuvering around Roberto.

Things, it seems, are never as simple as they first appear. Rosa's gesture of friendship contained within it a small hint of its opposite: their relationship, one might say, was glancing over its shoulder at an image of its own inversion. That inversion is like an inoculation that will keep their friendship healthy. One can see in this a dim acknowledgment that the saving lie is a lie, that the lie's facade conceals not the truth, but an alternative lie, and that saving lies are fragile. One would like to have had a more detailed account of Nuer conduct as they enacted it, not only of the dominant egalitarian structure but also of the submerged nonegalitarian structure which Evans-Pritchard bracketed out of his model. How did an ordinary Nuer, whose "derisive pride amazes a stranger," conduct himself in the presence of a "bull"? Was everyone always straightforward and straight-faced? Humor has the peculiar capacity to notice the contradictions in our social life and at the same time diminish them, easing the tension and suggesting that, in the end, it is all a joke. Humor takes away the terror that comes from realizing, momentarily, that a saving lie is a lie. Ridicule, on the other hand, directly challenges the lie.

Recall the vignette of the shepherd telling Roberto's old mother what she would be doing "come the revolution." Those words, on the surface, appear to present overtly the structure that the lintel owner so elaborately concealed (and yet made plain) in pantomiming the conventions of *signorilità*. The shepherd also was pantomiming, probably with the opposite intent, certainly with the opposite effect. He used humor, not ridicule. He was offering a prestation of friendship, and claiming (notwithstanding the directly voiced threat of revolution) that he and Roberto's mother were *paesani*, and the politics of class difference did not define their relationship. Analytically, he talked class conflict; at the same time he enacted the moral equivalence of *paesani*, of neighbors (and, I would guess, of old age).

Nothing seems to stay simply itself. The simplicity of a money transaction (cash for the lintel or coins for the beggar) in both cases segued swiftly into the higher reaches of morality, where the situation was again simplified as inclusion in, or exclusion from, a moral community. When people compete to define a situation, they subdue complexities by acting as if they do not exist. Humor pushes in both directions. On the one hand it simplifies, because it puts an end to critical thought, to cerebration: to laugh is at least to suspend, if not to end, reasoning and calculation. On the other hand, humor also points to things that are not in the open; it points to unspoken complexities and uncertainties, and thus reveals the fragility and unreality of a saving lie. Structures, whether enacted or presented in analytic form, seem never quite to cleanse the situation of their contraries. In neither case can a structure be usefully understood without recognizing the background presence of its alternatives.

## Cross-talk

My mentor on the Indian train, teaching me how to deal with beggars, realized that I could not read signals about dharma. So he communicated in the neutral language of transactions, pointing out that it cost very little to buy off a beggar, and then added a mildly ironic sugaring of morality—my payoff would include spiritual merit. The language of transactions is universally understood, even when not accepted: I understood what the mentor said; the peasant understood Roberto's offer of money for the lintel. Transactional discourse is relatively simple: it brackets away the multiple alternative structures that might have been offered to define a situation. Each different structure has its own dialect; transactionalism is a lingua franca.

*Alternative* suggests contraries: *paesani* values (including *signorilità*) are logically incompatible with the values of class conflict: both cannot be fitted into a single structure. But they can be enacted in one and the same situation and used tactically to subvert one another, even to subvert themselves. To deploy different structures in a single situation one must follow rules of strategy that state what may be said or done by whom, to whom, in what circumstances, and with what consequences. In this section I will inspect a small sample of these rules.

The strategy of claiming the high moral ground, one might at first think, could only be effective when both parties adhere to the same moral values. The cases given above seem to show this. The beggar, by putting the match between his teeth, invoked notions of dharma, expecting that I would be moved to join him on that moral high ground and give him his due. But the strategy failed because I knew nothing of the dharma. Out of that example emerges a simple hypothesis (the M-rule): Strategies that use morality as a persuasive device are effective only within the appropriate moral community, that is, between people who share the same beliefs and values.

The logic of that proposition is impeccable. A moral rule influences those for whom it is a moral rule; a circle is round; it is a matter of definition. But, although valid, the proposition cannot make sense of contests to define a situation, because it assumes a single regnant morality. Situations, before they are defined, are not structured by a single morality; to assume so is an unrealistic oversimplification of the concept *moral community*. Moral communities are arenas in which people argue about what should be the regnant morality. The M-rule therefore is valid (in Friedman's sense) but not always applicable.

Another hypothesis, which is about the significance of power in strategies of persuasion, fails in a similar way. It is the P-rule: Higher-ranking persons, when dealing with their subordinates, use command strategies rather than persuasion. Persuasion does not use the imperative mood; it is optative or subjunctive, expressing a wish or a contingency, indicating something that might happen but is not certain because the persuadees still have the capacity to decide for themselves. The command strategy states the rule directly: "This is the right thing to do!" The best of my teachers used to direct his students and junior colleagues to find what was good in a seminar presentation before trying to shred it.[19] According to the P-rule, he could do that because he was our teacher; he had the power. This rule (like the M-rule) is a convention derived from the tautology that those who have the power give the orders. If we defied him (we sometimes did), that would not break the "grammatical" connection between rank and the imperative mood, but would simply be evidence that the situation was not defined by the structure that gave him authority.

The P-rule, like the M-rule, assumes a single regnant structure and does not address inchoate situations in which structures are contested. Power does not derive only from position (of teacher or wealthy man) in a single regnant structure; it can also be drawn from alternative structures that the parties invoke to define the situation. Each exchange is potentially an occasion on which the power that goes with a particular rank in a particular structure is put on test. In other words, the connection between power and strategy can go both ways. Sometimes the powerful person (my teacher) can give direct moral com-

19. Max Gluckman.

mands; in that case strategy is a function of his status in a regnant structure. But strategy can also be used to challenge a status and therefore also to challenge the structure that sustains it. (When we did defy our teacher we generally did so on the grounds of either collegial equality or of cold rationality—he was sometimes given to unrealistic enthusiasms.)

Look again at the complexity of the lintel story. Roberto not only had the higher rank but was also, in general, much the more powerful person. Yet the lintel owner gave him a "no." We could say, lawyerlike, that the law specifically did not permit the peasant, as a coparcener in the property, to dispose of any part of it for his personal advantage; therefore the law gave him the power to refuse Roberto's offer. But a legalism of that kind leaves most of the tale untold. The peasant did not invoke the law; he appealed to custom and morality.

Furthermore, his "no" seemed to be equivocal. He was (ostensibly) polite and deferential and would, he said, have liked to be in a position to do what Roberto wanted. The P-rule would fit that conduct: being gratuitously disobliging to a rich and powerful neighbor is both "ungrammatical" and likely to have a negative payoff. Conceivably that could have been the reason why the peasant's refusal was very much in the subjunctive mood, which makes it appear to be the strategy of a weak person.

But it was not. The peasant was in fact gratuitously disobliging to a rich and powerful neighbor; he skewered him and he got away with it. To understand why is to look at the encounter's most interesting complexity, which is cross-talk. The peasant was empowered because, in that single situation, he could call on several structures. He put three of them to use: the moral equivalence of *paesani* (E) and *signorilità* (S), and, on the other hand, class conflict (C) which denies any moral equivalence between himself and Roberto. He used the first two to assert the third, and in the process strengthened it and weakened them. In talking of his obligation to his brothers, and hinting that Roberto's offer was therefore inconsiderate and improper, he was invoking E, and, secondarily, S (Roberto was not behaving in the way that a gentleman should—the deferential form of address was an indirect comment on this lapse). By piling on the ridicule he was upholding C as the contrary of both E and S, and at the same time diminishing them. In short, he made overt use of the E and S moralities in order to subvert them and to make C regnant. Strategies overtly deploying particular moralities were effectively used to promote a structure that had a contrary morality and was never openly named.

Note, in fact, that not one of these three structures was ever explicitly identified by giving it a "local habitation and a name." Roberto throughout was fed allusions and left to make his own inferences about what the message was. How is that indirection to be explained? The P-rule might seem to apply: it is not appropriate for the lowly to pitch homilies at their superiors. The more open a rebellious act, the more it is likely to have painful consequences if it fails. But the P-rule does not fit the situation. Certainly the peasant presented himself as acting from a position of inferiority, using rhetorical devices that are typically the resort of the weak. But that was mockery; in fact he turned out to be in command. He talked brotherhood and (deviously) appealed to fraternal values (including the *paesani* values that embraced Roberto) in order to come off best in their encounter. Roberto accepted the unspoken definition of their situation.

Are there other ways to make sense of this maneuver? A structural functionalist might suggest that these were not examples of cross-talk at all. In particular, the *paesani* symbolism and the peasant's deferential manner could have been simply an attempt to restore an equilibrium by reinvolving Roberto in the moral community (E) after his money-offer gaffe, which was an offense against E. I floated a similar suggestion that perhaps the beggar was trying to domesticate me. But, as I said, in both cases the notion of good intentions seems quite Panglossian; a put-down through ridicule is much more persuasive.

People who are monolingual cannot enter a cross-talk arena, although they may feel the effects of another's cross-talk and eventually come to realize that there are other designs for living besides the one they assume to be dominant. For cross-talk to happen, at least one party has to be bilingual. The beggar confronted me directly in the single register of Hindu values. I riposted, directly, in the single register of a transactional (non-)exchange. Neither of us attempted cross-talk; we did not communicate. Cross-talk entered because the audience, my mentor, knew what both the beggar and I, in our different ways, were trying to say. The result was my discomfiture when I realized that a structure to deal with the situation did exist and I did not know what it was. Cross-talk opens the mind to alternative structures and is a step toward putting saving lies to the test.

## Assertion and Suggestion

There are differences between analytic exchanges (Chapters 2 through 6) and enacted exchanges (Chapters 7 and 8) with respect to indirection as a strategy. Directness—by that I mean the use of logic and the syllogism to support propositions—is only effective when there is a prior agreement on premises. Indirection, involving cross-talk and sometimes humor, dominates the stories of enactment, because all of them concern inchoate situations in which there is no prior agreement and more than one structure is at hand. In the lintel case, plain direct talk appears only at the outset when Roberto makes an unadorned transactional offer. Once that is turned down, prestations take over and nothing is straightforwardly said; the peasant's messages are transmitted in a variety of allusions and they terminate in farce. Trying to ignore the beggar, I too was unequivocally transactional, and my response projected him into pantomiming the dharma. Rosa, acknowledging a favor done out of friendship, made a joke, offering a nonexistent payment, as if to convert the friend into a hireling—a prestation into a transaction. *Complimenti*, sugary words, enact a relationship that is intendedly sour. The peasant used deferential forms to convey disrespect. Why could they not be direct? What messages does avoiding plain talk and using humor convey? That question will lead us eventually back to saving lies.

Indirection and humor (but not ridicule or the more combative forms of irony) invite complicity. To provide a significant fragment and to invite the other person to reconstruct the whole, is, as I said, a persuasive device. It encourages alter to take some credit for the whole that is created; it makes it his (or hers) as well. It is a hint: "You and I think alike." It is a prestation, a claim about a relationship. Humor likewise constructs a community of understanding: we *share* a joke; the joke annuls both distance and authority. Humor also disinvites criticism because it downplays commitment and intensity—it negates fanaticism. It is a softener—it takes away the hard edges.

In this book indirection and humor have appeared only in its third part, which concerns the *enactment* of structures, not their analysis. Chapters 1 through 6, which are about models and their applicability, noticeably lack humor. Messages are directly and assertively delivered. If humor does appear, it is more often as open ridicule than ironic indirectness. Ridicule, of all humor's forms, is the one that comes closest to the imperative mood, being dismissive and authoritative. There is, of course, a sense in which Friedman, Coase, Evans-Pritchard, and the rest want to "persuade" their readers of the truth of what they are writing, but their delivery is less that of a pleader than of a bishop or a professor (which those three were) speaking ex cathedra, with authority, as an expert (or even a sage).

To write with the ethos[20] of authority is implicitly to deny that one's "truth" could ever be a saving lie and therefore might have valid

---

20. *Ethos* is a rhetorical presentation of the self (of one's character) in a way that will appeal to the audience. The word in this sense is a more general equivalent of *pathos*, which is the arousal of pity or sadness. The Greek word *ethos* also means "custom," something normally and rightly done; from it we derive *ethics*.

contraries. In ex cathedra writing, contraries are either ignored or (sometimes) confronted and purportedly demolished. That kind of academic discourse about social systems constructs a wonderfully simple world: there is *one truth*, and it is found by seeking out and exterminating other would-be truths. Yet often, as I pointed out, rival truths are not allowed to run the course and the favorite is then declared winner by default; what looks like a debate is a set-up. From that aspect, academic discourse is devious. The participants are concerned not with truth but with victory.

From another point of view, analytic discourse is straightforward because, unlike enacted exchanges, it lacks cross-talk. The reason is that analytic exchanges purport to be *transactions*: what is supposed to matter is the thing exchanged (information and ideas), not the relative status of the exchangers. Any indication that an analytic exchange has been tainted by status is a mark against it, because status gets in the way of truth. Enacted exchanges, on the other hand, which are prestations, are not about truth, but about relative power. They are negotiations: truth cannot be negotiated, but power can. Indirection, and especially humor (including ridicule), are clear signs of a concern with status, and they transform what is supposed to be a transaction into a prestation. They put status ahead of truth and so they turn the search for truth into a joke or make it ridiculous. Status should have no place in truth seeking.

A second reason for the absence of cross-talk, humor, and indirection from the first two parts of the book is the ivory tower. Analytic debate is further from praxis—from putting theory into practice—than is an enacted exchange, not only in the sense of empirical remoteness suggested by Evans-Pritchard's "imaginative constructs" or his disdain for applied anthropology, but also because enacted exchanges require rapid responses: willy-nilly, there is a more or less instant feedback. These are the occasions when structure is being negotiated, when one cannot be sure that everything is fixed and tied down and the ground will not shift under one's feet. Enacted messages can, of course, be assertive and hortatory, but such messages are effective only when the performer already enjoys an edge of power. Without that edge, the response is likely to be ridicule. Those who must rely on persuasion are apt to feel—and for tactical reasons often display—some measure of diffidence, an admission that they are not in full control of the situation, and that the contrary of what they want cannot be casually dismissed from the scene, because what they want has, like any definition of a situation, the status of a saving lie. They know they may have to compromise. Indirection and humor leave that path open. If the contest is for power, then compromise is a possibility; but "truth" does not admit of compromise. Enactment, in short, can be tentative. Analytical discourse, in contrast, normally is assertive.

Indirection and humor minister to our need both to recognize and simultaneously deny life's uncertainties, to admit that the stories we tell to make the world understandable might yet be mistaken, and that there are other ways to define the situation besides the regnant one. Indirection, the failure to make the direct assertion, leaves open the possibility of denial, of compromise, and therefore of change. Humor, the indirect admission that no one is being or need be serious, that nothing is firm, fixed, sacred, and indisputably self-evident, has the same effect; it leaves matters open and postpones the amen that marks an assertion of one structure over another.

## Conceptualizing Structure

Leach, whose Kachin book launched me into ideas about multiple structures, insisted (not without rhetorical panache)[21] that multistructuralism was not only *his* analytic construct, it was also the way the Kachin themselves saw their sociocultural world. Likewise, I assume that Roberto and the peasant could model their world as a repertoire of alternative structures. The peasant speaks of *paesano* values—he means class antagonism. Roberto essays a market structure. Obviously they are reflexively aware (not tacitly, like M. Jourdain) of those and of other structures.

In the place where and at the time when I was introduced to social anthropology (Oxford in 1949), structural functionalism prevailed. "Functional unity," to quote Radcliffe-Brown again, was "a condition in which all parts of the social system work together with a sufficient degree of harmony or internal consistency, i.e. without producing persistent conflicts which can neither be resolved nor regulated." The word *structure* could be used in the singular and attached to a particular society by the definite article, as in "*the* social structure of the X." A higher-level coherence—a monostructural integrity—was taken for granted, at least heuristically, and sometimes predicated not only with a conceptual but also a real existence.[22]

21. "Thus described my method sounds like a scholastic device of the purest pedantry" (1954, 285–86). The technique of argument is procatalepsis—anticipation, or smiting the critics before they can criticize.

22. Conceptual existence is apparently predicated in Radcliffe-Brown's remark about "internal consistency," but when he writes of regulating or resolving "persistent conflicts" he seems to give a behavioral concreteness to the idea of structure. Certainly it was

Data gathered in the field (in India) soon showed that there were multiple versions of the social reality, none of them dominant enough to eliminate the rest, and that a monostructural model would cause the data that interested me (on social change) to be bracketed away. At that time I knew of two ways to model social structure. Both presuppose that structures are guides for action. If it is then assumed that a higher-level structural coherence is realized in conduct, so that people in fact generally observe *one* set of such rules, which constitute *the* structure, it follows that a social system can be adequately represented by a description and analysis of that integrated conceptual whole. The classic monographs of structural functionalism, for example *The Nuer*, are modeled in that way. The second model, developed by Leach, does not make that assumption and takes into account a plurality of alternative structures, each one of which exists in the frequency with which its rules are followed. If, for instance, one could count how often Konds made appeals to tribal principles as against the principles of caste, one would have a statistical measure of the relative prevalence of those two structures (Bailey 1960). The problem of course is that in practice it is difficult to decide what precisely to count.

There remains the agency question: What goes on when people choose between structures? That suggests a third interpretation, in which structures are modeled neither as objective, quasi-statistical accounts of what people do, nor as an ordering of the rules that guide their actions, but as repertoires or folders that store the *claims* people make to justify, condemn, or in other ways influence actions, opinions and attitudes. That, more or less, is the model used in *Tribe, Caste, and Nation* but not, I now see, sufficiently exploited.

To make sense of such claims I again have two basic models, which are complementary and not exclusionary (unlike the one structure/ many structures alternative). The first, which I used in that book and which was in tune with contemporary concerns about the way the world was changing, describes the various contradictory structures about which claims are made, and then asks which claims prevail, what circumstances allow them to prevail, and what are the consequences. In that model, structures are social formations and social process is a partly evolutionary, partly designed operational selection between them. *Tribe, Caste and Nation* was written as a description of the shift between structures caused by people in the Kondmals trying to cope with problems and seize opportunities that arose from changes in their political and economic circumstances.

---

interpreted that way by, for example, Leach, who, as I noted earlier, complained about a "deep-rooted" confusion in social anthropology between the idea of structural equilibrium and a stable society (1954, 7).

The second model, inadequately explored in *Tribe, Caste and Nation* but providing the main frame for this chapter, focuses not on outcomes but on agency, specifically on the rhetorical strategies that people use in order to prevail in arguments. It links rhetorical techniques with the contexts—structures and motives—that give the techniques substance and meaning. That procedure radically alters the concept *structure*; it is no longer seen as a social formation (whether the outcome of action or the goal of action) but as a conceptual resource that can be used to confound an opponent. *In this model,* rhetorical techniques are disconnected from their effect on social formations; they cease to be instruments and become virtual ends in themselves. Rhetoric is then a game that is played with structural forms. For the players, the ostensible purpose of rhetoric—persuasion used to promote adherence to a particular structure—is incidental to the main purpose, which is the pleasure of winning the game. For the observers, attention shifts from the structural consequences or functions of the game to the game itself.

Chapter 8 of *Tribe, Caste and Nation* contains an extended account of a dispute in which the three structures epitomized in the book's title were invoked. At the time, I assumed that the wrangling was done for practical ends (to get the better of a petty official who had pocketed someone's tax payments, and, on the side, to grind a few political axes) and that its (latent) function was, in a rather remote way, to uphold or diminish one or other of the three structures. I did not appreciate, although it was very much on the surface, the gamesmanship that was going on, and I believe now that the players would have been quite disappointed if the official had simply returned the money and not given them (especially those who had reputational axes to grind) a chance to show off their rhetorical mettle. Rhetoric, in other words, has not only a persuasive but also a palaestral (or epideictic—showing off) aspect. What is gained or lost by *modeling* that to be its significance will now be considered.

## Agency Models

I will begin by marking again the word emphasized in the preceding sentence. Models are models; a method is a method and not a collection of truths. As Giddens puts it, one should not to confuse "methodological procedures" with "ontological reality" (1984, 285). Models give limited access to reality. They are not its facsimiles—they are tools. An analytic or descriptive apparatus is not the same as what is being analyzed or described. Models have a limited application and are not necessarily invalidated when shown not to address whatever reality is beyond their scope.

Now recall the tale of the lintel. Roberto came out of the encounter partly amused, partly bemused, seeing himself not so much mugged as outmaneuvered by an agile shape-shifter, and regretting that he had not used Vincenzo as his cat's-paw in the first place and so spared himself the hassle. He did not tell the story in the manner of someone brainwashed, Socratic fashion, and on his way to believing that class antagonism was the dominant structure in Losa. He understood very clearly how the peasant saw (or implied he saw) life in Losa, but there was no sign that he himself, Roberto, as a result of the encounter, was moved to see it in the same way. He was not persuaded. Nor, I think, was the peasant trying to foist on Roberto the thesis that Losa was structured by class antagonism. Certainly he enacted his own hostility toward Roberto and other rentiers. But that is not the same as promoting Roberto's acceptance of a class antagonism definition.

In the end, the encounter did not have much to do with persuasion. This was not Mark Anthony's rhetoric deployed to turn the Roman mob against Caesar's assassins. Mark Anthony shifted the foundations; the peasant had no such agenda. Nor was he trying to put his ideas across as "truth." Rather he intended to "provoke or confound an antagonist," to put Roberto into the position of having no words to argue back. Essentially he was defining their *immediate* situation by defining himself as smarter and therefore superior. The complex deployment of *paesano* and *signorilità* values, to be "unfolded" by Roberto into class antagonism, was a convenient vehicle for a display of rhetorical skill. Those structures entered the situation not as definienda but as contextual resources—weapons—that allowed the peasant to get the better of Roberto. The reward for winning was not a convert, but the winning itself—having the satisfaction of contemplating his victim knocked off balance, subtly but indisputably insulted, and quite unable to do anything about it. A bumpkin look-alike, a moralizing innocent apparently so anxious to please, revealed himself to be an artful and punishing strategist, happy to spike Roberto, not just because Roberto belonged to the rentier class, but also because spiking is a manifestation of palaestral skill, which can be an end in itself.

A game played for its own sake may or may not have an effect on structures. But even if it has no effect, structures remain an integral part of agency models, not as explananda but as resources. Structures are like cards in a card game; without them the game cannot be played at all.

I said earlier that the model I would use is intentionalist; it concerns people's understandings and the ways in which they try to control situations. Since the best-laid schemes "gang aft agley," no intentionalist model, by itself, can make sense of unintended consequences.[23] A fortiori neither can the study of rhetoric (or any other agency model). Even when the rhetorician is successful, as Mark Anthony was, and the intended consequences are the actual consequences and might not have happened if the speaker had been less persuasive, the events for sure had other causes besides the speaker's way with words. Events are always over-determined. Certainly, up to a point, rhetoric is a maker or breaker of social structures. But those structures are also the outcome of an evolutionary process and of a vast number of other, more immediate nonrhetorical variables. Churchill's wartime orations in Parliament, on the radio, and reported in the press certainly raised morale and helped to win the war; so also did cracking the Enigma code, the entry of the Americans, the tenacity of the USSR, some of the strategic decisions that Hitler made, and thousands and thousands of other contributing causes. If we study Churchill's oratory, it is not only—or mainly—to decide how much his speeches contributed to victory; it is to uncover the techniques that he used to make those speeches effective in defining situations.

In these two chapters I have assumed that the study of agency (in this case rhetoric) can be legitimately centered on agency itself rather than on the social formations that it may serve to create or to undermine.[24] From this perspective, rhetoric is a kind of competitive sport, and its central question (for me) is "What do people think they have to do in order to win and why do they think it?" This seems to be a straightforward marking out of a field of investigation, without prejudice to other kinds of inquiry, and therefore it should be generally acceptable. But this has not always been the case, and I feel obliged to defend my presuppositional boundary as a Goffmanesque "membrane" within which the concept of agency can develop.

23. This feature of our lives is nicely caught in one of the many meanings of the word *irony*—the unintended outcome that seems to mock our best intentions, the irony of fate. Such events, of course, are open to rhetorical analysis, not to explain why things turned out the way they did, but to identify the ironic element and to show how it was or could be exploited to excite pity for the victims' suffering or scorn for their hubris.

24. Booth writes of "the borderline where irony ceases to be instrumental and is sought as an end in itself," adding that the "functional" view of irony (and therefore of rhetoric) held the field from Quintilian's day and earlier until "well along into the eighteenth century" (1974, 139). Form without function or a function that is trivial still occasion some unease. In their introduction to *Irony in Action*, Fernandez and Huber write, " . . . irony can be a confirmation of unequal power rather than effective resistance to it. Irony may give a brief sense of mastery over forms intended as a means of control, but, because it does not have to be acknowledged, it can contribute to the perpetuation rather than the eradication of a sense of victimization" (2001, 27). I agree; irony itself does not make a revolution or unseat the powerful. But it can make the powerless feel good and the powerful frustrated.

An interest in agency and strategies (and, by entailment, in rhetoric) goes along with a Machiavellian turn of mind, and Machiavelli generally has a bad press. "A handbook for gangsters," was Bertrand Russell's verdict on *The Prince*.[25] Machiavelli justified his attention to the techniques of winning on the perfectly logical and (from the point of view of a collectivity) perfectly moral ground that only those who knew how to win could put an end to the violence and disorder that afflicted the Italy of his day. That aspect of his work, however, has not commanded popular attention because, I suppose, in *The Prince* he does mostly write about how rulers can win by force or by deception—*per forza o per frode*.

A long time ago I wrote *Stratagems and Spoils*. As the title suggests, the book has a narrow focus on political maneuvering. I made its limits clear, but critics (including, ironically, the person who translated the book into Italian and gave it that same Machiavellian title—*per forza o per frode*) complained that there was more to politics than tactics and strategy. The book, they said, took no account of the logic of higher-level structural coherences, nor did it consider the evolution of political forms. It was too much directed at the micro side of the micro/macro divide and disregarded the structural and historical contexts that gave actions their significance. That comment, although it correctly identifies the book's target, misses the mark, because it is impossible to discuss actions without placing them in a context. The critics were in fact complaining that my contexts were not the "important" ones they would have chosen.

Importance? What stands out in the story of the lintel is its utter triviality. Nothing substantial was accomplished. I am sure the participants thought so too. Roberto, had he been speaking my variety of English, might have remarked, apropos the peasant, "That was quite a performance!" *Performance* is an interesting word. It has a place in the world of authenticity, as when one speaks of the performance of a duty; it also suggests (as it does in the present context) play-acting and the world of pretence. It then shades into insincerity, fakery, and doing something that is not what it seems to be because it has a form that is not its substance (as in the case of a rhetorical question which is not

---

Function apart, I am arguing that irony (and rhetoric generally and therefore agency) merits study also as "an end in itself."

25. This is according to Isaiah Berlin (1980, 35). Russell's own account (1946, 525–32) is more judicious, as is the long essay by Berlin himself, in which he remarks on the extreme diversity of verdicts on *The Prince* and on its author's morals, including one that wrote off *The Prince* as intended irony, as satire. Noticing a preponderance of disapproval, he links it to Machiavelli's refusal to fudge a compromise between public and private moralities in order to falsely present the social world as "a single intelligible structure" (1980, 25–79).

a question). It is a sort of play. It lacks weight—it is not to be taken seriously because it is inconsequential. There was no noticeable rearrangement of power in Losa as a result of the encounter. None was intended. Nothing was at stake, other than, perhaps, one person's enhanced and another's mildly bruised amour propre.

One could say something similar about the scope that I have given to the word *rhetoric*: it reaches down toward the trivial. The Greek word *rhetor* indicates a person who speaks in public, who orates. For sure there was a simulacrum of grandiloquence—a touch of the soapbox—in the peasant's protests (that was part of the mockery), and he certainly made use of devices conventionally classified as rhetorical, but this was not oratory, not a polished speech like Mark Anthony's podium-style oration to a mass audience. The encounter over the lintel was one-to-one, pseudoprivate, pseudoinformal, less oratorical than phatic.[26] Yet I have treated it as rhetoric and thus implied that Ciceronian orations before the Roman courts or in the Senate, Winston Churchill's or Roosevelt's broadcast talks during the Second World War, Hitler pumping up the party members at Nuremberg rallies, and Castro's marathon harangues all go into the same box with the lintel owner's verbal games. I think they do, so long as the question remains "What did they think they had to say in order to prevail?"

I thought that the critics of *Stratagems and Spoils* failed to look beyond the evolution of political forms, did not understand microprocess, and had no grasp of what could be learned from agency models. Some were obsessed with moral issues; others were inebriated with Louis Dumont's visionary transcendences, his quest for "wholes" and "global, unified pictures."[27] They forgot that these same political forms are created and re-created by the use people make of them, that is, by enactment, which has discoverable patterns of its own.

It is not the events recounted in the story of the lintel that matter; they had no consequential importance—they are indeed trivialities. (That is one reason why I selected this tale.) The events are of interest to me because they exhibit patterns of rhetorical conduct which invite generalization beyond particular occasions and particular cultures. To speak of universals in cultural anthropology may still, I suppose, be

26. This is Malinowski's word for communication that does not convey information but defines the quality of the relationship between the speaker and the audience—in other words, a prestation. The verb from which *phatic* is taken, *phanai*, covers any kind of speech, formal or informal, whatever the number of people involved.

Then does rhetoric occur in arguments with oneself? I think so. Do we not use rhetoric to persuade—or even to intimidate—ourselves into acting on a belief that we know is either false or shameful or both?

27. I have in mind his *Daedalus* essay (1975).

considered a near profanity, but the concept can be made respectable by replacing an existential with a heuristic format: a universal is nothing but a question generated in one situation (or in one culture) and asked again in another, and so on until one has assembled a repertoire of strategies and attached each of them to whatever contexts give it meaning and make it effective. The product of such inquiry is not, of course, a set of universal naturalistic laws but rather an analytic compendium of the conventions that rhetoricians follow. The way forward is the way of comparison.

Finally, there is a moral dimension—Bertrand Russell's over-hasty "handbook for gangsters" gibe. What does the palaestral model (or rhetoric or any agency model) have to say about right and wrong? To found the inquiry on the question "What must be done in order to win?" would place it with the neoclassical economists and other rational-choice theorists, and so model agency as something close to a natural system and therefore blind to the actors' moral sensibilities. But in fact my question is different: "What *do people think* they must do in order to win?" We are looking for patterns in beliefs about social behavior, not laws that govern it. These patterns, obviously, can include what people think about good and evil. No less obviously, they do not include *our own* judgments about good and evil. Nor do I think they should.

Not everyone agrees. My own view, I suspect, might be considered pseudoscientific and outdated. Fernandez and Huber, in their introduction and again in a coda to the essays in *Irony in Action*, anticipate the chill wind of disapproval that blows around many (but not all) forms of irony. An ironic view of life may also be a cynical view that ends in nihilism; it may both misrepresent the "moral imagination" of the people studied and excise the moral capacities of those who study them. Irony points the scholar toward a "detour from rather than a route to responsibility"(2001, 262–63). It indicates a "suspension of commitment" and so undercuts moral standards and moral responsibility (2001, 15).[28] What is to be done? Their answer, which has an appropriate whiff of manifesto, is this: "While the moral imagination may not be much easier to define than irony itself, we would like to suggest a simple enough definition relevant to those who work in the human sciences: the creating of as clear an image, or set of images, as possible of existing social conditions in their positive and negative aspects, along with an image or set of images of one's own obligations for achieving through practical action better conditions for all concerned. In other words, scholars, like professionals more generally,

28. They also note, with less evident anguish, that irony likewise subverts the Enlightenment "belief in progress through reason."

have a set of responsibilities in the world, not just to their own fields" (2001, 263). They go on to say, rather weakly in the light of the remark quoted in note 24 above, that irony can at least be used to take the wind out of "powerful persons" who are being "repressive."

I would buy that more readily if they had also explained (1) why knowledge must be followed by good works, (2) how to keep knowledge from being skewed by "moral imaginations," (3) how to determine "better," and (4) how to make others accept that version of "better." My position is simpler. Agency models, including rhetoric and irony, deal with forms of human interaction about which we are seeking knowledge. That, in itself, is enough to justify the inquiry. What use is made of that knowledge, or any other knowledge—"achieving better conditions for all concerned" (a Pareto optimum shifted from economics into utilitarianism and every bit as impractical)—is an important but also an entirely separate issue. Evans-Pritchard (to say it yet again) got it right: "Knowledge of man and of society is an end in itself and its pursuit a moral exercise that gains nothing and loses nothing by any practical use to which it can, or may, be put."

# Conclusion:
# General Theses and Particular Cases

*Toleration is historically the product of the realisation of the irreconcilability of equally dogmatic faiths, and the practical improbability of complete victory of one over the other.*

—Isaiah Berlin, "The Originality of Machiavelli"

## The Itch for Totality

I cannot imagine that there could ever be a *theoretical* resolution between the tractable, entirely amoral expected-utility framework and the morality-assuming but wholly intractable paradigm of structural functionalism. Nor do I admire single-minded hierarchy-obsessed visionaries who, as Louis Dumont did, pursue in every situation the prodigiously imagined chimera that is *the* whole, *the* single structure in which all is encompassed. Such grand ideas, Foucault said, are a kind of "tyranny"; they blank out vast areas of experience; they inhibit inquiring minds.

At the same time, I know that there can be no understanding without imagined entities—categories, structures, and theories, which can themselves be presented only as if they were comprehensive wholes. The mistake is to ignore limitations. Expected-utility people are blind to morality, structural functionalists shy away from "divergent interests," and both conduct themselves as if their own model deserves exclusive possession of the field because what the other deals with is at least secondary, if not entirely irrelevant. Nor can I imagine any unfudged theoretical compromise that would present those two incompatible paradigms as "a single intelligible structure."[1]

To choose one model and exclude the other, or simply to be tolerant and acknowledge that each has its merits, is to sidestep the incompatibility. An agency model, on the other hand, confronts it and (in a

---

1. Gary Becker's *A Treatise on the Family* comes to mind again. It is a monstrous fudge.

practical way) resolves it by discovering what happens to ideas when they are put to use. To challenge an idea with reality is, as I construe the situation, to challenge a saving lie with its rivals; it is then tested less for its truth than for the clout that its backers command.

Foucault rejects "the tyranny of globalizing discourses" and favors an "autonomous, non-centralized kind of theoretical production" which, I assume, would be closer to the domain of practice. The choice, however, is not exclusionary; practice cannot function without some level of globalizing.

This concluding chapter repeats the book's theme: we cannot do without saving lies, but we can and should, by underlining their uncertain status, inhibit their tendency to tyrannize.

## General Theses and Particular Cases

Alexis de Tocqueville, writing about democracy in America, neatly summarizes the costs and benefits of these two modes: "The chief merit of general ideas is that they enable the human mind to pass a rapid judgment on a great many objects at once; but, on the other hand, the notions they convey are never other than incomplete, and they always cause the mind to lose as much in accuracy as it gains in comprehensiveness" (1994, 2:3).

The same two modes shape this book, and their difference rests in the level of abstraction. The unitary analytical fundamentalisms— Blake's "generalizing Demonstrations" or Foucault's "globalizing discourses"—of both expected-utility theorizing and structural functionalism, which require a high level of abstraction (Chapters 1-5), stand in contrast with the anecdotal, event-focused, fragmented particularism that seems to characterize the chapters on agency. In fact, although the book is divided in that way, it is also unified by one simple observation: the everyday world of experience puts all ideas, big and small, highly abstract and less abstract, at risk of being considered false or, if not false, of being written off as pointless or condemned as dangerous. How it does so is a more complicated matter than those words suggest, for three connected reasons. First, ideas are formulated at different levels of abstraction. Second, the phrase "everyday world of experience" requires (to quote Kenneth Burke again) that "we ask ourselves what complexities are subsumed beneath it." Third, it may not be clear whether the test concerns truth or power. Propositions made at a low level of abstraction more readily attract empirical truth-oriented examination. The higher the level of abstraction, the more likely is a proposition to be a function of power:

it is accepted to the extent that its backers are powerful and its acceptance enhances their power. I will come to power later; first I consider ways in which big (very abstract and general) ideas differ from small (more practical and particular) ideas.

In one stunning marathon sentence near the beginning of *The Hedgehog and the Fox*, which is an essay on Tolstoy's vision of how the world works, the mellifluous Isaiah Berlin describes, with an eloquence that calls on the reader's stamina and yet is sustaining, a distinction that, suitably unfolded, serves to mark the difference between the third part of this book and the two parts that went before it.

"For there exists a great chasm between those, on the one side, who relate everything to a single central vision, one system more or less coherent or articulate, in terms of which they understand, think and feel—a single, universal, organizing principle in terms of which alone all that they are and say has significance—and, on the other side, those who pursue many ends, often unrelated and even contradictory, connected, if at all, only in some *de facto* way, for some psychological or physiological cause, related by no moral or aesthetic principle; these last lead lives, perform acts, and entertain ideas that are centrifugal rather than centripetal, their thought is scattered or diffused, moving on many levels, seizing upon the essence of a vast variety of experiences and objects for what they are in themselves, without, consciously or unconsciously, seeking to fit them into, or exclude them from any one unchanging, all-embracing, sometimes self-contradictory and incomplete, at times fanatical, unitary inner vision." (1957, 7–8)

Those in search of a "unitary inner vision" are "hedgehogs"; those who "pursue many ends" and are content to find "the essence of a vast variety of experiences and objects" Isaiah Berlin calls "foxes," borrowing the metaphor from an enigmatic verse of the satirist Archilochus: "The fox knows many things, but the hedgehog knows one big thing." Tolstoy, a novelist of genius, a brilliant and ruthlessly insightful portrayer and analyst of complex and diverse situations in the small worlds of individuals, who are seen in all their many-sidedness, had the fox's talent. Nevertheless, Berlin insists, Tolstoy was all the time agonizingly in search of the "single, serene vision, in which all problems are resolved, all doubts are stilled, peace and understanding finally achieved" (120).

In "Two Types of Mind," a short confessional essay by F. A. Hayek, the economist who is an icon for true believers in capitalism and the free market, there is a related (but not identical) distinction. Hayek talks about himself and acknowledges (surely with tongue in cheek) that he cannot match "the stereotype of the great scientist" who "is seen, above all, as the perfect master of his subject, a man who has at his ready command the whole theory and all the important facts of his discipline and is prepared to answer at a moment's notice all important questions relating to his field." But, he continues, there are compensations for those who are not master scientists and have no exhaustive knowledge of the totality that is their discipline. Hayek is a fox: "It was because I did not remember the answers that to others may have been obvious that I was often forced to think out a solution to a problem which did not exist for those who had more orderly minds" (1991, 52). When he lectured on the history of economic thought, "what I told my students was essentially what I had learnt from those writers and not what they chiefly thought, which may have been something quite different" (51). Hayek is (his own terms) a "muddler" or "puzzler." "I owed whatever worthwhile new ideas I ever had to *not* being able to remember what every competent specialist is supposed to have at his fingertips." Muddlers and puzzlers, he implies, have, as Berlin put it, no "single central vision" that subdues and sets in order the "vast variety of things" contained in it; their attention is "scattered" and "moves on many levels."

In fact Hayek did have a single central vision, which pervaded and conditioned his scholarly endeavors. An economy, he believed, and indeed an entire culture (which he calls "traditions") is, for all intents and purposes, to be understood as a whole, as an *organism* (his word) that evolves of its own accord; it is not an *organization*, something intentionally designed. As with any evolutionary process, its product can sometimes be understood in a cause-and-effect framework, but only in retrospect; to foresee its patterning is impossible, and to plan its future is futile. For Hayek, the methodological consequence of this single central vision, although he does not say it in so many words, is, paradoxically, to aim lower, rely on serendipity, and deal with diverse problems as they arise—in other words to use one's talent as Tolstoy used his and be like the fox. The controlling vision—that an economic system must be left to evolve in its own way, since it will do so anyway—freed Hayek to follow his preferences. At the same time it turned him into a scholar with a message, a sermonizer if not a prophet, a moralizer whose convictions, even though he saw them as the product of objective scientific reasoning, were anchored in, and stated with, emotion.[2]

2. The single vision does not seem to have given him much serenity, if the contentiousness and the occasional angst in his writings are enough indication. He would have liked, he claims, to believe in that other vision: "From all considerations other than the purely scientific one I have every reason to wish that I were able to believe that a planned socialist society can achieve what its advocates promise." He describes the "process of disillusionment which led me to [my] present views" as "extremely painful" (1991, 46–47).

Tolstoy, also emotionally involved, as the second epilogue to *War and Peace* testifies, could not find the certainty—the "truth"—that Hayek did. Hayek did not reject the idea of an orderly world, only of one that is ordered by design. Order exists—the evolutionary pattern—but it is not a purposed order that is the product of planning. Tolstoy, much as he seemed to long for the "single, serene vision," could identify neither design nor pattern in the larger scheme of things. The ordered sequences and regularities that historians purport to find in historical events for him did not exist. He considered even more deluded those who, having fictionized a pattern in what happened around them, also believed they had themselves brought it about. Tolstoy saw, insistently and repeatedly, the confusions of events, which alone, for him, was the reality. He "could not justify to himself the apparently arbitrary selection of material, and the no less arbitrary distribution of emphasis, to which all historical writing seemed to be doomed" (Berlin 1957, 27). *War and Peace* contains many passages— particularly the battle scenes—that trumpet the disorder of reality, our reluctance to admit that such disorder exists, our need to find patterns, and our capacity to construct them as fictions. In 1805 Prince Bagration, the commanding general, visits the front at Schön Grabern: "Nor is the chaos of battle in any way made clearer either in fact or in the minds of the Russian officers by the appearance of Bagration. Nevertheless his arrival puts heart into his subordinates; his courage, his calm, his mere presence create the illusion of which he is himself the first victim, namely, that what is happening is somehow connected with *his* skill, *his* plans, that it is *his* authority that is somehow directing the course of the battle . . ." (1957, 28–29). "This, then, is the great illusion which Tolstoy sets himself to expose: that individuals can, by the use of their own resources, understand and control the course of events" (1957, 33).[3]

Hayek is less agonized; he has identified the "power" or "force" (Tolstoy's terms) that patterns history. Its principle (evolution by natural selection) can be understood, and its working out can sometimes be comprehended, but since the selection is natural, we can only wait and see how things turn out; the evolutionary process cannot be controlled. Hayek lives in a fox-world of serendipitous problem solving, the grand evolutionary design, not the doers' intentions, determining the outcome of whatever was rationally (that is, purposefully) done.

3. Tolstoy, commenting on the falsified tidiness of military historiography, wrote: "[I]n every description of a battle there is a necessary lie, resulting from the need [to describe] in a few words the action of thousands of men spread over several miles" (1957, vol. 3, 542). The engagement at Schön Grabern occupies Chapters 16–21 in vol. 1, book 2 of War and Peace.

What can be done does not go beyond working out why things happened the way they did and sometimes making small-world adjustments to designs for living—to structures—in response to events that were beyond anyone's control.[4]

By and large I think that fairly describes the experiences and attitudes of people in Losa. When I look back on the place as I knew it in the 1960s and '70s, I am struck by how small a hand its people had in their own fate. They did not design the larger frameworks that shaped their destinies; rather, things happened and they made what adjustments they could. Population in the mid– to late nineteenth century grew beyond the carrying capacity of the land; people emigrated. The growth was not anyone's intended outcome. The First and Second World Wars uprooted a quasi-feudal peasant social order, making room for class conflict, which in turn (after the Second World War) was made uncertain by the expanding European economy and by rampant consumerism. Losa people had a restricted choice in these matters. They did not cause the events to happen; the strategies that preoccupied them were those they devised to deal with and sometimes profit from upheavals.

These remarks make clear where the model of situation-defining strategies, outlined in the third part of this book, is focused and what its limitations are. It is the view of the fox, the view from where the action is. It is an agency view; it is not about patterns that might be discerned in the flow of history, except insofar as they impact upon everyday lives. Nor has it much to do with the outcome of grand designs directed toward planned macrochange—Mussolini's ambition to remake a Roman empire, Hitler's plan to dominate the world, the Bolshevik design to build a command economy, or even Keynes's "practical men" scrambling for strategies to control the whirlwind their laissez-faireism had reaped—until (and if) the designs begin to affect everyday life.[5] From this perspective, patterns in history come alive only in the actions of people who experience, categorize, and adapt to them by redefining their social order (or striving not to). The agency model is directed toward that kind of understanding.

In other words, Hayek's world of an outside-located one-way evolutionary causality, a purposeless universe that we experience but is not

4. That Hayek wanted some room for rational choice within the evolutionary constraints is made clear by the following (especially the words that I have emphasized): "Much that has been blamed on the capitalist system is in fact due to the remnants or revivals of pre-capitalist features; to monopolistic elements which were either the direct result of ill-conceived state action or the consequence of *a failure to understand that a smooth-working competitive order required an appropriate legal framework*" (1991, 71).

5. The model could, of course, be applied to the actions taken to implement the grand designs.

of our own making, is useful for understanding strategies only to the extent that it identifies, after the event, the limits of their effectiveness. To stay beside Hayek, the true believer in an evolutionary history that runs like a train on rails and therefore cannot be steered, is to turn away from the larger part of what we observe and experience in social interaction. It may indeed be the case that there is neither a steering wheel nor a track—that was Tolstoy's agony—but the conduct that we want to understand is the product of a Prince-Bagration conviction that we can control our destinies. Alternatively, it is the conduct of Hayek wearing the mask of "muddler" and "puzzler." Our model of strategy, like North's, is choice-theoretic; it is enough that people *believe* their choices matter. The question of whether or not this is a mistaken belief can, if one's goal is to understand the thinking that underlies strategic decisions, be put to one side.

## Knowledge and Know-How

Resignation to an all-controlling fate that has no meaning, although certainly not unknown, is for most people a last resort. Even when experience shows that they have been dealt a hand that is wholly unexpected, they still try to find meaning in the event by calling up a saving lie that will make sense of it. They derive these lies ultimately from some highly abstract faith-demanding "single central vision," which serves as an "amen construct" and "a place to stand." The expected-utility model and the structural-functional model are places to stand; so is the idea of evolution by natural selection. Below these are layers of derivative ideas that are less encompassing but still qualify as saving lies: the structured hierarchical relationship of principal and agent, residual rights of contract, gains from trade, the need to remove trade barriers or privatize public utilities or socialize private losses, and any other professed presuppositional construct. So also, in the world of Losa's everyday experience, ideas of *signorilità*, class struggle, or consumerism are amen constructs. So is anything that can be advanced as a structure qualified to define a situation, whether with the intention of manipulating it or just to understand it—Kachin notions of *gumsa* and *gumlao*, or the beggar invoking the dharma, or Coase insisting that transactions do have costs. All those ideas, greater and lesser, are places where people are ready to take a stand, their ultimate justification being that where they stand is (or is a derivative from) a fundamental, unquestionable single central vision.

A generalized vision of that kind has an obvious failing when it comes to praxis, which is the application of a theory to particular problems in the real world. Evans-Pritchard, you will recall, claimed that a structural description allows one to see what Tolstoy could not see—"the society in its essentials and as a single whole." The claim, as I said, is misleading, because it assumes a general agreement about what is *the* essence. There generally is no such agreement, and therefore a single central vision has limited practical use because it leaves out of account diverse and contradictory visions, which also can be presented as single and central. That was Leach's message. So how are ideas connected—in either direction—to the everyday world of experience?

The process that converts experience into ideas, called "unfolding" in Chapter 8, both widens the applicability of an idea and at the same time removes it further from the multiform reality from which it was extracted and which it purports to represent. The outcome, as Evans-Pritchard said, is an imaginative construct, which, taken from its original context and re-discovered in different settings, enhances our knowledge by making it more comprehensive—providing, of course, that in the new settings the unfolding is put into reverse and the imaginative construct is tested to see if it is as applicable there as it was in the original setting. In that way ideas are reconnected with and tested against experience. Elements that were overlooked or were simply dumped into the ceteris paribus box are reintroduced. That is what happened when Coase noted that transactions have costs, or Herbert Simon pointed out that rationality is bounded, or Leach demonstrated that Kachin have alternative structures on which to call.

To put it another way, testing an imaginative construct (a saving lie) involves *know-how*, which converts abstract knowledge into praxis by taking account of other saving lies that are present in the same situation. What then occurs, willy-nilly, is a contest (between different visions or structures) which is functionally equivalent to the discussion—more likely, as you will see, the negotiation—that takes place between experts in different fields when they seek a practical solution to an administrative problem. That dialogue between different visions, which occurs in the everyday world of experience, is the defining feature of praxis. In short, to confront a structure with reality is to confront it with alternative structures, which are its possible replacements.

This, in one construal, is the straightforward and perfectly rational procedure entailed in the idea that problems in social life, whether of action or understanding, call for the use of diverse kinds of expertise. When solutions that take account of only one kind of knowledge are put to the test, they are likely to fail. In the provision of health care, what a fundamentalist neoclassical economist might offer as the appropriate policy would be less than adequate—or might invite disaster—because political, cultural, psychological, and even medical variables, which also enter into the situation, had been overlooked. That is a lesson to be drawn from the first two parts of this book: only by combining different kinds of knowledge can one arrive at the know-how needed to work on the world.

## Knowledge and Power

Certainly that is the case, but it is a case presented from a narrowly scientific and consciously experimental perspective, which presupposes that all those involved are concerned only with scientific truth. There is another perspective that, through the idea of enactment, gives know-how—practical knowledge—a different significance. I wrote in the introduction that theories can be evaluated in two contexts, one intellectual and the other political. Scientific procedures determine (supposedly) the truth of a theory—whether or not it is, as its upholders claim, the case. Enactment, by contrast, reveals how much clout its backers have.

Administrative consultation issuing in enactment is a contest, for which the word *discussion* is too formal, too tidy, too suggestive of science, order, and rationality; the word hints at truth searching and it belongs with the chapters on expected-utility theories and structural functionalism. The chapters on agency are not about purported scientific truth; the actors are not in search of truth, even when they claim to be; they are out to win. Roberto and the lintel owner were not debating the relative truth-value of class struggle and *signorilità* as descriptors of social relations in Losa. They were making instrumental use of those and other structures, which are available to characterize Losa, by deploying them in a contest to define their immediate situation.

Notice what was happening. The encounter was not about the truth-value of the concepts *signorilità*, *paesano* moral standards, consumerism, and the class war, but about their effectiveness as rhetorical weapons. In such encounters, analytic constructs are taken out of their sheltered ambiance (where other things are equal) and deployed in a field of social relationships, where they are tested against other such constructs not for their truth but for their backer's clout. In practice, expected-utility theories and structural functionalism and other analytical forms of knowledge are tested in the same way; power makes the decision, not truth. In theory, of course, any saving lie that can be rewritten in a testable form—the proposition, for instance, that free-market privatization and deregulation will increase productivity and make everyone better off—can be subjected to an empirical, strictly scientific test of its truth. Does productivity go up and is everyone better off, and if so, does the credit go to privatization and deregulation?

In practice, however, people fall to arguing about how to measure productivity and what precisely should "better off" mean, and the occasion turns out to be less an inquiry into the proposition's truth than a contest decided by the relative power (both material resources and adversarial skills) of the disputants. This is hardly unexpected, since a single central vision, such as market freedom, is not an ontological reality (although often presented rhetorically as such), but a presuppositional idea, more or less grand, about the nature of things. It is not open to empirical truth testing nor is it acquired epistemologically by commonsense observation of events and systematic abstraction of their intersubjectively agreed ("self-evident") features, as Robbins suggested; it is the product of someone's imagination pouncing on a vision that looks likely to pay off.

Both *War and Peace* and Hayek's essays were concerned more with the truth of ideas than with their adversarial use and their relevance to power. Foucault faced the other way: truth is secondary, power is primary, and too much effort goes into constructing "global systematic theory" and not enough into understanding "the specificity of mechanisms of power." "The role for theory to-day seems to me to be just this: not to formulate the global systematic theory which holds everything in place, but to analyze the specificity of mechanisms of power, to locate the connections and extensions, to build little by little a strategic knowledge."[6]

Under the superabundance of Foucault's verbiage, there is a terrain that looks familiar. In question-and-answer sessions reported in *The Foucault Effect*, an interviewer talks of him "breaking up existing self-evidences to show both how they are produced and how they are nevertheless always unstable" (1991, 82). The "existing self-evidences" (also called "objectifications") are *saving lies*, forms of discourse intended not to welcome questions, but to inhibit them. They turn away criticism: they "anaesthetize" it. He describes (55) an episteme (a body of organized knowledge) as "a complex relationship of successive replacements," and talks (76–78) of "discontinuity" and "eventalization." His "events" are my *encounters*, occasions when structures may be shaken loose, and "successive replacements" occur when one saving lie supplants another. Discontinuity characterizes an "event"; something unexpected has taken place, something not "self-evident." Therefore there is a problem: "to recognize a discontinuity is never anything more than to register a problem that needs to be solved." Problems in "de-eventalized history" are ironed flat by some grand saving lie and

6. 1980, 145. The translator's "strategic knowledge" is the French word *savoir*, which I have construed as "know-how."

therefore never faced or solved. History is thus impoverished in order to present "the most unitary, necessary, inevitable and (ultimately) extra-historical mechanism or structure available," which is, in other words, a hedgehog's "single central vision." Tolstoy, refusing to produce a pattern in history by arbitrarily highlighting some features and suppressing others, was rejecting "de-eventalized history."

The sermon against single central visions runs through Foucault's writing just as it runs through *War and Peace*. In *Power/Knowledge* (1980, 81) he writes, ". . . the attempt to think in terms of a totality has in fact proved a hindrance to research." Big theories—expected utility, structural functionalism, natural selection—take attention away from the "local level"; they inhibit those who, like Hayek, make their contribution to knowledge by muddling and puzzling. Foucault advocates ". . . an autonomous, non-centralized kind of theoretical production, one, that is to say, whose validity is not dependent on the approval of the established regimes of thought." He talks of "subjugated knowledge" (82) and of "the tyranny of globalizing discourses" (83).

The connection between knowledge and power (ideas are weapons) is identified: "[W]e cannot exercise power except through the production of truth" (1980, 93). Those who produce "truth" (who define the situation) thereby exercise power. Truth is not "the ensemble of truths which are to be discovered and accepted" but "the ensemble of rules according to which the true and the false are separated and specific effects of power attached to the true." The battle, he states, is "about the status of truth and the economic and political role it plays" (132).

" 'Truth,' " he continues, "is to be understood as a system of ordered procedures for the production, regulation, distribution, circulation and operation of statements" (133). This definition is made in the explicitly political context of an essay entitled "Truth and Power," but if the political intent is put aside, the proposition restates Popper's "Scientific objectivity can be described as the inter-subjectivity of scientific method." Popper's "ordered procedures," however, include "free criticism" and "recognizing experience as the impartial arbiter of . . . controversies," and he can therefore make a distinction between objective truth and enforced or negotiated truth. Foucault chooses not to do so; he does not believe in impartial arbiters.[7]

So, yet again, what is truth? I said at the outset that those who claim to have found *the* truth were usually mistaken; their truth is likely to be only one among several competing truths. Recall Christopher Fry: "There may always be another reality / To make fiction of the truth we

---

7. Douglass North likewise (mutatis mutandis) noted the absence of impartiality, and treated it as a "disturbing cause"—a major flaw—in the model rather than as an inescapable feature of all claims to scientific truth. See Chapter 3.

think we've arrived at." To believe this—to be methodologically sceptical of received wisdom—is not to be nihilistic or subversive of social
and intellectual order. It is simply to recognize what can happen: an
idea holds up until people, putting it into practice, come to realize—or
are persuaded—that it does not or has ceased to deliver what is expected; then they try to replace it with another idea, which they are persuaded will better serve them because it is nearer to reality. The soothing
cigarette of the forties and fifties is now unambiguously a slow killer.

Such revisions of "the truth" are generally anything but smooth.
Nor are they decisively guided by the canons of scientific objectivity.
Active steps, over many years, were taken by the tobacco industry to
impede that particular revision, but eventually Popper's "intersubjectivity of scientific method" and the "test of experience" amply demonstrated that cigarettes cause lung cancer and other ailments and that
nicotine is addictive; that is hard science. But hard knowledge does
not easily survive outside the laboratory. If the knowledge is to be put
to use—as distinct from being tested by the methods of science—a
know-how process must transport it into the domain of political and
economic relations and into the social domain of moral responsibility,
where its status as hard truth is softened by interested parties competing to redefine the situation in ways that will be to their advantage.

Most people think the tobacco barons were lying when they swore
under oath that they believed their product not to be addictive, because to admit that they knew the damage it did and yet continued to
manufacture and sell it would make them liable at law. But the claim
that they lied is not a scientific fact; it is an opinion, and its accuracy is
tested not in a laboratory but in a law court, where truth is decided
not by the intersubjectivity of scientific method but, Foucault-style and
adversarially, by "a system of ordered procedures for the production,
regulation, distribution, circulation and operation of statements." The
addictive quality of nicotine, which in the domain of science is a fact
validated by "recognizing experience as the impartial arbiter of . . .
controversies," has become, when the knowledge is shifted to the domain of praxis, a series of moral issues. What is the responsibility of
the manufacturers? Of the advertisers? Of the retailers? Of the individual smoker? Moral issues, however, are not decided by scientific
methods.[8] Anyone who tries to do that is cheating—recall Friedman's
attempt to subordinate normative economics to positive economics.
The ultimate truths of morality cannot be defended by reason; the appropriate weapons are persuasion, assertion, or force. In short, the
"truth" of moral questions is not discovered but negotiated or enforced.

8. "Moral distinctions [are] not derived from reason" (Hume 1940, 2:165).

## Global and Local Knowledge

There is in Foucault's writing a continuing note of indignation about "the tyranny of globalizing discourses" that stifle the "non-centralized kind of theoretical production." He is not alone in seeing tyranny flow from the realm of theoretical discourse into political actions. A similar case is argued in a book by James Scott, *Seeing like a State*. He, too, deplores the injustices that result when grand regimenting ideas are put into practice. His critique, however, is less moralistic than it is positivist and rational: grand schemes derived from single central visions— forced collectivization in the Soviet Union; resettlement schemes in Tanzania; scientific forestry in Prussia and elsewhere; new capital cities like Brasília and Chandigarh, or rationally reconstructed old ones (Baron Haussmann's nineteenth-century Paris is his example)—often do not work. Local-level diversity reasserts itself, and when it does not, the consequence may be an even greater disaster. Local knowledge contains local know-how, and the grand universalizing schemes, exactly because they rest on one-size-fits-all reasoning, falter when diversity is encountered. As Scott explains, planners with a central vision try to change local conditions to fit the Plan, instead of adapting the Plan to local conditions. The planners may have an effect, but the outcome of their designs, like those of Prince Bagration, is rarely what they intended.[9]

A similar vision—big is bad (as Callimachus the bibliographer said of books)—has until recently dominated cultural anthropology. Clifford Geertz, anthropology's late-twentieth-century champion of "minutely organized Particulars," which (following Gilbert Ryle) he calls "thick description," in the 1970s and '80s preached the doctrine of relativism and campaigned to drive positivists out of the temple. Their sin was to define the study of society as a single-vision generalizing science that would produce sociological laws by "careful examination of diversities to discover underlying uniformities" (in Radcliffe-Brown's words). Geertz's particularistic anthropology has been center stage in cultural anthropology for two decades.[10] Foxiness, in other words, has been in fashion; Radcliffe-Brown's hedgehogs, "underlying uniformities" and "grand theory," have been shelved to make room for "local knowledge" and an "autonomous, noncentralized kind of theoretical production."

Neither position (universal or local), if taken by itself, can adequately

9. One theoretical alternative to centralized planning is no planning at all. In other words, listen to Hayek and let the market be the "natural" allocator of resources, because the market, supposedly, does respond to local knowledge and preferences.

10. There is an extensive literature. It can be sampled (for anthropology) in Geertz 1983 and 1984, Spiro 1986, Keesing 1987, and Strathern 1987.

model ideas that guide social interaction, because everyone in fact takes both positions. We all, in all that we do and say, make use both of universals and of particulars, and each has its benefits and its costs. To be a hedgehog, a universalist, is to feel secure, because it is to have at hand—in the form of an all-commanding vision—an amen structure, a fundamental saving lie, and a place to stand. Tolstoy and Hayek, each in their different way searching for security (and in Hayek's case discovering it), seem in their preoccupation with that quest to testify, albeit not in words, that a single central vision is not an intellectual problem-solving tool—always translatable into a procedure or an algorithm that will explain why the car won't start, why you have a headache, or why economies go bust, and having that as its function—but rather, as I suggested in Chapter 6, a means to satisfy a craving for the peace of mind that comes from being able to make sense of life and its experiences. The vision may be spelled out in intellectual terms and rationalized as the starting point for a chain of reasoning, but at the same time its basic function is the gratification of an emotional need. Such models are sustenance for the psyche, serving it as food serves the body. Therefore, whether for good or for ill, grand, all-embracing saving lies have always been an intellectual staple and always will be.

So there is no one who is not at least some of the time a hedgehog, sustained by saving lies. But the rest of the time that person must be a fox, attending to the practicalities and particularities of everyday life. The binary division between hedgehog and fox does not bring into existence two perfectly and wholly distinct types of person, as one might think when Isaiah Berlin says firmly that Dante was a hedgehog and Shakespeare a fox, and then assigns a score more writers to one or the other category. In social interactions everyone plays both hedgehog and fox; we shift between the two modes of thinking according to the situation in which we find ourselves and the way we wish to have it defined. A hedgehog vision that works well in one context may be found wanting when the context changes, and to arrive at a new and better vision calls for the fox's muddling and puzzling. (Hedgehog and fox, as must by now be obvious, is a figure of speech for models of structure and models of agency.)

If we leave aside the purity of high abstraction and, foxlike, attend instead to situations, the style of questioning that has come to the surface repeatedly in this book prompts us to ask, of any situation, how salient in it is either element. The simple binary opposition between local and universal—one or the other but never a mixture of both—is clearly over-simple. Totalities are forms of knowledge that are always undone if submitted to the test of experience. On the other hand

Hayek-like or fox like muddling and puzzling always builds in hedge-hog features; it is itself a gradation—steps in a staircase—from "solutions" that are grand saving lies at the top (having the status of a religion) down to others that become progressively more insecure as one descends the stairs and brings them closer to the test of experience, which requires progressive localization and therefore introduces progressive diversity. That model fits a variety of contexts. The central planners who designed Brasília, or the Soviet officials who planned and executed rural collectivization, were single-vision hedgehog people, removed from the reality of implementation; they had the luxury of bracketing away "disturbing causes." When leaders in Delhi made a policy decision about, say, land tenure reform, they enjoyed the hedge-hog's privilege of seeing the matter clearly and simply. But when the same policy passed down the chain of administrative implementation, from the federal level to the states, to the districts, and to the local communities, foxlike qualities were ever more needed to adapt the plan to the diverse conditions that each new level introduced.

A similar pattern of increasing engagement with the complexities of the real world appears in this book as we move from Friedman, first to Coase, and then to North, or from the austere tidiness of Evans-Prichard's "imaginative construct" of Nuer social structure to Leach's Kachin, who push and shove to impose on each other alternative definitions of the local situation.

So do we ever arrive at the truth? One might imagine that each step downward toward the empirical reality must be a step nearer to The Truth, as those two words seem to imply—truth is whatever is the case, whatever is reality. In the imagined world of hard science that is the model of how things work: truth is uncovered by discovering what objectively is the case. But objectivity, even in hard science, seems not to be quite what the word suggests. Popper again: "Scientific objectivity can be described as the inter-subjectivity of scientific method." In other words, objectivity is a saving lie agreed upon by qualified people. "Qualified" suggests not only knowledge but also people who have no axe to grind. Such people exist in the image that the practitioners of hard science have of themselves. Do they continue to exist when they enter into the actuality of politics and economics and social matters generally? For that to happen we are in need of an "entity" that, like North's third-party enforcer of contracts, will serve as an honest and disinterested arbiter of Truth. But in politics the truth arbiter, like the contract enforcer, is an entity that "no one at this stage in our knowledge knows how to create." Today's "qualified" people may tomorrow be reckoned to have been incompetent and prejudiced.

In that context, truth becomes a function of power and the useful sociopolitical question is not what the truth *is* but rather how it is negotiated. How are saving lies defended? How are they assailed and toppled? How are they used? What are the outcomes? And, of course, there is the inescapable question: Who benefits?

# References

Asad, Talal
 1973 (ed.) *Anthropology and the Colonial Encounter.* New York: Humanities Press.
Bailey, F. G.
 1960 *Tribe, Caste and Nation.* Manchester: Manchester University Press.
 1969 *Stratagems and Spoils.* Oxford: Blackwell.
 1971 (ed.) *Gifts and Poison.* Oxford: Blackwell.
 1993 *The Kingdom of Individuals.* Ithaca, N.Y.: Cornell University Press.
 1994 *The Witch-Hunt.* Ithaca, N.Y.: Cornell University Press.
Bannock, Graham, R. E. Baxter, and Evan Davis
 1992 *Dictionary of Economics.* London: Penguin Books.
Barth, John
 1960 [1958] *The End of the Road.* New York: Avon Books.
Barzini, Luigi
 1966 *The Italians.* London: Hamish Hamilton.
Becker, Gary
 1981 *A Treatise on the Family.* Cambridge, Mass.: Harvard University Press.
Berlin, Isaiah
 1957 *The Hedgehog and the Fox.* New York: Mentor.
 1980 *Against the Current.* New York: Viking.
Bernstein, Basil
 1964 "Elaborate and Restricted Codes: Their Social Origins and Some Consequences." *American Anthropologist* 66 (6, pt. 2): 55–69.
Blaug, Mark
 1985 [1962] *Economic Theory in Retrospect.* Cambridge: Cambridge University Press.
 1992 [1980] *The Methodology of Economics: Or How Economists Explain.* Cambridge: Cambridge University Press.
Bloch, M.
 1990 "The Symbolism of Money in Imerina." In J. Parry and M. Bloch, eds., *Money and the Morality of Exchange.* Cambridge: Cambridge University Press.
Bohannan, Paul
 1955 "Some Principles of Exchange and Investment among the Tiv." *American Anthropologist* 57: 60–70.

Booth, Wayne C.
   1974   *A Rhetoric of Irony*. Chicago: University of Chicago Press.
Brown, Richard
   1973   "Anthropology and Colonial Rule: Godfrey Wilson and the Rhodes-Livingstone Institute, Northern Rhodesia." In Talal Asad, ed., *Anthropology and the Colonial Encounter*. New York: Humanities Press.
   1979   "Passages in the Life of a White Anthropologist: Max Gluckman in Northern Rhodesia." *Journal of African History* 20: 525–41.
Bryson, Gladys
   1968 [1945]   *Man and Society: The Scottish Inquiry of the Eighteenth Century*. New York: Augustus M. Kelley.
Burke, Kenneth
   1969a [1945]   *A Grammar of Motives*. Berkeley: University of California Press.
   1969b [1950]   *A Rhetoric of Motives*. Berkeley: University of California Press.
Coase, Ronald
   1937   "The Nature of the Firm." *Economica* 4: 386–405.
   1960   "The Problem of Social Cost." *Journal of Law and Economics* 3: 1–44.
   1991   "The Nature of the Firm: Meaning." In Oliver E. Williamson and Sidney G. Winter, eds., *The Nature of the Firm: Origins, Evolution and Development*. New York: Oxford University Press.
Colson, Elizabeth
   1962   *The Plateau Tonga of Northern Rhodesia: Social and Religious Studies*. Manchester: Manchester University Press.
   1974   *Tradition and Contract: The Problem of Order*. Chicago: Aldine Press.
Devons, Ely
   1950   *Planning in Practice*. Cambridge: Cambridge University Press.
Dumont, Louis
   1975   "On the Comparative Understanding of Non-Modern Civilizations." *Daedalus* 104 (2): 153–72.
Evans-Pritchard, E. E.
   1937   *Witchcraft, Oracles, and Magic among the Azande*. Oxford: Clarendon Press.
   1940   *The Nuer*. Oxford: Clarendon Press.
   1948   *Social Anthropology: An Inaugural Lecture*. Oxford: Clarendon Press.
   1951   *Social Anthropology*. London: Cohen and West.
   1956   *Nuer Religion*. Oxford: Clarendon Press.
   1962   *Essays in Social Anthropology*. London: Faber.
   1970   "Social Anthropology at Oxford." *Man* (n.s.) 5: 704.
Faris, James
   1973   "*Pax Brittanica* and the Sudan: S. F. Nadel." In Talal Asad, ed., *Anthropology and the Colonial Encounter*. New York: Humanities Press.
Fernandez, James W., and Mary Taylor Huber
   2001 (eds.)   *Irony in Action: Anthropology, Practice, and the Moral Imagination*. Chicago: University of Chicago Press.
Fortes, M.
   1940   "The Political System of the Tallensi of the northern Territories of the Gold Coast." In M. Fortes and E. E. Evans-Pritchard, eds., *African Political Systems*. London: Oxford University Press.
Fortes, M., and E. E. Evans-Pritchard
   1940 (eds.)   *African Political Systems*. London: Oxford University Press.

Foster, Brian L.
    1974   "Ethnicity and Commerce." *American Ethnologist* 1: 437–48.
Foucault, Michel
    1980   *Power/Knowledge: Selected Interviews and Other Writings 1972–1977.* Ed. Colin Gordon. New York: Pantheon.
    1991   *The Foucault Effect.* Ed. G. Burchell, C. Gordon, and Peter Miller. London: Harvester Wheatsheaf.
Frankenberg, Ronald
    1989 [1957]   *Village on the Border.* Prospect Heights, Ill.: Waveland Press.
Friedman, Milton
    1953   The Methodology of Positive Economics. In *Essays in Positive Economics.* Chicago: University of Chicago Press.
Friedman, Milton, and Walter Heller
    1969   *Monetary versus Fiscal Policy: A Dialogue.* New York: W. W. Norton.
Geertz, Clifford
    1983   *Local Knowledge.* New York: Basic Books.
    1984   "Anti-Anti-Relativism." *American Anthropologist* 86: 263–78.
Giddens, Anthony
    1984   *The Constitution of Society.* Berkeley: University of California Press.
Gluckman, Max
    1955a   *The Judicial Process among the Barotse of Northern Rhodesia.* Manchester: Manchester University Press.
    1955b   *Custom and Conflict in Africa.* Oxford: Blackwell.
    1958 [1940 and 1942]   *Analysis of a Social Situation in Modern Zululand.* Manchester: Manchester University Press.
Goffman, Erving
    1961   *Encounters.* Indianapolis: Bobbs-Merrill.
    1970   *Strategic Interaction.* Oxford: Blackwell.
Hayek, F. A.
    1988   *The Fatal Conceit: The Errors of Socialism.* London: Routledge.
    1991   Two Types of Mind. vol. 3 of *The Collected Works of F. A. Hayek,* ed. W. W. Bartley III and Stephen Kresge. Chicago: University of Chicago Press.
Herskovits, M. S.
    1960   [1952] *Economic Anthropology.* New York: Knopf.
Herzfeld, Michael
    2001   "Irony and Power: Toward a Politics of Mockery in Greece." In James W. Fernandez and Mary Taylor Huber, eds., *Irony in Action: Anthropology, Practice, and the Moral Imagination.* Chicago: University of Chicago Press.
Hirschman, Albert O.
    1979 [1970]   "The Search for Paradigms as a Hindrance to Understanding." In Paul Rabinow and William M. Sullivan, eds., *Interpretive Social Science: A Reader.* Berkeley: University of California Press.
Hobbes, Thomas
    1946 [1651]   *Leviathan.* Oxford: Blackwell.
Hobsbawm, Eric, and Terence Ranger
    1983 (eds.)   *The Invention of Tradition.* Cambridge: Cambridge University Press.
Hume, David
    1940 [1738]   *A Treatise of Human Nature.* 2 vols. London: Dent.

Hutcheon, Linda
    1995    *Irony's Edge*. New York: Routledge.
James, Wendy
    1973    "The Anthropologist as Reluctant Imperialist." In Talal Asad, ed., *Anthropology and the Colonial Encounter*. New York: Humanities Press.
Keesing, Roger M.
    1987    "Anthropology as Interpretive Quest." *Current Anthropology* 28: 161–76.
Keynes, John Maynard
    1932    *Essays in Persuasion*. New York: Harcourt Brace and Company.
    1947 [1936]    *The General Theory of Employment, Interest, and Money*. London: Macmillan.
Kuper, Adam
    1983    *Anthropology and Anthropologists*. London: Routledge and Kegan Paul.
Laidlaw, James
    2000    "A free gift makes no friends." *Journal of the Royal Anthropological Institute* 6 (4): 617–34.
Larrabee, Harold A.
    1952 [1824] (ed.)    *Bentham's handbook of Political Fallacies*. Baltimore: The Johns Hopkins Press.
Leach, Edmund
    1954    *Political Systems of Highland Burma*. London: Bell.
    1961    *Pul Eliya: A Village in Ceylon*. Cambridge: Cambridge University Press.
    1977    "In Formative Travail with Leviathan." *Anthropological Forum* 9 (2): 54–61.
Liddell, Henry George, and Robert Scott
    1890    *A Greek–English Lexicon*. 7th ed. Oxford: Clarendon Press.
Lienhardt, Godfrey
    1974    "E-P, a Personal View." *Man* (n.s.) 9: 299–304.
Mauss, Marcel
    1990 [1923–24]    *The Gift: The Form and Reason for Exchange in Archaic Societies*. Trans. W. D. Halls. New York: W. W. Norton.
McCloskey, Deirdre M.
    1998 [1985]    *The Rhetoric of Economics*. Madison: University of Wisconsin Press.
McCloskey, Donald M.
    1994    *Knowledge and Persuasion in Economics*. Cambridge: Cambridge University Press.
Moe, Terry M.
    1984    "The New Economics of Organization." *American Journal of Political Science* 28: 739–77.
    1995    "The Politics of Structural Choice: Toward a Theory of Public Bureaucracy." In Oliver E. Williamson, ed., *Organization Theory*. New York: Oxford University Press.
Moraes, Frank
    1973    *Witness to an Era*. New York: Holt, Rinehart and Winston.
Muecke, D. C.
    1969    *The Compass of Irony*. London: Methuen.

Nelson, Robert H.
  1991    *Reaching for Heaven on Earth: The Theological Meaning of Economics*. Savage, Md.: Rowman and Littlefield.
North, Douglass C.
  1990    *Institutions, Institutional Change and Economic Performance*. Cambridge: Cambridge University Press.
Parry, J.
  1986    "The Gift, the Indian Gift and the 'Indian Gift.' " *Man* 21: 453–73.
  1990    "On the Moral Perils of Exchange." In J. Parry and M. Bloch, eds., *Money and the Morality of Exchange*. Cambridge: Cambridge University Press.
Parry, J. and M. Bloch
  1990    (eds.)    *Money and the Morality of Exchange*. Cambridge: Cambridge University Press.
Popper, K. R.
  1966 [1945]    *The Open Society and Its Enemies*. 2 vols. London: Routledge and Kegan Paul.
Radcliffe-Brown, A. R.
  1952 [1935]    *Structure and Function in Primitive Society*. London: Cohen and West.
Richards, I. A.
  1936    *The Philosophy of Rhetoric*. New York: Oxford University Press.
Robbins, Lionel
  1937 [1932]    *An Essay on the Nature and Significance of Economic Science*. London: Macmillan.
Rosenau, Pauline Marie
  1992    *Post-Modernism and the Social Sciences*. Princeton, N.J.: Princeton University Press.
Russell, Bertrand
  1946    *A History of Western Philosophy*. London: George Allen and Unwin.
Scott, James C.
  1998    *Seeing like a State*. New Haven, Conn.: Yale University Press.
Simon, Herbert A.
  1976    "From Substantive to Procedural Rationality." In S. J. Latsis, ed., *Method and Appraisal in Economics*. Cambridge: Cambridge University Press.
  1986    "The Failure of Armchair Economics." *Challenge* November/December: 18–25.
Smith, Adam
  1909 [1776]    *An Inquiry into the Nature and Causes of the Wealth of Nations*. New York: Collier.
  1966 [1759]    *The Theory of Moral Sentiments*. New York: Kelley.
Spiro, Melford E.
  1986    "Cultural Relativism and the Future of Anthropology." *Cultural Anthropology* 1: 259–86.
Strathern, Marilyn
  1987    "Out of Context: The Persuasive Fictions of Anthropology." *Current Anthropology* 28: 251–81.
Sugden, Robert
  1986    *The Economics of Rights, Cooperation, and Welfare*. Oxford: Blackwell.

Tocqueville, Alexis de
    1994 [1835, 1840]    *Democracy in America*. New York: Knopf.
Tolstoy, Leo
    1957 [1868]    *War and Peace*. Trans. Louise and Aylmer Maude. 3 vols. London: Oxford University Press.
Williamson, Oliver E.
    1995 (ed.)    *Organization Theory*. New York: Oxford University Press.
Williamson, Oliver E., and Sidney G. Winter
    1991 (eds.)    *The Nature of the Firm: Origins, Evolution and Development*. New York: Oxford University Press.

# Index

Motivation, 107–9; and contracts, 33–36; of economists, 109–18; and Friedman, 25–26; and North, 53–62; of social anthropologists, 118–23. *See also* Enlightened self-interest
Muecke, D. C., 161 n.7, 166 n.14
Mussolini, Benito, 1n, 159, 190

Natural, ambiguities of the term, 114
Natural law, 87, 114, 116
Natural-science models, xiii, 3, 67–88, 107–9, 196–200; and economics, 6–9, 15–62, 109–18; and social anthropology, 68–78
Natural selection. *See* Models, evolutionary
NEO (New Economics of Organization), 30–45. *See also* Adverse selection; Cheating; Contractual model of organizations; Free loading; Opportunism; Principal/agent models; Trust
Neoclassical economics. *See* Expected-utility models
Neoclassical economists, xii, 7–9, 15–23; amorality of, 108–17; imaginary worlds of, 8, 21; Keynes on, 1, 114n; and power, 115–16. *See also* Free-market economies
NIE (New Institutional Economics), 46–62. *See also* Economic efficiency; Enlightened self-interest; North, Douglass; Organizations; Regulatory organizations
Nonconformity, 145–51
Normative claims, 4, 103–5, 196. *See also* Moral imagination; Moral judgments
North, Douglass, 13, 47–62; and choice-theoretic models, 54–60; on institutions, 53–54; and the negative-sloped curve, 59–60; on regulatory organizations, 55–59
Nuer, 74–77, 92, 95–96, 101
*Nuer, The,* 74–78, 118, 123, 176; causality in, 80–82; contents of described, 80–81; and expected utility, 74–78, 80–82; externalities in, 91–96; guiding question of, 92–93; and leadership, 77–78, 94–102. *See also* Evans-Pritchard, E. E.; Nuer
Numen, 132, 149–50

Objectivity. *See* Experience; Intersubjectivity; Positivism

Observed behavior. *See* Experience; Positivism
Old Adam, 7, 7n, 33, 37, 47, 56–57, 132; and Nuer, 76, 96n. *See also* Economic man.
Opportunism, 31–32, 35–40, 44, 57–58. *See also* Postcontractual opportunism
Optimizing. *See* Rationality, bounded; Utility-maximizing
Order, psychological need for, 107–8, 127–28, 187–91
Organizations, xiii, 15–23; and change, 53–59, 150; and institutions, 20 n.6; and markets, 23–43. *See also* Institutions; Regulatory organizations

*Paesano,* 158–75
Paradigms, xii–xiii, 16, 22. *See also* Models
Parry, J., 138n.
Particulars, 14, 101, 127, 165
Patterns, xii, 4, 185–86; in history, 188–89, 194–95; versus laws, 78–86
Peasants, 156–58; caricature of, 161. See also *Paesano*
Performance, 4–6, 161–65, 180; of economies, 46–62. *See also* Agency; Knowledge, practical
Persuasion, 39–40, 128–29, 146; and force, 167, 167 n.18; by selective omission, 165. *See also* Rhetoric
Plautus, 6
Political economy, 16–20, 47, 69
*Political Systems of Highland Burma,* contrasted with *The Nuer* and *African Political Systems,* 98–105
Politics of identity, 110, 148n
Popper, Karl, 3, 195–99
Positivism, xiii–xiv, 6–9; and economics, 8, 23–29, 110–12; and social anthropology, 78–87
Postcontractual opportunism, 35, 40, 40n, 44
Postmodernism, xiii–xiv, 107–8, 108 n.2
Power: balance of, 72–74; discretionary, 38, 113; and economics, 23–29, 31, 38, 55–59, 114–17; and knowledge, 193–96; and truth, xi, 115–17, 174–75, 193–200
Pragmatism, 3–4
Praxis, 4–5, 174, 191–92, 196. *See also* Knowledge, practical

# Acknowledgments

For their comments on one or more of the several recensions of this book I am grateful to Susan Love Brown, Roy D'Andrade, Dan Doyle, Michael Meeker, Eloise Meneses, and Don Tuzin.